THE FAMILY
BOOK OF
GAMES

This edition published 1994 by Brockhampton Press,
a member of Hodder Headline PLC.

© Sceptre Books, Time-Life Books B.V.

All rights reserved. No part of this publication may
be reproduced, stored in a retrieval system, or
transmitted, in any form or by any means,
electronic, mechanical, photocopying, recording
or otherwise without the prior permission of the
copyright holder.

ISBN 1 86019 021 9

Printed and bound in U.A.E.

THE FAMILY BOOK OF GAMES

DAVID PRITCHARD

BROCKHAMPTON
PRESS

793
PRI

CONTENTS

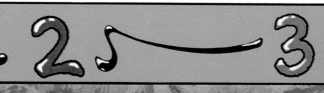

CARD GAMES

CHILDREN'S GAMES

GAMBLING GAMES

ACKNOWLEDGEMENTS

Many of the games in this book are protected by trade marks and copyrights. These are acknowledged below. In some cases acknowledgements are made to a manufacturer or distributor who is not the copyright owner. The publishers express their appreciation to all concerned for approval to reproduce illustrations and other matter used.

Black Box, Cluedo, Hare and Tortoise, Lexicon and *Monopoly* are marketed in the UK by Waddingtons, House of Games, Oulton, Leeds.
Pit is manufactured by Parker Bros, Salem, Mass., USA, who also distribute *Risk (Risiko)*, a Miro (France) Game. Both games are marketed in the UK by the Palitoy Company, Coalville, Leicester.
L-Game is copyright by Edward de Bono and is protected in all Berne Convention countries.
Master Mind is an acknowledged trade mark of Invicta Plastics Ltd, Oadby, Leicester.
Diplomacy and *Kingmaker* are manufactured by Gibsons Games, Littlers Close, London SW19.
Othello is a trade mark of Peter Pan Playthings Ltd, Peterborough.
Scrabble is the registered trade mark owned in the USA and Canada by Selchow and Righter Co., New York, in Australia by Scrabble Australia Pty Ltd, and in most other countries by members of the J.W, Spear & Sons plc, Enfield, Greater London Group.

Focus is manufactured in the UK by J.W. Spear & Sons plc.
Rummikub is a brand name of Lemada Light Industries Ltd, Tel Aviv.
Connect 4 is a trade mark of Milton Bradley Co.
Marrakesh is the copyright of Xanadu Leisure, Hawaii, USA.
Acquire and *Twixt* are Bookshelf Games of the Avalon Hill Co. of Baltimore, Maryland, USA.

The playing cards illustrated are by John Waddingtons. Tarock cards are by Piatnik (Vienna).
The publisher would like to thank Just Games, 62 Brewer Street, London W1, for the generous loan of games and equipment used in many of the illustrations in this book.

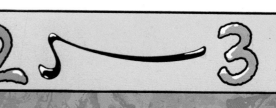

INTRODUCTION

Man has never shown so much imagination, observed the German philosopher Leibniz, as in the various games he has invented. This book is full of that imagination, drawn from many cultures and spanning most of recorded history.

The early games inventors, who bequeathed us such masterpieces as Chess and Go, and who in the sum have enriched our leisure as few other artists have done, go unrecorded. And yet little has changed: the inventors of today's great games are similarly unacknowledged except by a knowing minority who eagerly seek out their creations.

No attempt has been made to make *The Family Book of Games* comprehensive, for that would require a volume many times this size. Instead, selection has been restricted to representative games from all parts of the world and to games of outstanding merit, regardless of their origin. Those that call for physical skills have been excluded partly because their number would impose an unacceptable dilution. Games have been grouped in sections for convenience. Inevitably these divisions are arbitrary and in a few cases a game could with equal justification be placed in a different section – Pontoon, for example, is a card game as well as a gambling game.

The essential rules of each game are explained clearly. Detailed rules, which cover such points as who sits where, who plays first and what penalties are enforceable if, say, a card is inadvertently turned over or a board is wrongly set up, have been omitted as unnecessary for the enjoyment of the games. A little common sense takes care of all of them.

A feature of the book is the emphasis given to strategy. There is advice on how best to play a game, and not just how to play it, for satisfaction is to be derived from playing a game well, apart from the pleasure of winning it.

The aim throughout has been that the description of each game should stand by itself. Most strategy games have developed from common roots, however, and in this instance good starting points are Alquerque and Chess because many games are related to them.

The increased popularity of indoor games in recent years has stimulated the growth of the specialist games shop. This is the place to go if you cannot find the game you want locally. But even the specialist games shop will not stock all the strategy games described here. Fortunately, and without exception, those that cannot be obtained can be easily made or assembled.

TABLE AND STRATEGY GAMES

Games of strategy have been played since earliest times. Many of these games are still played today and are immensely popular. It is an astonishing commentary on their endurance that their strategies are disputed as fiercely as ever, as much as a millennium or two after their invention. Of course, several old games have been modified over the centuries but many, like Go and the Mancalas, are structurally so simple that the way they are played now must be essentially the way they have always been played.

The games in this section have in most cases a long ancestry. They can be divided into three groups: race games like Backgammon and Pachisi, games of configuration of which Nine Men's Morris is an example, and games of conflict.

The conflict games predominate, reflecting man's heritage of struggle. Mostly these are board games for two players who start from an even position, the aim of each player being to vanquish the other. Play is along the lines of the board or in the cells formed by the lines. The men tend to be uniform and are generally moved orthogonally (up and down or to left and right) or diagonally, or a combination of these movements.

Three types of capture are commonly met. The oldest is by enclosing, either by surrounding (as in Go) or by flanking, found in the games of the Tafl family. The second type – the system with which we are most familiar – is by displacement. In a displacement capture the capturing man takes the place of his victim, who is removed from the board. Chess is the best-known of the games that use this type of capture. Lastly, there is the leap capture, employed in Draughts, which is probably more recent than the other two but is still at least a thousand years old and possibly much older.

It is usual to play all conflict games on the principle of 'touch and move'. This is a recommended discipline, even for friendly games within the family.

ALQUERQUE

Alquerque is a very old game for two players. A game much like it was played by the ancient Egyptians. It is the first known game to use the short-leap form of capture and is the parent of many popular board games including Draughts (Checkers). Alquerque was introduced to Spain by the Moors, who called it Qirkat, and the rules were recorded in a famous thirteenth-century manuscript.

PLAY

The board is a 5 × 5 grid with the medians and the main diagonals added. Each side has 12 men arranged at the start as shown in figure 1. The centre point is vacant.

A move is to an empty adjacent point along any line of the board. Whoever starts thus has a choice of four moves.

If an adjacent point is occupied by an enemy man and the point immediately beyond it is vacant, the man can be captured by leaping. Further captures can be made in the same move provided all captures are by the same man and each capture is along a line of the board. The capturing man can change direction after each capture.

Prisoners are removed from play and the winner is the player who takes all his opponent's men. Captures, including subsequent captures if possible, are compulsory but if there are alternatives the player can choose between them.

STRATEGY

An advantage of one man is usually enough to win: forces can be reduced until two men are left against one, when the lone man can be driven into a corner. White's winning position is shown in figure 2, the second White man being at any of the points marked with a cross. Black to play is forced to move to 4, when White's second man is played to 9. Now Black must take and is himself taken next move. White to play in this position simply marks time.

The only difficult position is that in

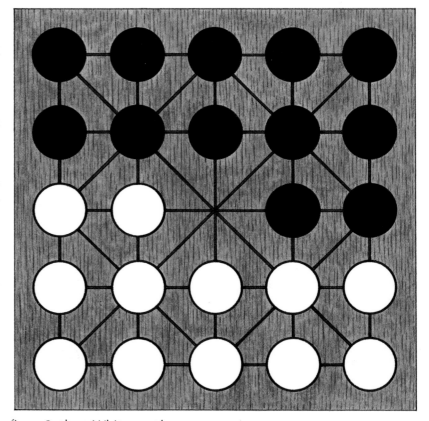

Figure 1
The starting arrangement

figure 3 where White must lose a move to win. After Black moves to 9, play continues: White 19; Black 15; White 24; Black 10; White 25; Black 15; White 8; Black 10; White 20; Black 5; White 15 (now we are back to figure 2); Black 4; White (8) 9; Black (captures) 14; White (captures) 13.

Notice the weakness of points 8, 12, 14 and 18. Here a single man can be trapped in mid-board by two opposing men. Draws are less frequent in Alquerque than appears likely.

Figure 2

Figure 3

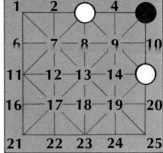

FIGHTING SERPENTS

Fighting Serpents is a two-player game of skill played by the Zuni Indians of New Mexico, to whom the snake symbolizes the Sun-God. It is probably derived from Alquerque, which was introduced to North America by the Spaniards, and bears a marked similarity to Draughts (Checkers).

PLAY

The game is played on a board, sometimes embellished with serpents, and each side has 23 men, in contrasting colours. The starting position is shown in figure 1. Board designs vary, and the game has been played with as few as 12 men a side; a circular board, though not of Zuni origin, has 34 men a side.

The players move in turn and the object of the game is to capture all the opponent's men. A move consists of playing a man along a line to an adjacent empty intersection. Thus at the start the first player has a choice of six moves.

Captures are made by leaping over an adjacent enemy man to an empty point immediately beyond. Multiple captures are permitted, but each capture must be by the same man and always along a line of the board. An example of a multiple capture is shown in figure 2. White to play can take all five black men by following the sequence shown. Capturing is compulsory, but if two or more men can make a capture, the player can choose. Captured men are removed from play. Draws are quite common.

Figure 2
A multiple capture

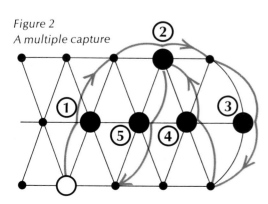

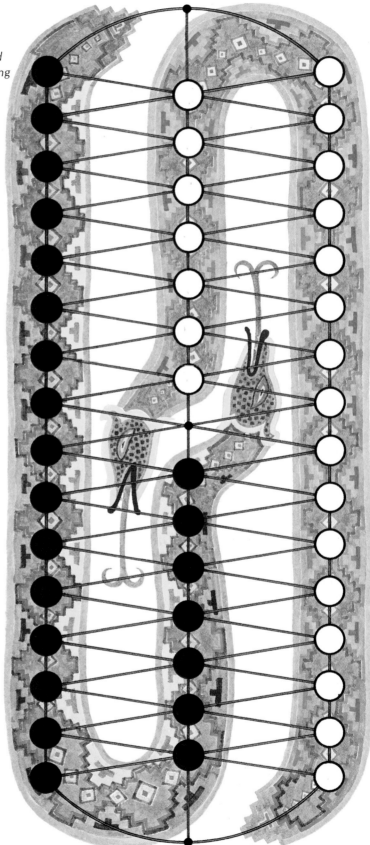

Figure 1
The board and starting position

SEEGA

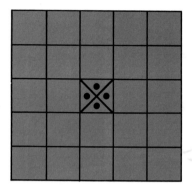

Figure 1
The board

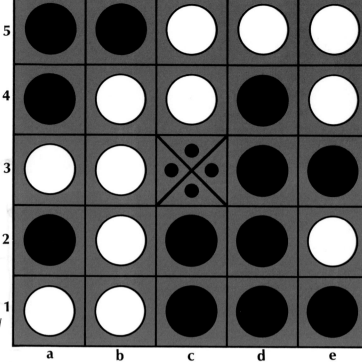

Figure 5
The board dressed
for play

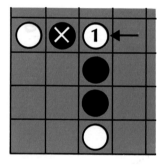

Figure 2
A capture

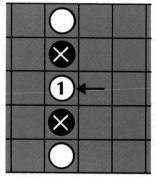

Figure 3
A multiple capture

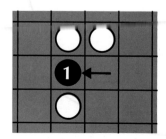

Figure 4
No capture

Seega is derived from a two-player Roman game and is played over much of north-east Africa.

PLAY

The square board is divided into 5 × 5 squares, with the centre square sometimes marked (figure 1). Each side has 12 men, in contrasting colours. (Sometimes the game is played on a 7 × 7 board with 24 men a side.)

Play starts with the board empty. Each player in turn puts two of his men on empty squares until the board is filled, the centre square being left unoccupied. The board is now dressed for play.

A turn consists of moving a man orthogonally, i.e. in a straight line forwards, backwards or sideways, to an adjacent empty cell. Clearly the first player must move into the centre. Men are captured by the escort (or custodian) method: if a man is trapped between two enemy men, it is captured (see figure 2). Multiple captures of single men are possible (figure 3) but only one man can be trapped in any one direction, and a man may safely move between enemy men (figure 4). Capturing is compulsory and if the man played can then move to make a second capture, and so on, it must do so. If one side has made a move that leaves the other side unable to move, the first side moves again to allow his opponent space.

A player wins by capturing all his opponent's men (Major Victory) or, if there is an impasse, for example where one player forms a barrier and moves back and forth behind it, the player with the most men remaining is the winner (Minor Victory). Draws are frequent.

STRATEGY

The outcome of a game depends largely on the initial arrangement so the board should be dressed with care. First plays are commonly at the perimeter. It is advisable to separate pairs by placing the men on opposite sides of the board.

Figure 5 shows a typical arrangement. There are three points to observe: perimeter squares are equally divided; there is symmetrical deployment on the eight squares around the centre point; and the four men orthogonally adjacent to the central cell (i.e. those that can move) are supported behind by a man of like colour.

The first move is usually a considerable advantage. With the arrangement shown in figure 5, if Black had the first move he would play d3–c3 and then move again (since White is without a move); if Black opened c2–c3 he would lose two men if White played b2–c2. Similarly, White would play b3–c3 and move again, and for the same reason since to play c4–c3 would mean losing two men if Black played d4–c4.

NYOUT

This simple Korean race-game is perhaps a thousand years old. It is still much played in Korea today, often for money, and is suitable for two, three or four players.

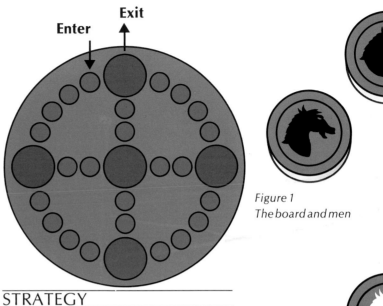

Enter · Exit

PLAY

The board is formed by 29 points regularly arranged in a circle divided into quadrants, the centre and cardinal points being larger than the others and sometimes carrying decorative ideograms (figure 1).

The men are horses (*ma*) of different colours; four each for the game with two players, three each for three players, two each for four players. Moves are governed by the casting of two-sided dice (*pam-nyout*) but an ordinary die can be used instead.

Horses enter at the point shown, move counter-clockwise and exit to the north. A player moves one man a turn the number of spots on his die-roll, 6 not counting (roll again). However, every roll of 4 or 5 gets an extra throw, when the player has the option of moving one or more men accordingly.

A man ending its move, or notionally landing after a roll of 4 or 5, on a cardinal point (other than the exit) may subsequently follow the central arm, pivoting if desired on the centre point. Thus a player fortunate enough to start with a 5 (roll again), a 4 (roll again) and a 3 or more may enter a *ma*, turn at the first cardinal point, turn again at the centre point and bear off.

A man that completes its move on a point occupied by an enemy sends the enemy man back to the start and takes another turn. A player may have all his men in play at the same time. If two men of the same side occupy the same point they may move thereafter as one but they may also be captured as one.

In the partnership game a player may elect to move one of his partner's *ma* in preference to his own. The player or side that first exits all its *ma* is the winner.

Figure 1
The board and men

STRATEGY

It is dangerous to be in front of enemy *ma*. Consider figure 2. If yours is the front *ma* here and you roll a 1, turn left even though the route is longer. To play ahead would give the opponents an excellent chance of kicking you (landing on your *ma*) – remember that a player who rolls a 4 or 5 completes his rolls before nominating the man or men to be moved.

It is risky to keep a man back at the end to chase the opponent's last *ma* – you may never catch it.

Figure 2
A game in progress

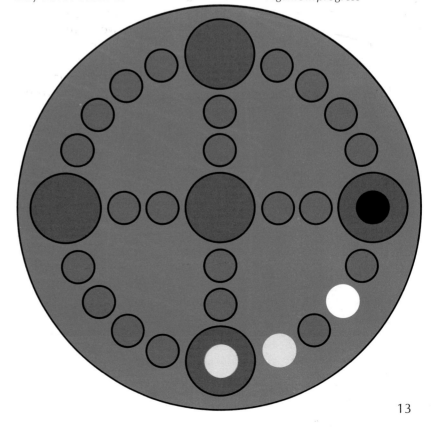

PACHISI

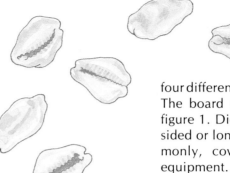

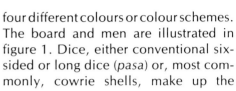

This is an old race game which, in its simplified form, everyone knows as Ludo. Pachisi ('Twenty-five') is almost a tradition in India where it is now largely played by children. The Mogul emperor, Akbar the Great, had Pachisi boards inlaid in his palaces and used slave girls for pieces. Today, communal boards are often to be found in Indian villages, crudely scratched on stone.

There are no approved rules for Pachisi, and many variations of those given here are practised. It can be played by two but is best as a partnership game for four.

EQUIPMENT

The board is usually made of cloth and is cruciform in shape. Each arm is made up of 24 alternately coloured squares, three of which are marked with crosses and are known as forts. The centre of the board is similarly marked and is called the *char-koni* or throne. Sixteen dome-shaped wooden pieces are used, four of each of four different colours or colour schemes. The board and men are illustrated in figure 1. Dice, either conventional six-sided or long dice (*pasa*) or, most commonly, cowrie shells, make up the equipment.

PLAY

Partners sit opposite each other and are designated North/South (red and green men) and East/West (yellow and black men). The object of each side is to enter all their men, complete a circuit of the board with each man, and be the first to bear all their men off. Each player has four men (eight in the two-player game) and moves only his own.

All the men start in the *char-koni*. A player brings his men on down the centre of the arm facing him, moves them anti-clockwise round the board and back up the centre of the arm to be borne off to the *char-koni* (figure 2).

Moves are determined by cowrie or dice throws. If cowries are used, each

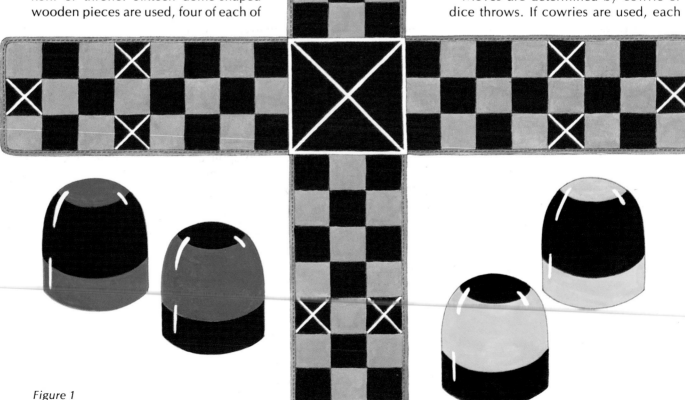

Figure 1
The board and men

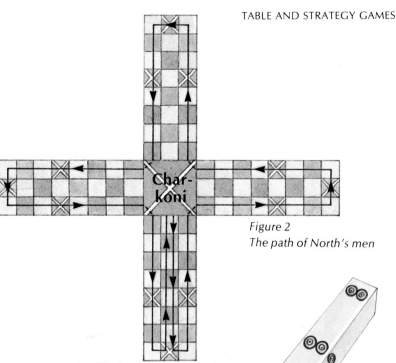

Figure 2
The path of North's men

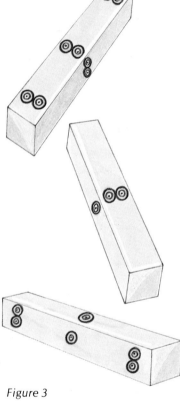

throw allows a man to be moved the number of squares shown by the cowries:

    0 mouths up 25*
    1 mouth up 10*
    2 mouths up 2
    3 mouths up 3
    4 mouths up 4
    5 mouths up 5
    6 mouths up 6*

The asterisked numbers indicate 'entry and grace' throws which alone can be used to bring on men (after the first) and also earn an extra throw.

Each player may bring a man on from the *char-koni* with his first throw. Thereafter men may only be entered with one or other of the permitted throws, which alternatively can be used to move men in play. A grace throw may be used to move the same or a different man. A player may elect not to move after throwing, but cannot move part of his entitlement. To bear off a man the throw must be exact: if it overshoots, then that man cannot be moved.

Two or more men of the same side may occupy the same cell, and a player (not a side) who has two or more men in the same cell may move them as one man. Opposing men can never occupy the same cell. A man (or men) is captured when an opposing force *of at least equal strength* lands on that square. The 12 forts are, however, havens: no man can be captured in a fort and hence a fort occupied by one side is automatically closed to the other. Captured men are returned to the *char-koni* and must start again. A player making a capture has an extra throw.

STRATEGY

A basic principle is that one should always bring a man into play, given the opportunity, rather than move a man already in transit. In theory the more men you have in play, the greater your options.

Usually when you are pursued you should run: to sit still is to invite the

opponent to sit still also until he gets the right throw. The alternative strategy is to bring up a man behind to threaten him in turn.

The forts are clearly desirable stopping places. There one can lie in ambush for an opponent's man to pass and then move out behind it with the aim of sending it back to the *char-koni*. The key forts are those at the extremities. If you reach one on the penultimate arm you can wait there until you throw the cowries 'mouths down' for a 25 – the count needed to bear off. Similarly, you can hold a key fort for your partner or deny it to the opposition.

One strategy is to get all your men in the same cell of your central column, where they are invulnerable, before moving them as one piece round the board. You can only do this by refusing a lot of turns, which tends to spoil the game, and many players permit no more than two men to move as one or bar multiple moves completely.

RELATED GAMES

These are too numerous to mention and most differ only slightly one from the other. Amongst the older Indian games, Chaupur and Chausar are played with long dice. These dice have a number, indicated by circles, on each of the four long sides. The numbers vary according to the game for which they are intended. Chausar uses three long dice, each numbered 1 and 6, 2 and 5 (figure 3). These dice are often included in Pachisi sets.

Figure 3
Long dice used for Chausar

HNEFATAFL

Hnefatafl ('the king game') is the ancient board game of the Norsemen. It was taken with them on their voyages and was later adopted by the Saxons. The game was almost certainly derived from the Roman *Ludus Latrunculorum*, which has a similar form of capture. Many different boards have been recorded (a number have been found in Viking grave-mounds) and the rules probably varied also.

PLAY

The board is marked with an 11 × 11 grid. The centre square is the throne. The defenders are the Vikings, grouped around their king who occupies the throne. The attackers are the foe – the Muscovites or whoever the Vikings were fighting at the time. For convenience, the two sides are here referred to respectively as Black and White. The starting arrangement is shown in figure 1.

White's aim is to capture the king. Black's aim is to get his king to any perimeter square. All men move in the same way – like a rook in Chess – that is, orthogonally (in straight lines forwards, backwards or sideways) over any number of vacant squares. The king, however, may only move up to three squares at a time, and only the king may move on to or through the throne square. There is no diagonal movement.

Men are captured by the custodian or escort method: two men flank the victim. A simple capture is demonstrated in figure 2A. More than one man may be taken at a time: figure 2B shows how this can happen. In the case of a multiple capture, each man must be flanked on either side by an enemy. However, a man may move safely between two enemy men – see figure 2C. Captured men are removed from play.

The king is captured when he is surrounded on all sides by the enemy or when his only escape is to the throne square (figure 3). The king may not assist in a capture.

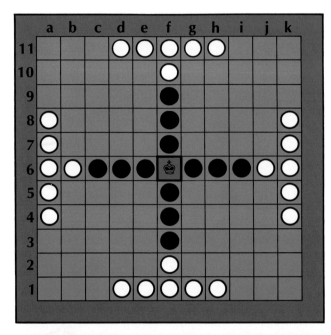

Figure 1
The starting position

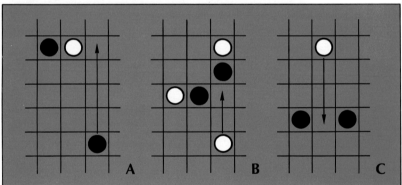

STRATEGY

White should advance gradually on all sides. He must quickly cover the exposed corners – the four doubled men can be usefully deployed there. At this stage White can afford few losses, otherwise the king will slip through a gap in the cordon. A defender roaming behind the lines can be dangerous and should be contained if possible.

Later, when the cordon is tighter, exchanges may be tolerated but generally the more defenders there are, the harder it is for the king to move about. White should make all his men work: an attempt to storm the centre with a few men is easily repulsed.

Figure 2
The escort capture

Figure 3
Capturing the king

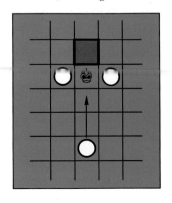

Figure 4 A draw

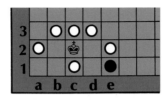

Figure 5 Final position

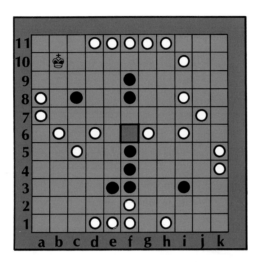

*Figure 7
A variant using a larger
board*

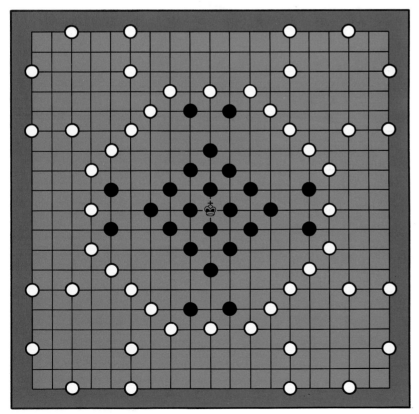

Black should switch his king from one part of the board to another in order to throw White off balance. If the king can get near the edge, a draw can result. In figure 4, White cannot stop this; e.g. e2–d2, Kc2–b2; c1–b1; Kb2–c2, etc.

The following is a short game between beginners. (Between experienced players games last much longer.) White starts.

```
 1  a4–d4, e6–e3;
 2  a5–c5, f7–c7;
 3  a7–b7, c7–c8;
 4  l7–c7x, d6–c6x;
 5  b7–c7x, Kf6–f7;
 6  k6–k7, Kf7–j7;
 7  l8–j8, j6–j3;
 8  l6–j6, Kj7–g7 (the king was
     threatened);
 9  f10–j10, g6–c6x;
10  g1–g6x, Kg7–e7;
11  d4–d6x (a bad mistake: d4–d7 was
     necessary), Ke7–b7;
12  a6–a7, Kb7–b10 wins.
```

The final position is shown in figure 5.

RELATED GAMES

A smaller board with a similar deployment was used in Lapland (figure 6). Another version of Hnefatafl was played on the intersections of an 18 × 18 board though the balance of the forces was preserved (figure 7). Both of these variants are well worth trying.

Figure 6 A variant using a smaller board

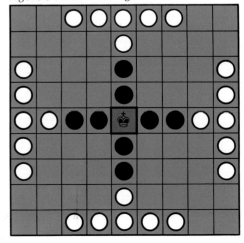

MANCALA

Mancala is not a game but a family of games of ancient ancestry. In one or other of its uncounted versions it is played throughout Africa, in parts of Asia, the Caribbean and elsewhere, varying from country to country, region to region and even village to village. Mancalas are games of pure skill for two players.

EQUIPMENT

The Mancalas require that pebbles or similar small objects such as shells, seeds, beads, beans or buttons are distributed in a series of holes. The players take it in turns to redistribute the stones according to the rules of the game being played, usually with the object of capturing the majority of them.

Mancala boards vary from elaborate, hand-carved affairs, usually in wood, down to a small cleared area of earth or sand in which holes have been scooped by hand. An adequate substitute is a strip of card on which holes are represented by circles.

Wari

This version of Mancala is popular in West Africa and boards are freely available in games shops. The board has two rows of six holes or cups and a reservoir or store at either end. The board is placed lengthways between the players and initially four stones are placed in every cup; the stores are reserved for captured men. The line of six holes nearest the player belong to him and the store to his right is for the stones he captures.

Either side starts. The first player lifts all four stones from any one of the six cups on his side of the board and sows them anticlockwise, one at a time, in successive cups, continuing round his adversary's side of the board if necessary; the store is ignored. Figure 1 depicts a Wari board on which White with his first play has just sown the contents of one of his cups. It is Black's turn.

Play alternates. A player on his turn

must empty one cup on his side of the board and sow it in like manner. When a player drops the last stone from the cup he is distributing into a hole on his *opponent's side* of the board that has exactly *two* or *three* stones in it, including the one sown, he picks them up and puts them in his store. These are his prisoners. If the preceding cup likewise has either two or three stones in it, then these too are prisoners, and so on until a cup is reached which has less than two or more than three stones, when the player's turn ends.

If a player sows from a cup that has 12 or more stones in it, then when he circuits the board and reaches the cup again he leaves it empty, dropping his next stone in the cup immediately beyond it.

You must leave your opponent with a play. If, at the end of your turn, there is no stone on your opponent's side of the board so that he is unable to move, he lifts all the stones remaining on your side and adds them to his store, thus ending the game. The game also ends when no more meaningful plays are possible. The players pick up their remaining stones and add them to their respective stores. The player with most stones is the winner.

Solitaire Wari

Put four stones in each of the cups plus four in one store. The second store is not used.

Pick up the stones from any hole and sow anticlockwise in the usual way except that a stone is also dropped in the store when passed during the circuit. If the last stone of a sowing is dropped in an occupied cup, the contents of the cup are then picked up and sown. If the last stone falls in the store, the contents of any cup may be picked and sown. The object is to get all the stones in the store. If the last stone of a sowing falls in an empty cup, the solitaire has failed.

An easier version allows the sowing to take place in either direction.

Figure 1
*Wari board after a first play
by White*

Mweso

There are many four-row Mancalas, one popular variant having a total of 112 (4 × 28) cups. Mweso is a four-row Mancala indigenous to East Africa and although using a small board is a difficult game to master.

There are four rows of eight cups, comprising two closed circuits, each player using only the circuit (two rows)

nearest to him. Each player starts with 32 stones. The first player distributes these in his cups as he pleases. It is advisable to leave one cup of each pair empty, as will be seen. A typical starting array might be:

    Row 1:   0 2 0 0 0 0 1 0
    Row 2: 1 4 0 3 3 0 0 0   0

The second player now has an equal freedom and distributes his stones. Captured stones are re-entered in the captor's circuit (hence the absence of stores) and the aim is either to win all the opponent's stones or to immobilize them. Stones are sown in the usual way but you may never sow from a cup that has only one stone left. Thus if all your stones are singletons you are immobilized.

If the last stone of a play is dropped in a cup that has one or more stones in it, the contents are emptied and are also sown,

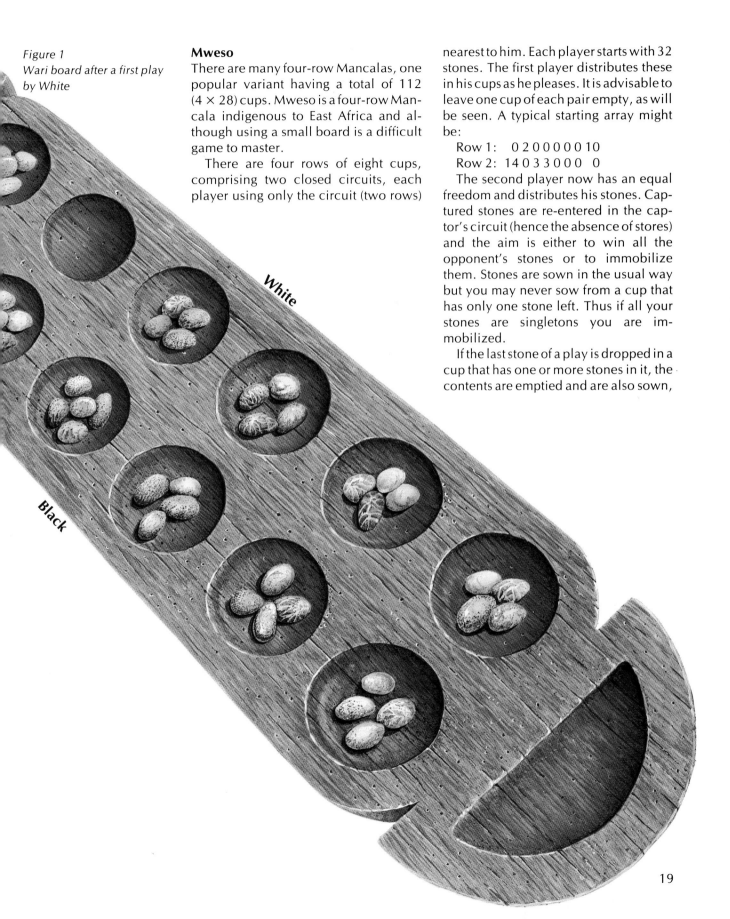

White

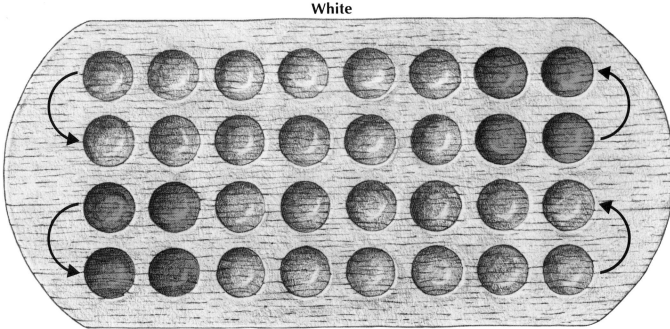

Black

and so on, until the last stone of a move is dropped into an empty cup, when the turn ends.

Movement is normally anticlockwise. The four holes on each player's left are, however, 'privilege' cups and have a dual significance. If a player sows the stones from one of these holes, he has the option of sowing them clockwise if, and only if, a capture is thereby made. If all the stones in the opponent's privilege cups are captured in a single turn of play, the game is won. The board is shown in figure 2.

The method of capture is quite different to that of Wari. In Mweso, stones can only be taken when they are in 'opposition'. Opposition is defined as the situation where the player has an occupied cup on his near row and both the opponent's cups on the same file (column of four) are also occupied. The opponent's stones are captured if the player drops his last stone into his occupied cup. It is irrelevant whether or not the player's inner cup is occupied. Thus in figure 3 if Black's last stone of a sowing is dropped into his occupied cup, then he captures the opponent's seven stones. These he now lifts and distributes in his own circuit in the usual manner,

starting in the cup immediately after the cup he vacated to sow the stones that resulted in the capture. It should now be clear why, when dressing the board, players prefer an arrangement that leaves one cup of each pair vacant: there is no 'oppositon', so all the stones are safe.

Mweso is also played with an initial dressing of four stones in each of the inner cups.

Gabata

Gabata is a three-row Mancala endemic to north-east Africa. The board comprises 18 cups, each player owning the row nearest to him and also the right half of the middle row. There is a store at either end. The board is dressed with three stones in every cup.

The first player picks up the contents of any of his cups and sows them in the sequence shown in figure 4. If the last stone of a sowing falls into an occupied cup, then the contents of that cup are scooped up and the sowing continues. If the last stone of a sowing is dropped into an unoccupied cup, the turn ends unless the cup is one of the column of three at the extreme left of the player, or a cup in the two columns (six cups) at the extreme

Figure 2
Mweso board showing direction of play and privilege cups

Figure 3
Mweso: White's stones are vulnerable

White

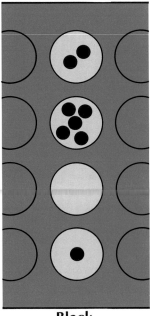

Black

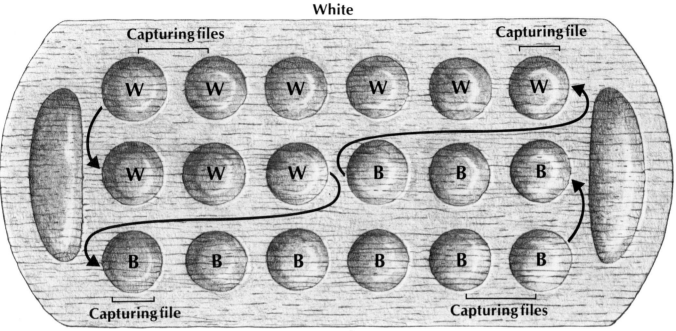

White

Capturing files

Capturing file

Capturing file

Capturing files

Black

Figure 4
Gabata board showing
direction of play

right, when any stones in the opponent's cup(s) in the same column are captured. Captured stones are transferred to the player's store, but the stone that made the capture is picked up and dropped into the next cup, which leaves three possibilities:

1 If the cup is occupied, sowing continues;

2 If the cup is unoccupied and is on the player's side of the board, then captures are made in the opponent's cup(s) in the same column, as previously;

3 If the cup is unoccupied but there are no stones to capture or the cup is in the opponent's half, then the turn ends.

Play continues until one player's side is empty. The second player then adds any remaining stones on his side to his store. This ends the round.

Now the player with the majority of stones dresses his board as before, putting the surplus into his store, while the second player fills his board, starting with the leftmost cup and putting three stones in each hole as far as he is able, and putting the odd stone(s), if any, in the final hole; he is likely to start the next round with several empty cups. The winner is the player who finally wins all his opponent's stones.

STRATEGY

All the Mancalas are games of calculation. In the early stages the possibilities are astronomical but as the game progresses the alternatives are reduced until a stage is reached where it is possible to foresee the outcome of any play.

In Wari, it is customary to build up strength in one's right-hand cups before assaulting the opponent's position. Aim to get several, if not all, the opponent's cups under attack.

Any cup which, if emptied, would result in the last stone being sown on the player's side of the board (or in other than the end columns in Gabata, for example) is inefficient since it poses no threat. Try to create and maintain these cups in your opponent's board and eliminate them in your own.

A cup with two stones in it in Wari is vulnerable. There are three methods of defence: empty the cup, empty a cup that will result in a stone being added to the threatened cup or play so as to add to an opponent's cup that is threatening yours, thereby creating an overshoot. An empty cup is also vulnerable. Drop a stone in on one sowing and harvest the next.

21

BACKGAMMON

Backgammon is a fast-moving game of skill and chance for two players. Its ancestry can be traced back to early Mediterranean civilization but the doubling die, responsible for Backgammon's popularity as a gambling game, was only introduced in modern times. The game is much played by socialites and the international circuit attracts a professional elite. This does not diminish its standing as a first-class family entertainment played for fun rather than money.

PLAY

Play is on a Backgammon board (figure 1), often in the form of a hinged box. The board is marked with 24 saw-tooth 'points' in two alternating colours (the points are numbered in the figure for ease of reference) and is divided into twin 'tables', an inner and outer, by a central partition called the bar. The inner, or home, table is traditionally closest to the light source. The board is placed lengthways between the players, who are referred to for convenience as Black and White.

Each side has 15 tablemen (or simply, men) similar to draughtsmen, in contrasting colours. Dice, and if desired a doubling die, are also necessary. The men move from point to point according to dice rolls and in opposite directions, those of one side moving clockwise and those of the other moving anticlockwise. The object is to be the first to bear off (remove) all of one's men from the board. The starting position is curious: only two of the 15 men occupy the initial point on each side, the remainder being distributed in three groups round the board (figure 2).

Play begins with each player rolling a die into the inner table. The player throwing the higher number starts (if equal they roll again) and moves a man or men of his choice the total shown on both dice. For example, White throws a 4 and Black throws a 2. White starts and

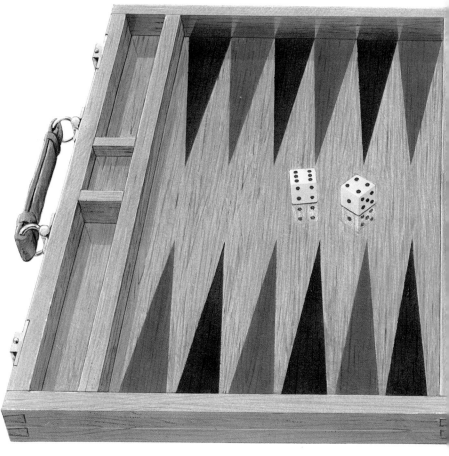

Figure 1
The board

Figure 2
The starting position

may either move one man four points and another man two points or a single man six points. Counting starts at the point next to that on which the man to be moved stands. If White decided to move a man from B12 a count of six in the example quoted, he would play it to W7.

A man may be moved to any vacant point, to a friendly point regardless of the number of men occupying it, or to a point occupied by one man, but never more, of the enemy.

Where a man is moved the total of two dice, it touches down at the intermediate point. Thus a throw of 5:3 could not be used to move a man eight points unless either the third or fifth points were available.

A point with only one man on it is known as a blot. If an opposing man lands there, even on the intermediate stage of a combined move, the blot is hit and the man is moved to the bar. A player with one or more men on the bar must, before making any other moves, bring his man or men back into play. Entry is through the opponent's inner table (the first point, corresponding to a roll of 1 on the die, is B1 for White and W1 for Black). If he cannot enter a man, because

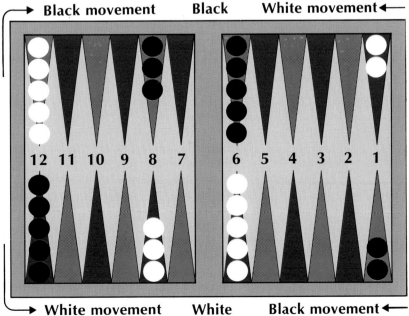

Black movement → **Black** **White movement** ←

12 11 10 9 8 7 6 5 4 3 2 1

White movement → **White** **Black movement** ←

the points indicated by the dice are occupied by two or more of the opponent's men, he loses his turn.

Consider figure 3. If White here rolls 5:4, he can move the man from B2 to B11 hitting the blot on B6 on the way. The black man is put on the bar and if Black is now unfortunate enough to roll 6:5 he cannot play as both these points (W6 and W5) are controlled by White.

After the first roll, players throw two dice alternately into the inner table and move accordingly. A player cannot decline to move. If like numbers are rolled – e.g. 3:3 – this is called a doublet and the player moves *four* times the number in any legal combination of moves (3,3,3,3; 3,3,6; 3,9; 6,6; 12).

A player may not bear off until all his men are in his inner table. If, during the bearing off, one of his men is sent to the bar, he cannot bear off any more men until the man has been re-entered and brought round the board into his inner table again. A man is borne off by taking it at least one point past the first point (W1 for White, B1 for Black). A man that is borne off is not used again.

Bearing off is optional: a player may move a man within his inner table instead of bearing off if he wishes. He must however always make *maximum* use of a roll. For example, if, during bearing off, a player had men on the 6, 5 and 4 points and he rolled a 6, he must use it to bear off a man from the 6 point. If he had no man on the 6 point, then he must bear off a man from the 5 point, and so on. If, at any stage of the game, a player can make use of one but not both of the dice rolls, he must play the higher number.

Figure 4 shows a not unusual situation. Black is bearing off and has already taken 10 men off the board. White, who cannot yet start bearing off because all his men are not in his inner table, has left behind a man in Black's home table and is here rewarded with a throw of 5:2. He hits the blot on B3 and continues to B8. Now Black cannot re-enter his man because all the points in White's inner table are closed to him. (Where six consecutive points are controlled by one side it is known as a prime – a prime obviously cannot be passed.) There is therefore no point in Black rolling. White will continue to roll and bring all his men into his inner table and then start bearing off, if possible leaving his prime intact until he has three men off. So a position that looked hopeless for White has turned round. White could easily win.

Scoring

Scoring is uncomplicated. A player who bears off all his men before his opponent has borne off any, and while he still has one or more men in his inner table or on the bar, scores a *backgammon*, or triple game. If the opponent has no men on the bar or in his inner table but has not borne off any men, the player scores a *gammon*, or double game. If the opponent has borne off one or more men, the player scores a single game. Whoever wins the game in figure 4 will therefore score a single game.

The doubling die may be used if desired. The die is six-sided and is numbered 2, 4, 8, 16, 32, 64. To start the game the die is placed beside the board

Figure 3

Black

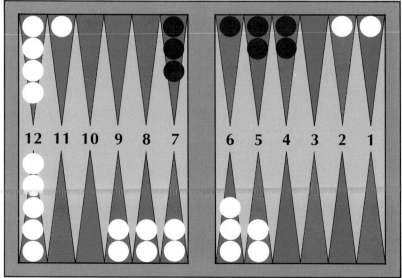

White

with the 64 uppermost. At any time in the game either player may pick up the die, turn it 2 uppermost, and place it in front of his opponent. This indicates that the stakes are doubled. The opponent can decline to accept the die, in which case the game ends and the opponent pays the single stake. If the die is accepted, the second player retains the right to redouble at any later stage by placing the die 4 uppermost in front of the first player. The right to double passes back and forth like this. It is possible to lose a triple game (backgammon) with the doubling die at 64 – 192 times the original stake!

Chouette

Backgammon can be adapted for three or more players in a version known as Chouette. Each player rolls a die in turn and the one throwing the highest number plays alone against the next highest, who has the rest of the players advising him. At the end of a game, the solo player pays or is paid by each of the others. If the solo player wins he continues solo, and the next player in turn is his opponent; if he loses he is replaced by the winner.

STRATEGY

Fortunes can change rapidly in Backgammon and strategy is a lot deeper than may appear. The strategy of both sides is likely to be dictated by the early dice rolls but since the situation can change dramatically at almost any time, you should be ready to alter your strategy.

The simplest approach is the running game when you race to get your men into your home table ready for bearing off as soon as possible. You try to avoid leaving blots but otherwise give little heed to what your opponent is doing. A running game would recommend itself if, for example, you started off with a roll of 6:6, particularly if your opponent threw low; the theory is that you have a useful lead and the odds are on you keeping it.

A deeper strategy is involved in the back game, which might suggest itself if

you had a succession of bad rolls. In this, you hold back men in the opponent's home table, typically the two 'runners' (the men that start there) together with other men brought in from the bar, with the intention of punishing the opponent's men as they arrive in the home table for bearing off. The ideal is to hold two points in the table, preferably the first and third. The position in figure 4 could have arisen from a back game.

The third major strategy is the blocking game. In this, a block – preferably a prime – is set up with the object of shutting one or more of the opponent's men behind it. In practice, the distinctions between the different types of game are likely to be blurred.

It is most important to use your men efficiently. This is done by making points where possible (to make a point is to gain control of it) since you not only secure your own men but restrict your opponent's choices. However, you should not overload a point as this is uneconomical – the spare men are needed to make points elsewhere.

Certain points are particularly valuable; the bar point (B7, W7) and the 5 point (B5, W5). Do not occupy any of the

Figure 4

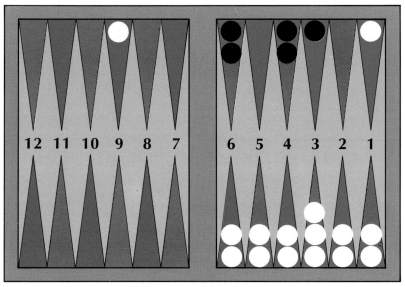

Black

White

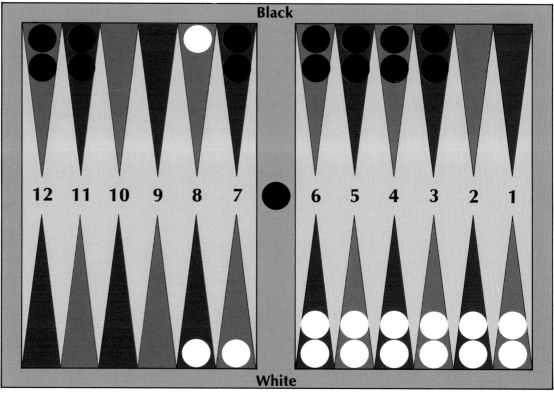

Figure 5

first three points in your home table until late in the game unless by so doing you form a prime. Do not be afraid to leave blots if re-entry is not likely to be a problem, for example, if your opponent has only two points in his inner table.

The good player is alert to the chances of any particular dice combination coming up. You can be too: there are only 36 possibilities. Briefly, any specific double has only one chance in 36 of turning up, but any other combination of two dice (e.g. 4:2) has one chance in 18, whereas one specific number (e.g. 5) has nearly one chance in three. A blot is most vulnerable when it is six points from an opposing man – one chance in two of being hit: slightly less vulnerable if closer, but much less if farther away.

It is an advantage to start first and the opening possibilities for each side have been analysed extensively. The best opening plays from White's viewpoint are given below; there are alternatives in one or two instances. (The equivalent moves are equally recommended for Black.) No doublets are possible.

6:5	B1-B12	
6:4	B1-B11	
6:3	B1-B7	B12-W10
6:2	B1-B7	B12-W11
6:1	B12-W7	W8-W7
5:4	B12-W8	B12-W9
5:3	B12-W8	B12-W10
5:2	B12-W8	B12-W11
5:1	B12-W8	W6-W5
4:3	B12-W9	B12-W10
4:2	W8-W4	W6-W4
4:1	W12-W9	B1-B2
3:2	B12-W10	B12-W11
3:1	W8-W5	W6-W5
2:1	B12-W11	B1-B2

In a middle-game situation it is often impossible to rule on a 'best move' since much will depend on style (do you gamble or play safe?), the doubling die, state of the match, and so on. In the ending, however, it is usually possible to be positive. Even simple-looking positions can mask subtleties. Look at figure 5 and notice that the men of both sides are efficiently employed, mostly in groups, two per point. White, who must surely win, here rolls 2:1. At first glance it seems not to matter how the moves are apportioned providing the stragglers are brought up, since Black with a man on the bar will not be able to move until White breaks the prime. Not so: B8-B10 and W8-W7 are necessary. White has now increased his chances of passing the Black block with his back runner but, more important, if he had instead moved one or both men on W7 and W8 the total

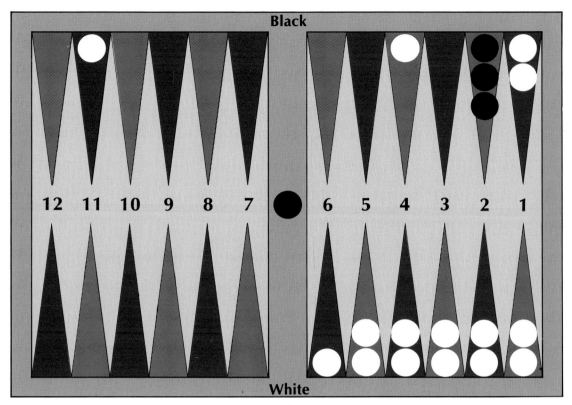

12 11 10 9 8 7   6 5 4 3 2 1

White

Figure 6

of the dice roll, then on his next roll a 4:4 would compel him to break the prime. If Black were then able to enter his man from the bar, the White straggler B8 would likely be doomed and it is Black who would be winning.

A decision is called for in the ending in figure 6 where White rolls 4:4. The position is not as hopeless as it looks even though Black has only three men to bear off. White has two aims: to maximize the chances of a hit and to minimize the chances of a backgammon. The temptation to play B11-W6 to make a prime, or B1-B9 × 2 (remember, White plays the 4 *four* times), must be resisted. Play B1-B9, B4-B8 and B11-W10. This leaves a blot on B1 but if Black hits it and takes a man off (unless it was 1:1, Black would be compelled to bear off a man from the 2 point) White, on the bar, would be odds on to hit one of the two black men. More than most games, Backgammon is not lost until it is won.

RELATED GAMES

Backgammon has quite a family of relations, many from the Mediterranean lands. *Plakato* is a Greek game in which all 15 men start on the opponent's first point. The bar is not used; instead, when

a blot is hit the man is imprisoned ('pinned') until the opponent moves off. Other rules are unchanged.

Gioul is a wicked version in which chance can play a big role. The board is dressed as in Plakato and the only other difference is in the application of doublets. In Gioul, a player is entitled to the doublet thrown and all doublets above it; thus a throw of 1:1 earns the thrower a massive six doublets, a total of 84 moves. However, if at any stage the player is unable to use a move then the opponent takes over until he is unable to move, and so on.

The Turkish *Moultezim* reverses the board layout so that Black's home board is White's outer board and vice versa. All men start on the opponent's 12 point and move the full 24 points anticlockwise. A player must get one man into his inner or outer table before he can move the others. Control of a point is exercised by a single man (again, the bar is not used) but a player may not command more than four points in his own outer table.

In *Dutch Backgammon*, all men start on the bar and enter in the usual way but no man may be moved twice until all men have been entered. A player cannot hit a blot until he has advanced a man to his home table.

NINE MEN'S MORRIS

This game of alignment for two players has a history that is probably as long as any board game. The name 'morris' is a corruption of merels from the Latin for counter. Merels has been played in many forms over at least 3000 years and was particularly popular in the Middle Ages. The version given here is perhaps the best known.

PLAY

The board (figure 1) is square and is marked with a pattern of squares joined by four lines at right angles to them such that every side is bisected, each of the 16 lines has three points (intersections) and each point is common to two lines. The points are lettered (omitting I and O) in the figure for reference.

The two sides each have nine men in contrasting colours or designs. Play starts with the board empty and each player in turn puts one of his men on any vacant point. The object is to form a mill – three men in a row along any line. When a mill is made, the player pounds (removes from the board) one of his opponent's men. However, he may not remove a man from a mill unless no other man is available.

When both sides have entered all their men, the second phase of the game begins. Now each player in turn moves one of his men along a line to an adjacent empty point. The object is still to form mills. A player can break his own mill and move back to re-form it on the following play. When a player is reduced to three men he may move anywhere on the board – he is not confined to points adjacent to his remaining men. A player loses when he has only two men left or is unable to move on his turn.

STRATEGY

The advantage of the first move is considerable. The initiative should not be ceded lightly, even to gain a mill. However, the direct approach can recoil.

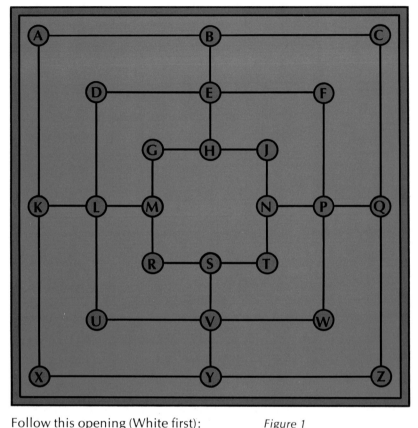

Follow this opening (White first):

1 A, K;
2 B, C;
3 E, H;
4 F, D;
5 P, W;
6 Q, N.

The initiative passes to Black who has double threats at J, L and U: see figure 2.

Figure 1
The board

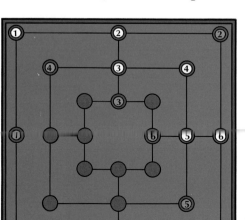

Figure 2
Position after Black's 6th play

There are only four distinct opening moves, bearing in mind the symmetry of the board: a corner play at A or D or a centre play at K or L. Superficially, L looks the most attractive since it, and its corresponding points E, P and V, can be extended in any of four directions.

The critical stage in any game is where one player is reduced to four men. The other player must time his next mill carefully since the freedom to move at will confers much power – mills are easily made and remade and vital points can be blocked. At least a four-man advantage is necessary to force a win. First, the stronger side should group his men together, at the same time keeping the weaker force split. Then multiple threats must be set up and finally one of the remaining four men captured. The following game exemplifies these strategies.

1 A, G;
2 X, K;
3 Z, M (yielding the first mill, but if Black at Y, White at C);
4 Y(xM), M (Black re-enters M to force a mill – a common tactic);
5 C, L(xC);
6 R, D;
7 U, E (Black's men are well concentrated but they need space to move for the second phase);
8 S (a sacrifice: White does not want his men split further), F(xS);
9 S, V (Now the movement phase starts);
10 Z-Q, E-B;
11 Q-Z(xB), G-H;
12 Z-Q, H-E(xQ);
13 A-B, F-P;
14 S-T (White is helpless). P-F(xU);
15 T-N, F-P;
16 B-C, L-U (opening four ways to a mill instead of taking a mill at once);
17 C-Q, D-L(xQ);
18 N-T, L-D;
19 Y-Z (White keeps his men on two lines in the hope that when Black captures he can make a mill at once, but . . . P-W(xT) (if White forms a mill Black will next play into L, so . . .);
20 R-L, W-P.

Black wins: the double threat is fatal. The end position is in figure 3.

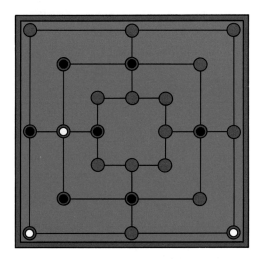

Figure 3 *End position*

RELATED GAMES

Three Men's Morris uses a nine-point board (figure 4) and is a trivial game if played without restriction, as the first player has only to enter the centre point to win. Twelve Men's Morris uses the same board as Nine Men's Morris with the addition of diagonals (figure 5) and is played to the same rules.

These and related games of alignment are known under many names and board design sometimes varies.

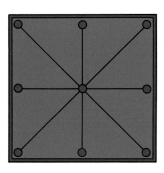

Figure 4
Three Men's Morris board

Figure 5
Twelve Men's Morris board

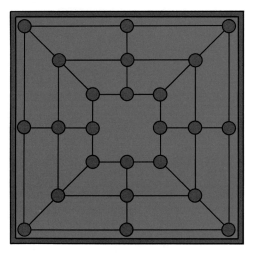

DRAUGHTS

Extravagant claims have been made for the ancestry of the two-player game of Draughts (or Checkers as it is known in North America) but it is now well established that the game, which borrows freely from Alquerque and Chess, was invented in Europe, probably France, during the twelfth century. As Draughts spread, the rules were frequently changed with the result that today many countries practise their own versions of the game which are sometimes further confused by regional variations.

No attempt has ever been made to bring these various forms together into a single game with unified rules in the way that Chess has been standardized. It would not now profit to do so since the three most widely played games, Anglo-American, Continental (also called French or Polish) and Turkish (also known as Greek) Draughts are manifestly different, each with its own developed strategy, literature and traditions. These three games are described here.

ANGLO-AMERICAN DRAUGHTS

The game is played on an 8 × 8 board chequered alternately light and dark. Only the dark squares are used. The board is placed between the players so that there is a dark square in the left-hand corner nearest each player, with the 'double corner' at the right. That is practice: for clarity of illustration, the board is turned and play is shown on the light squares. This in no way alters the game.

Each side has 12 draughtsmen: circular men of wood or plastic, about one centimetre thick and of uniform design. The men of one side are light-coloured, the other dark. The men are set up initially on the first three rows of each player, as shown in figure 1. The notation commonly used to indicate squares and moves is given in figure 2.

Figure 1
The starting position

Figure 2
Notation

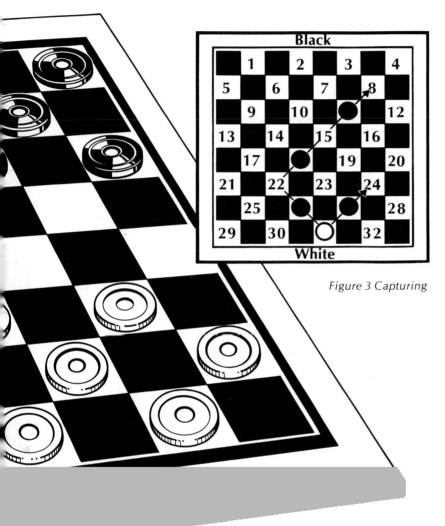

Figure 3 Capturing

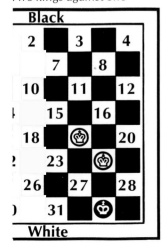

Figure 4
Two kings against one

Black starts and play alternates, one move per turn. All men move in the same way – one square diagonally forward; each side therefore has a choice of seven moves on the first play.

Men are captured by the short leap, diagonally forward over an adjacent enemy man to an empty square immediately beyond. The captured man is removed from the board. More than one capture can be made in a turn if the situation permits. In figure 3 the white man on 31 can leap to 22, taking the black man on 26, then to 15, capturing 18, and finally to 8, capturing 11. This counts as one move.

Capturing is compulsory but the player can choose between alternative captures. For example, in figure 3 White

could play 31–24, capturing 27, instead of taking the multiple capture. However, if after making a capture a further capture is possible, then this must be made. Thus once having played 31–22 (taking 26) in figure 3, White must continue to capture until he reaches 8.

A man attaining the end rank (the opponent's first row) is promoted to king. Thus Black promotes on any of the squares 29–32 and White similarly on squares 1–4. A king moves and captures in the same way as an ordinary man except that it can go backwards as well as forwards. When a man becomes a king another draughtsman of the same colour is put on top of it to indicate its new status. Promotion ends the move, so a man that promotes with a capture cannot continue with a further capture as a king on that turn.

Huffing, in which a player who fails to make a capture when able to do so has the offending man removed as a penalty, is no longer practised. The opponent can require the move to stand or to be withdrawn and the capture made.

The object of the game is to take all the opponent's men or, much harder to achieve, to deprive the opponent of a legal move by blocking the position. Draws are frequent between equally matched players and a game can be abandoned at any time if both players agree the result.

It often happens that a game is reduced to two kings against one. This is always a win for the stronger force. The lone king is easily driven to the temporary sanctuary of the double corner, when it can be forced out and captured. It is essential to understand this basic manoeuvre. In figure 4, Black plays first:

1	32–28	24–27
2	28–32	19–23
3	32–28	27–32
4	28–24	32–28
5	24–20	23–18
6	20–16	18–15
7	16–20	15–11

and the black man falls.

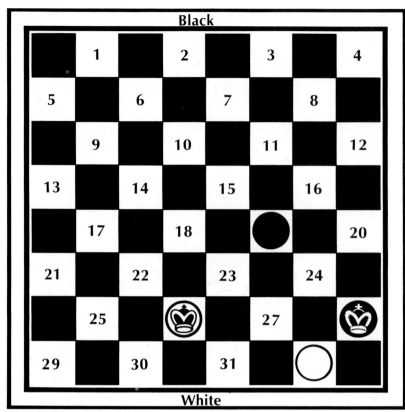

Black

White

A win by blocking starts from figure 5. White plays 32–27 and there follows 28–32 (otherwise Black must surrender a man, allowing the position in figure 4 to be quickly reached), 27–24, 19–28 (Black has no option), 26–23, when the black king is forced to vacate the double corner with 32–27 and White plays 23–32, leaving the remaining black man without a move.

There are a number of standard end-game positions and a half-hundred classified openings. Traps in the openings are not uncommon. Here is a classic. Black starts, remember.

1	11–15	24–20
2	8–11	28–24
3	9–13	23–19
4	4–8 (a blunder: see figure 6)	
		20–16
5	11–20	22–17
6	13–22	25–4

and White will win.

STRATEGY

Draughts, played properly, is a game of position, not the series of tactical moves favoured by the beginner. General guidelines, like playing towards the centre rather than the sides, directing your attack at the double corner, forcing

Figure 5
White wins by blocking

Figure 6
White wins

a man through to promotion, not advancing too many men to start with and not allowing your forces to be scattered and uncoordinated, are sound as far as they go but must be rejected where they conflict with the requirements of the position.

It is usually safe to bring two of your back-line men forward and it is certainly a mistake to try to keep the row intact to prevent your opponent promoting.

The sacrifice is an attractive device where used for positional ends, but more common is the temporary sacrifice in which the material given up is forcibly recovered with profit.

CONTINENTAL DRAUGHTS

The game is played on a 10 × 10 board chequered alternately light and dark. The squares of one colour only are used and the board is placed between the

Black

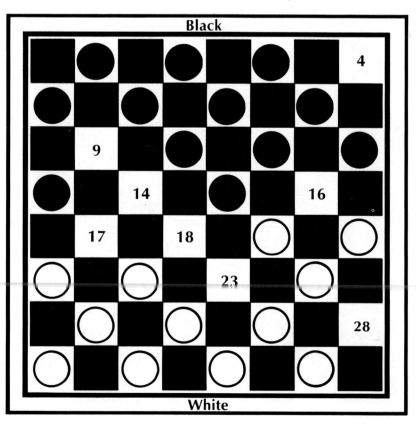

White

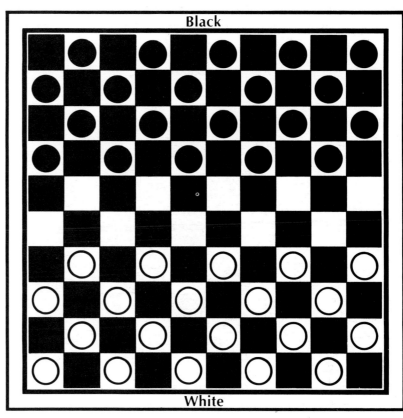

Figure 7
The starting position

Figure 8
Queen captures

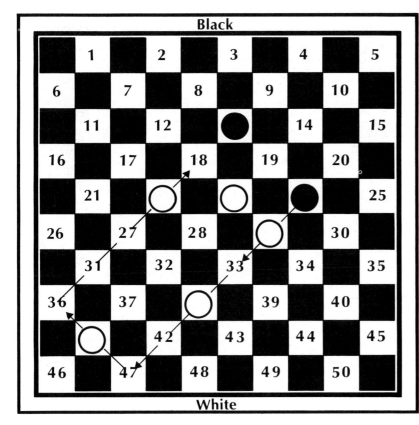

players with the double corner at the right. Each side has 20 men in contrasting colours, usually black and white. The men are deployed initially in the four ranks nearest to each player (figure 7).

The men move one square diagonally forward. Capturing is compulsory and is made in the same manner as in Anglo-American draughts but can be either forwards or backwards or a combination of both in the case of a multiple capture. Where alternative captures are possible, that which takes the greatest number of men must be played. Captured men are not removed until the move is complete, but a man once jumped cannot be jumped a second time in the course of a multiple capture.

Promotion to queen takes place on the end rank, but if a man reaches it in the course of a jump and a further capture can be made, it must continue the move and is not promoted on that turn.

A queen moves diagonally over any number of vacant squares and captures by leaping over an opposing man to any vacant square beyond. A queen may make multiple captures but cannot leap over more than one man at a time or over a man already captured. Figure 8 shows a sequence of queen captures. The man 23 cannot be taken because 29 has not been removed. The black queen will now fall to the man on 23.

A game is won by taking all the opponent's pieces. The movement of the queen makes it hard to catch: if one player is left with a bare queen and the other player has three pieces of which at least one is a queen, then unless the stronger side can force a win quickly the game is drawn.

STRATEGY

The axioms of the Anglo-American game are generally valid for Continental draughts but the bigger board, the power of the queen and the backward capture make for greater complexity and, in the views of many, the better game. Continental draughts is rich in stratagems which must be mastered by the aspiring player. One of these, which exposes the vulnerability of an unsupported row, is the spectacular Royal Coup. It can appear in many forms, one of which is

Figure 9
The Royal Coup

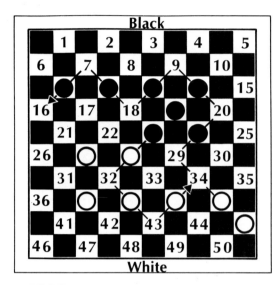

Figure 10
The starting position

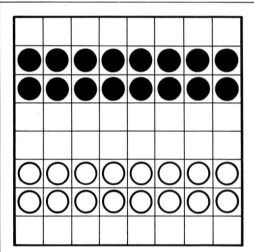

Figure 11
Movement and capture

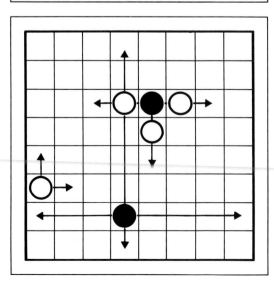

demonstrated in figure 9. White has just played 32–28. Now Black has three possible captures – 23–21, 23–41 or 23–34 – but is obliged to take the last because it is the most numerous. White then devastates Black by capturing six men with 40–16.

TURKISH DRAUGHTS

Turkish draughts uses a plain 8 × 8 board with 16 men on either side, arranged as in figure 10. All 64 squares are used in the game. Men move one square forwards or sideways to an empty square. There is no diagonal or backward movement. Captures are made by the usual short leap but in one direction of movement only. Capturing is compulsory and, as in Continental draughts, the longest captures must be taken where there is a choice. Pieces are removed as they are taken.

A man reaching the end rank is promoted to queen and thereafter moves like a rook in Chess – straight forwards, backwards or sideways over any number of vacant squares. A queen captures by leaping to any vacant square beyond its victim but cannot leap over a second man to reach it. The first player to capture or immobilize all the opponent's pieces, or reach an ending where he has a queen against a lone pawn, wins the game. Figure 11 shows examples of these plays.

STRATEGY

Opening play tends to be on the flanks. A strong column (three men) offers good chances of a breakthrough. A standard strategy is to deflect the leading defender sideways with a sacrifice, then confront the second defender, who will be obliged to leap, when your second man will recapture and advance to queen. A queen is worth about four men. In defence, a compact square of four is strong.

SURAKARTA

Surakarta is a little-known Indonesian strategy game for two with an unusual, and possibly unique, form of capture. The game is named after a city in Java.

PLAY

The board with the two sides, each of 12 men, arranged in the starting position is shown in figure 1. Sets are difficult to obtain at present but you can use a piece of card, suitably marked, and draughtsmen or counters. The object of the game is to annihilate the opposition, and, if this is not possible, then to have more men on the board than the opponent when the game ends.

All men move alike: one point in any direction, forwards, backwards, sideways or diagonally. The circles may not be used for moves. To capture, a man must go round at least one circle, entering and leaving by a tangential line. To do so, the man may travel over any number of vacant points both before and after circling, but no jumping is allowed. Capturing is by replacement and is optional; captured men are removed from play.

Figure 2 gives an end position. White, to play, can capture the man on c2 in any of four ways:

1. a4-circle c6-c2
2. b1-circle a2-c2
3. f4-circle d6-d1-circle f3-a3-circle c1-c2
4. b6-circle a5-f5-circle e6-e1-circle f2-c2

After the capture, Black will be compelled to move to e6, e5 or f5 with his remaining man, when White will again capture, this time having two ways of doing it.

If a position is reached where neither side can make headway, the game is terminated by agreement. Each player scores the number of counters he has left on the board. A match is best played to a fixed number of games or to an agreed total, the player with the higher score winning.

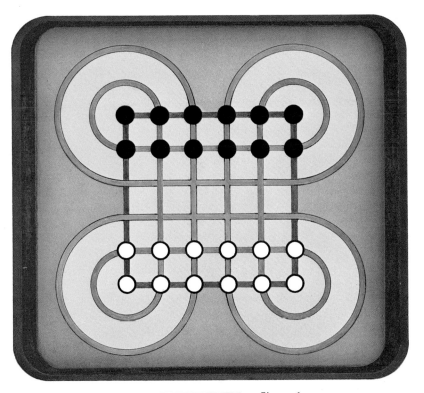

Figure 1
The starting position

STRATEGY

There are two capturing circuits, an inner and an outer. These are shown respectively in red and green in figure 3. Every point of the board is on one or the other or both, except the four corner points.

The key points are those that give access to both circuits. There are eight of these: b3, b4, c2, c5, d2, d5, e3, e4. Notice that it is not possible to switch from one circuit to another in the course of a move.

All attacks are mutual: if man A threatens man B, then man B also threatens man A.

The best strategy is to try and gain control of one or both circuits by occupying key points with your men supporting one another. Do not capture if this means surrendering a circuit.

Men in the corners must be brought out quickly—if the opponent controls the inner circuit, corner men cannot be moved without loss, as demonstrated in figure 2.

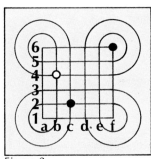

Figure 2
An end position

Figure 3
Capturing circuits

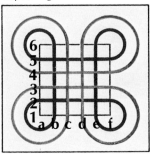

FANORONA

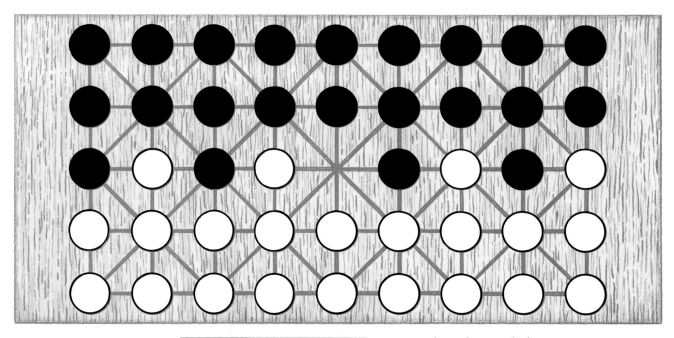

Figure 1
The starting position

Figure 2 Notation

This Malagasy two-player strategy game was once part of court ritual and is still popular in Madagascar today. It was certainly developed from Alquerque (the board is two Alquerque boards joined down the middle). An extraordinary feature of Fanorona is the *vela partie* — the 'debt' game after victory.

PLAY

The board dressed for play is shown in figure 1. Each side has 22 men. The central point is vacant.

The object is to take all the opponent's men or to prevent him from moving on his turn. A man moves one point along a line of the board in any direction.

There are two methods of capture: by approach or by withdrawal. In capture by approach, a man is moved one point next to an enemy man *on the line of movement*. The captured man is removed from the board. Capture by with-

drawal is made by moving a man one step back from an adjacent enemy man; again, the man moved, the empty point it moves to, and the man captured must be on the same line.

All men in sequence on a line behind a captured man are also captured, whether by approach or withdrawal. Capturing is compulsory but the player is free to choose between alternatives.

A series of captures may be made by the same man on a turn, as in Draughts, with this difference: at any time after the first capture, the player may decline to continue to capture. There is one restriction: a man may not return to any point it occupied in that turn, including the starting point, so that in a series of captures a man must change direction after each capture.

A game starts with one player occupying the central point — 23 in figure 2. There is a choice of four moves but of five captures because the men 22 and 24 can capture either by approach or withdrawal. The remaining three possible moves all result in two men being captured by approach. Since a man may not go back to its starting point, no further play is possible and the turn passes to the second player.

A decisive game is followed by a *vela partie*. The loser of the previous game starts and must take one man each turn for 17 consecutive moves. The winner may not take any man in this phase but must give men for his opponent 'to eat'. After the first player's seventeenth move he will have all his men on the board while the second player will have but five. Play now reverts to normal. The second player often wins! If he does, the custom is to subject the first player to an even more humiliating *vela partie*.

STRATEGY

Fanorona is a game full of snares and surprises, and to eat well (take a lot of men) early may mean starving later.

It is important to appreciate the arrangement of the board. Of the 45 points, 11 have eight connections, 8 have five, 10 have four and 16 have three. Generally, the points with the most connections are the strongest but it is often control of points in combination that is significant. Look at the remarkable end position in figure 3. Black appears to have a decisive advantage but White has only to move his man 11 backwards and forwards to 19 and Black cannot approach. Draws like this are quite common between skilled players. In general, a man ahead in the end position is not enough to win.

Here is an annotated game to clarify the play. White starts.
W1 32–33 (x14,5)
B1 15–5 (x25,35,45), 5–14 (x23).
This is known as the Vakiloha Miforitra — all the openings and the points of the board have names.
W2 22–23 (x24), 23–32 (x14).
B2 21–22 (x20). Notice here that Black could have taken four men had he wished.
W3 33–25 (x17,9), 25–24 (x26), 24–15 (x6), 15–14 (x16). With his last play, White could have opted to take 13,12,11,10.
B3 7–17 (x27)

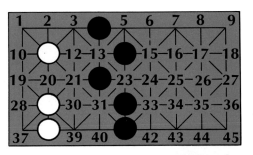

Figure 3
A drawn game

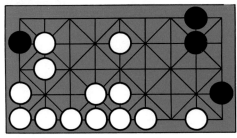

Figure 4
The position after White's 6th play

Figure 5
The end position

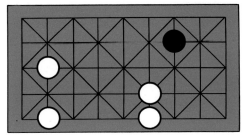

W4 29–20 (x11,2), 20–21 (x22), 21–11 (x1).
B4 18–27 (x36), 27–35 (x43), 35–36 (x34).
W5 30–21 (x12,3), 21–29 (x13).
B5 4–13. He has no capture.
W6 29–21 (x13), 21–20 (x19). The position is now as in figure 4.
B6 10–19 (x28, 37), 19–29 (x39), 29–30 (x31,32).
W7 14–15. A sacrifice to disturb the Black position. White has seen through to the end.
B7 17–16 (x15).
W8 44–35.
B8 36–27.
W9 35–43 (x27)
B9 8–17.
W10 43–33.
B10 17–25 (x33,41).
W11 11–21. The point behind W10.
B11 30–39 (x21).
W12 40–41 (x39), 41–33 (x25). White wins. Figure 5 shows the end position.

REVERSI

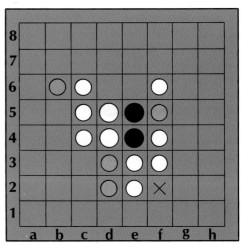

Figure 3 A multiple capture

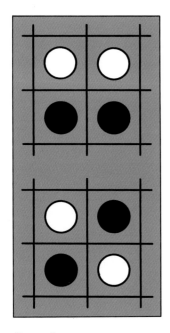

Figure 1
Dress formations

Reversi is a two-player abstract game that is at present enjoying a revival in a slightly modified form as the proprietary game Othello. It is quick to play, with simple rules yet profound strategy.

Reversi was invented in England towards the end of the last century. An early rule book claims that Reversi 'may now be fairly said to have taken its place as one of the – if not the – most popular of indoor games'.

PLAY

The board is marked with 64 squares in a regular 8 × 8 grid and is uncoloured or of a single colour. The men are discs, usually of plastic, black on one side and white on the other, and should sit comfortably within the board squares. There are 64 discs, shared between the players.

White starts and places a disc, own colour uppermost, on one of the four central squares. Black does likewise and these plays are repeated so that the four squares are filled. This is called dressing the board. Only two basic formations are possible, the parallel or the diagonal (figure 1). In Othello the board is always dressed before play in the diagonal formation, and Black then starts.

Play now alternates, each player in turn placing a disc, own colour uppermost, on a vacant square. Once a disc is placed it is never moved.

At least one disc must be captured at each turn of play. A disc is captured by trapping it between two of the opponent's discs, orthogonally or diagonally. The three discs must occupy consecutive squares. The captured disc is then turned over ('flipped') to become, for the present, the property of the player.

In any of the starting positions, the first player (i.e. the player who places the first disc after the board is dressed) will have a choice of four legal plays. Thus in Othello, Black could play at e3 or f4, in either case flipping e4; or at c5 or d6, in either case flipping d5 (figure 2). After

this play there will be four of the first player's discs on the board and one of the second player's. Nevertheless, the second player will always be able to make a capture with his first move.

Play now alternates and multiple captures quickly become possible. A multiple capture is made in the same manner as a single capture. There are two types:
1 Two or more discs may be trapped on the same line;
2 One or more discs may be trapped in two or more directions simultaneously.

An example of a multiple capture is shown in figure 3. In this position, Black to play can enter a man at f2 to capture simultaneously six white men – those on e2, e3, d4, c5, f3 and f4. Notice that the white man on f6 is not captured since it is not trapped between two black men.

Only the disc played determines the line or lines of capture. For example, when the white disc c5 in figure 3 is flipped, this does not result in the capture of the white disc d5 even though it now stands between two black discs.

If one side is unable to play because no capture is available, the other side continues to play until a legal move becomes available for the second player, when turns again alternate. The game ends when the board is full or neither player has a legal move. The winner is the player who has more discs of his colour uppermost.

Wins of 64–0 are quite common, particularly between poorly matched players. It is possible to complete a game in only nine turns. Look at figure 4; odd moves are Black's, even moves White's.

Figure 2
Possible first plays by Black

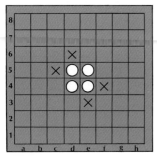

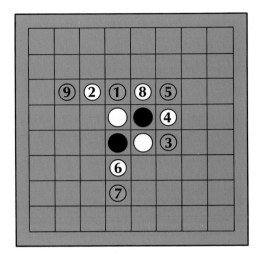

Figure 4 Black wins after nine moves

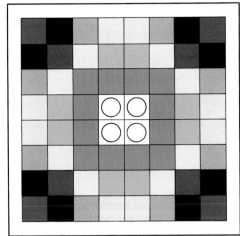

Figure 5 Relative values of the squares

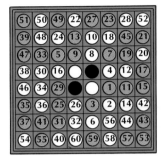

*Figure 6
Black wins 41−23*

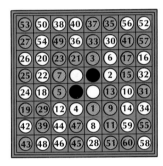

*Figure 7
Black wins 43−21*

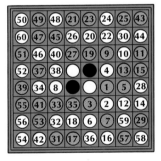

*Figure 8
White wins 53−11*

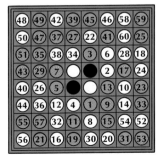

*Figure 9
White wins 33−31*

If you play the game through, remembering to flip the appropriate disc(s) at each turn, you will find that after move 9 all the discs are black and no further play is possible. This situation is known as a 'wipe out' and Black wins 64−0.

Handicapping

Badly matched players do not spoil a game: the stronger player will strive to maximize his score and not just win. The best way to handicap, since it does not interfere with the game, is to allow the weaker player to add an agreed number of points to his score. Another way is to permit him to occupy up to four corners before play starts.

STRATEGY

Reversi has only been seriously studied in recent years and there is no common view on correct strategy. Certain guidelines have however been established of which perhaps the most surprising is that it is a mistake to aim for maximum captures in the early and middle game. Rather the contrary; single captures are to be preferred since they cut down the opponent's options.

The relative values of the different squares are in dispute but it is accepted that corner squares are the most valuable since not only does a disc in the corner act as an anchor in three directions, but by definition it can never be captured — the four corners are the only really safe squares on the board.

Play moves out inevitably from the centre and the emphasis should be more on avoiding weak squares than capturing strong ones. The 12 squares surrounding the middle may be considered safe, but thereafter play becomes increasingly critical. The truly dangerous squares are those adjacent to the corners, since occupation of any of them may give the corner away.

An approximate guide to the relative values of the squares is given in figure 5. Red indicates the more desirable squares, black the less desirable, ranging from dark red (best) to dark black (worst). However, there is no consensus view and, as in most games of strategy, tactical considerations may disturb or even reverse general principles. An obvious objection to an early occupation of edge squares is that this strategy usually involves the flipping of a number of discs, which militates against the principle that one should try to minimize captures until late in the game.

However desirable the corners are, they are not the only key to success at Reversi. Discs stranded in the middle of enemy concentrations are strong since they cannot be captured and in the closing stages of a game can often be used to trap lines of enemy discs.

Examples of Play

Figures 6 to 9 show four games played in 1982 at the Othello Grand Master tournament in Japan. (Remember to flip the appropriate discs after each play.) Observe what is perhaps the distinguishing feature of the game — the repeated apparent reversals of fortune as first one side holds the majority, then the other.

39

LASKA

Laska is a modern abstract game for two with novel strategy. It was invented by Dr Emanuel Lasker, a world chess champion. The similarity to Draughts (Checkers) is illusory; it is a quite different game, although a Draughts set can be easily converted for playing Laska.

PLAY

Play is on the white squares of a 7 × 7 chequered board of which the corner squares are white. There are 11 men a side, distinguished by colour, known as soldiers. In the starting position these occupy the first three ranks of each side, as in Draughts. An elegant board can be made by omitting the unnecessary black squares and substituting circles for the white ones. Both designs, with the starting position, are illustrated in figure 1.

The moves are identical to Draughts — one square diagonally forward only. A soldier that reaches the end rank (opponent's first rank) is promoted to officer. The men have a spot on one side to denote the rank — the soldier is turned over on promotion. (If you use Draughtsmen, a dab of paint solves this.) An officer moves as a king in draughts — one square diagonally in any direction.

Capturing is also as in Draughts, by leaping over an adjacent enemy to a vacant square immediately beyond. Capturing is compulsory, including any subsequent captures by the same man, but if more than one capture is available, the player can choose between them. Promotion concludes a move: a soldier that captures on promotion cannot continue to capture as an officer on that turn.

In Laska, no men are removed from the board — all men stay in play throughout the game. A man making a capture picks up his victim beneath him to form a stack of two. Columns increase in size as further captures are made, captured men being placed beneath the pile each time. A stack is controlled by the man on top of it, known as the commander. If a stack commanded by a soldier reaches the end

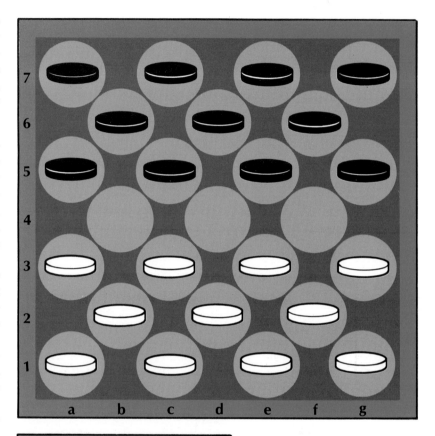

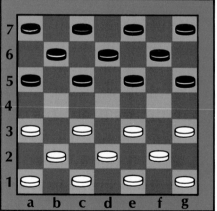

Figure 1
The two board designs and the starting position

rank, the soldier is promoted to an officer in the usual way. Officers keep their rank throughout the game.

Only the top man of a stack is captured, never the whole stack. The significance of this is shown in figure 2. The white soldier jumps the three-man column, capturing its commander, a black officer. The result is two stacks, both with white commanders. It is not

Figure 2
A capture by a white soldier

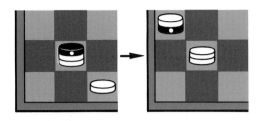

permitted to jump the same stack twice in a turn.

As play proceeds, the men are grouped into fewer and fewer stacks. The end is reached when one player cannot make a legal move, either because he is blocked or because all stacks are controlled by the other side.

Draws are impossible in Laska since there are no double corners in which a man can move back and forth, as in Draughts. If two stacks finally face each other, the side with the move loses. In theory, all men could end up in a single column but in practice stacks in excess of seven are rare.

STRATEGY

Consider the two white columns in figure 3. The left-hand stack is strong since it could be jumped four times and would still have a white commander. The right-hand stack is weak since it would only

have to be jumped once to release a powerful black force headed by an officer. White should use the strong column for attack while he should shield the weak column. In a sense – and this is a curiosity of Laska – the right-hand stack is valuable because it locks up nearly half of Black's army. A strong stack can be built feeding the opponent then removing the commander – it is tactics like this that make the game so entertaining.

A man in the corner can be lured out by a sacrifice – remember that captures are compulsory. Follow the sequence in figure 4. Notice that without the white soldier a5, Black would make a double capture.

Sometimes two columns have a running battle. Look at figure 5. White plays f2 and the stacks leap each other until the second position is reached. White has profited handsomely! You cannot jump your own men so you can only add enemy men to your columns, which is why sacrifices are such an important feature of Laska.

A final piece of advice. Keep a mobile position: the playing area is small and forced moves can mean ruin.

Figure 3
A strong and a weak stack

Figure 4
White lures a black commander out of a corner

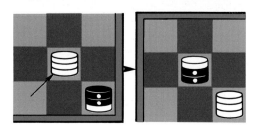

Figure 5
A running battle between stacks

RELATED GAMES

Pasta was invented by Alvin Paster and is a cross between Draughts and Laska but with its own strategy. It is a fast little game in which it is true to say that one player loses rather than the other wins.

The initial set up and moves are identical to Draughts (8 × 8 board, double corner on the right). However, as in Laska, a captured man is picked up by his captor. Men are not promoted but a stack is promoted when it is headed by two men of the same colour. The object is to be the first player to get a man on the opponent's first rank. If a column headed by a king reaches the end rank but is obliged to continue with a capture, this does not count since the move does not end on the rank.

CHESS

♟ **Pawn**　♞ **Knight**　♝ **Bishop**　♜ **Rook**　♛ **Queen**　♚ **King**

Chess, a game of skill for two players, is the world's most popular game. Nearly a hundred nations compete in the biannual Olympiads, but Chess is equally a family game, to be played for amusement – and five-year-olds are not too young to learn.

The game originated in India and is perhaps 14 centuries old, sharing a common ancestry with Shogi and Xiangqi. It was brought to Europe by the Moors but it was not until the fifteenth century that Chess as we know it today was played. It has flourished ever since, though it is only in recent times that the game has been popularized. In the last few decades it has enjoyed a remarkable expansion and is now dominated by youth – Chess is played and studied in schools and universities almost everywhere. Authority is vested in the Fédération Internationale des Echecs which pronounces on the rules, awards titles and manages international events, including the World Championship.

EQUIPMENT

Chess is played on a chessboard of 64 squares (8 × 8) coloured alternately light and dark. The board is set between the players so that each has a dark-coloured square in the near left-hand corner (figure 1).

Horizontal lines of squares on the chessboard are called *ranks*; vertical lines are called *files*; and diagonal lines, which may vary from two to eight squares in length, are called *diagonals*.

Each side has 16 men, eight pieces and eight pawns. One side has the light (white) men, and the other the dark (black) men. The players are usually referred to as White and Black.

Chessmen come in many designs but the Staunton pattern, named after a famous English player of a hundred years ago and shown in figure 2, is standard. Symbols for chessmen used in diagrams also vary, but are usually recognizable. Those used here are common.

PLAY

The starting position is shown in figure 3. Notice that the kings and queens stand on the central squares, the queens always on the squares of their own colour, and that both sides have a bishop on each colour.

Black

Figure 1 **White**
The board

Figure 3
The starting position

Black

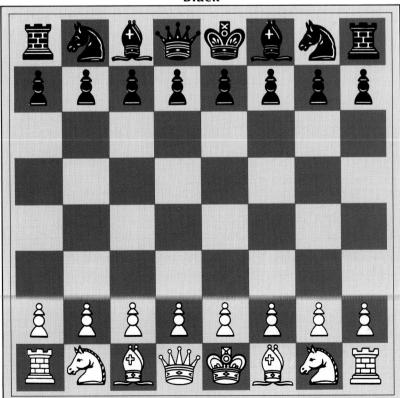

White

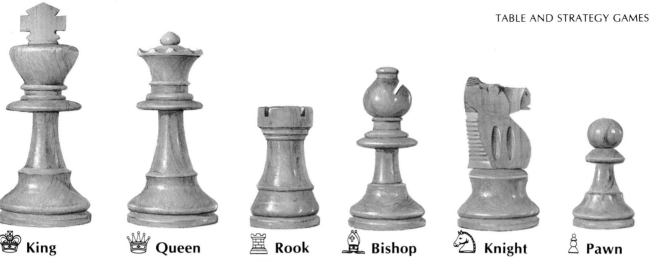

King **Queen** **Rook** **Bishop** **Knight** **Pawn**

Figure 2
Staunton chessmen and symbols

Figure 4
The king's move

Figure 5
The queen's move

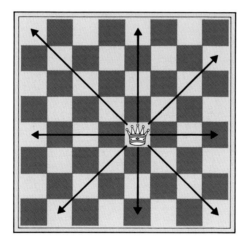

Figure 6
The rook's move

The left half of the chessboard seen from White's side – the half in which the queens stand in the initial position – is referred to as the queen's side, the right half as the king's side. The pieces in each half are identified accordingly as the queen's bishop, the king's rook and so on. These descriptions remain unchanged by subsequent movement.

Moves
The object of the game is to capture the enemy king. White always moves first, and play then alternates. A player can make only one move at a time and cannot opt not to move.

Each type of man has its own move, shown in figures 4–9. The king may move only to an adjacent square; the queen, rook and bishop may travel over any number of vacant squares but may not jump over men of either colour. Two points are worth noting: a bishop is confined to the squares of the colour on which it stands; and the power of the rook is not reduced, like that of the other pieces, on an edge square.

The knight's move is peculiar and for this reason is often feared by beginners.

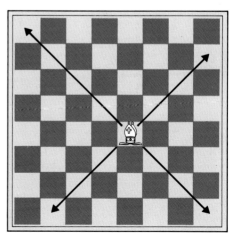

Figure 7
The bishop's move

Figure 8
The knight's move

Figure 9
The pawn's moves

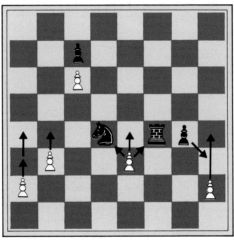

Figure 10
Pawn promotion

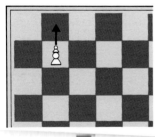

The starred squares in figure 8 show where the knight may go. Notice that the piece does not strictly cross the intervening squares, which can be occupied by men of either side. For this reason the knight's move is often described as a jump. Notice also that a knight can only ever move to a square of the opposite colour on which it stands.

No piece can change direction in the course of a move and only one man may occupy a square. Pieces are captured by displacement, that is, the man making the capture moves to the square occupied by the enemy man, which is then removed. All the pieces capture in the same manner that they move. A player may not, however, capture his own men.

The pawn is the humblest of the chessmen but has a variety of moves. Alone among the men, the pawn may only move forward – straight forward, one square at a time – except on its first move when every pawn has the option of moving two squares straight forward. Also, unlike the pieces, a pawn captures in a different manner to which it moves: the pawn attacks the two adjacent squares diagonally forward (but only one if it stands at the edge of the board).

There is a peculiar pawn capture that occurs occasionally called *en passant*. If a pawn advances two squares on its first move and the intervening square is attacked by an enemy pawn, then the advancing pawn may be captured as though it had moved one square. The rule only applies to a capture by a pawn, and furthermore the pawn must be taken on the next move. If another move is made, the right to capture the pawn *en passant* is forfeited.

Figure 9 gives examples of the various pawn moves. The pawn in the file on the extreme left stands on its original square and can therefore move forward one or two squares. The pawn next to it has already moved and can now move only one square at a time. The two pawns facing each other on the next file are blocked: neither can move. The white pawn in the centre can capture either the knight or the rook, or it can move forward a square.

The *en passant* capture is demonstrated far right. If the white pawn makes its initial double step, the black pawn can capture it as though it had moved one square.

Pawn promotion When a pawn reaches the end rank (the opponent's first rank), whether by move or capture, it is at once promoted to a piece, other than a king, of the player's choice. A queen is almost invariably picked because it is the most powerful piece. It is irrelevant what pieces are in play at the time, so it is quite possible to have four or even five queens on the board together. (Extra queens are not provided with chess sets and an inverted rook is commonly substituted, although a token will do.) Promotion ends the move but the promoted piece can give immediate check or checkmate (see below). The promotion sequence is shown in figure 10.

Relative values of the chessmen

It is only possible to ascribe rough relative values to the different men. The true value of a man is a reflection at any given time of its position and its potential. Thus a pawn on its starting square would normally be worth only a fraction of the value of a pawn that is but one square from promotion. Take the following ratings therefore as a guide only:

Pawn	1
Knight	3
Bishop	3
Rook	5
Queen	9

The king cannot be given a value because of his special role, but offensively he is about equal to a bishop or knight.

Check

A king that is attacked by an enemy, i.e. threatened with capture on the next move, is said to be in check. In friendly games, it is the practice to say 'check' when attacking the king.

A king in check must immediately be rescued. There are three ways to get out of check:

1 Capture the attacking man.
2 Interpose a man between the attacker and the king.
3 Move the king to a square where it is not attacked.

It is unlikely that all three possibilities will exist at the same time.

There are three types of attack on the king:

The simple check: the king is attacked directly by an enemy man.

The discovered check: the man that moves does not itself put the king in check but discloses the attack from a piece standing behind it.

The double check: this is a check by two pieces simultaneously and is necessarily a discovered check. The only defence against this type of attack is to move the king.

It follows that no move should ever be made that places or leaves one's king in check, nor may the two kings ever stand on adjacent squares.

Figure 11 shows the black king in check from the white rook. Black must now either capture the rook with the knight, interpose the bishop or move the king into the corner. Notice that Black cannot interpose with the rook as this move would expose his king to check from the white bishop.

Checkmate If a king cannot be rescued from check, i.e. its capture on the following move is certain, it is checkmate and the game is over. The side giving checkmate has won. Four examples of checkmate are given in figure 12.

Figure 11
Example of check

Figure 12
Four examples of checkmate

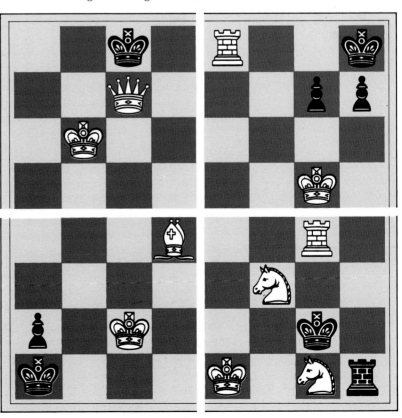

Figure 13
Castling

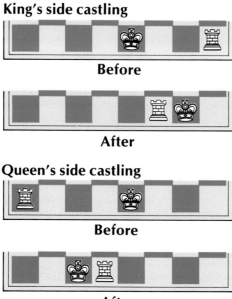

King's side castling

Before

After

Queen's side castling

Before

After

Castling

This is a manoeuvre involving the movement of two men, the king and a rook. Both sides are entitled to make this manoeuvre once in a game and it counts as one move. The king moves two squares towards the rook and the rook is then brought next to the king on the inside of it. The king is moved first.

The right to castle may only be exercised if all the following conditions are met:

1 The king and the rook have not previously moved.
2 The squares between them are vacant.
3 The king is not in check.
4 The king does not, in castling, cross over or move on to a square that is under attack.

Observe that the king may previously have been in check provided he did not get out of it by moving.

Castling may take place on either side of the board and is known respectively as queen's side castling and king's side castling. The purpose is twofold: to move the king to safety and to bring a rook into the centre. These manoeuvres are shown for both sides in figure 13.

Ending the game

Although a game may end with checkmate, a more common way for a game to conclude is by one player resigning. There is little point in continuing to play when the only remaining hope is that the opponent will make a bad mistake.

Similarly, a game may be drawn by mutual agreement, either because there is insufficient force for either side to checkmate – for example, if only the kings remain on the board – or because both sides see little prospect of forcing a win.

In addition to mutual agreement, there are three other ways in which a game can be drawn: stalemate, repetition of position and the 50-move rule.

Stalemate If a player whose turn it is to move and whose king is not in check has no legal move, it is stalemate and the game is drawn.

Repetition of position If a position is repeated three times in a game with the same player to move on each occasion, then either player may claim a draw. The commonest case is where one side forces a repeated sequence of checks ('perpetual check'). An example of this is demonstrated in figure 14. White checks (A) when the black king has only one square to escape, whereupon White checks again (B), and this sequence can simply be repeated indefinitely.

50-move rule If 50 consecutive moves have been made by both sides without a pawn having been moved or a capture made, either side may claim a draw. This rule is rarely invoked as draw by agreement is likely before the limit is reached.

Notation

Notation is a form of shorthand used to transcribe moves and positions, and is the common language of chessplayers. There are two main systems in use, the Descriptive and the Algebraic, of which the Algebraic is the most widely practised and is described here.

Algebraic Notation The files of the chessboard are lettered a–h and the ranks are numbered 1–8, as shown in figure 15. Any square can be defined by the combination of a letter and a number; for example, the top right square, on which Black's king's rook stands at the start of the game, is designated h8.

Individual men are referred to by initials:

K   king
Q   queen
R   rook
B   bishop
N or Kt   knight
P   pawn

Symbols are used to express the mechanics of play:

—	moves to
×	captures
+ or ch	check
e.p.	en passant
=Q or (Q)	promotion to queen
0–0	castles, king's side
0–0–0	castles, queen's side
!	good move
?	bad move

A move is recorded in the following sequence:

1 Initial of man moved.
2 Symbol for either 'moves to' or 'captures'.
3 Description of square moved to.
4 Other symbol if appropriate.

Thus, if White brings out his king's knight towards the centre at the start of the game, the move could be written down as N–f3; in practice, however, the 'moves to' symbol is often omitted and the move is written Nf3.

In further pursuit of brevity, it is common also to drop the initial 'P' for pawn. Thus, if White advanced the pawn in front of his king two squares, the move would be recorded simply as e4. There is no ambiguity: no pawn other than the pawn on e2 can move to e4.

Ambiguity is, however, possible in some situations, for example, when both rooks or both knights can move to the same square or when two pawns can make the same capture. In these cases, the man moved is identified by inserting after the initial the file or rank on which the man stands. For instance, Rad1 means that the rook on the a file (obviously on a1) moves to d1; exd5 means that the pawn on the e file (which must be on e4) takes the man on d5. Notice that a captured man is never identified: it is sufficient to indicate the square on which a capture is made.

The principle of notation is always to record a move as economically as possible consistent with clarity and lack of ambiguity.

Forsyth notation is used for recording positions where a diagram is not available. Starting at the top left of the board (a8), each rank is recorded from left to right and top to bottom. The men are denoted by their initials, capital letters for white men, lower case letters for black men. Empty squares are indicated by numbers, and ranks are separated by strokes, with two or more empty ranks grouped together as one. For example, figure 12 on the previous page could be recorded as a single position in Forsyth: 2k1R2k/2Q3pp/1K6/6K1/3B2R1/5N2/p1K3k1/k3K1Nr. The sum of squares and men must of course equal 64.

STRATEGY

It is a popular misconception that chess masters see a long way ahead. This is true in a few situations but mostly the experts follow a thought pattern that goes something like this: what are the strengths and weaknesses of the position? what therefore is the best plan? and what is the logical move to progress with this plan?

Chess is a battle of ideas. No move should be made without reason, and aggressive moves – like giving check – are useless unless they form part of a

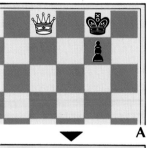

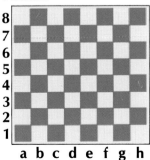

Figure 14
Perpetual check

Figure 15
Notation

Figure 16
Scholar's Mate

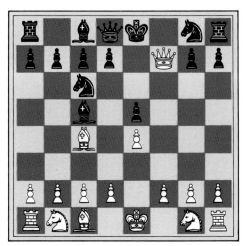

board-wide plan. On the other hand, aggression carries its own impetus while passive play is an invitation to disaster. It is important to keep objectives under constant review – plans will probably have to be changed many times in the course of a game.

A chess game commonly has three phases: the opening, the middle game and the end game.

Chess openings have been studied for hundreds of years. Few definite conclusions have emerged though two general principles can be said to be common to almost all openings: get one's pieces posted quickly on squares where they are effective, and strike, directly or indirectly, towards the centre of the board. It is usual also for both sides to castle early in the game. A beginner's error is to move the same piece – particularly the queen – repeatedly.

Most openings have names and thousands of books have been published on the subject. However, it is wiser to explore the ideas that lie behind openings rather than commit to memory whole series of moves.

The middle game is the main battle and begins as the opening phase closes. As men get captured and the board empties, the end game approaches. The end game is that phase where one or both sides probably have as their immediate objective the promotion of a pawn. Because the forces are diminished, the

kings can come out of hiding to use their offensive powers.

Many games do not go through all phases. Some are concluded in the middle game and some even in the opening (there are a number of opening traps familiar to experienced players).

Scholar's Mate One of the commonest short games which can catch the unwary is known as Scholar's Mate. This can arise in a number of ways. Here it is in simple form:
1 e4, e5;
2 Bc4, Nc6;
3 Qf3, Bc5;
4 Q×f7 mate (figure 16).
After 3 Qf3 Black could rejoice: White has exposed his strongest piece to attack and has taken away the best square for the king's knight. Black need only reply Nf6 to destroy White's attacking chances.

A chess game can be said to have three elements: time, force and space. Time is represented by the moves of the men, force by the power they exert and space by the territory they control. All of these elements are desirable: you lose time by having a piece driven back; you cede force when, for example, you give up a rook (value 5) for a bishop and pawn (value 4); and if you surrender space your position becomes cramped and your pieces interfere with one another. Mastery in chess belongs to those who know when to surrender one element in exchange for another.

Powers of the pieces
Every man has his strengths and weaknesses and should be handled accordingly. Pawns are sometimes despised, though never by strong players. Pawns in fact have several advantages, not least that pieces must give way before them. United pawns are strong in both attack and defence – and every pawn is a potential queen. A pawn can never retreat, so every pawn move is to this degree commital.

The knights, with their curious move, work best on a busy board where the other pieces get in one another's way. Watch out for knight forks – simultaneous attacks on two pieces, often the rook and king.

Bishops work best at long range and are usually stronger than knights in the end game. The weakness of the bishop is that it is confined to the squares of one colour.

Rooks are powerful, particularly when working together on the same file. A rook which penetrates to the seventh rank, where it is immune from pawn attack, can devastate the defence.

The queen is the strongest piece but has the paradoxical weakness of being obliged to retreat if attacked.

Recall that the king can prove useful in attack once the risk of checkmate has receded. At other times, it must be kept well protected.

Examples of play

Two games, each briefly annotated, are given below. They are in striking contrast. The first is known as the Immortal Game and was played in 1851. Both sides attack from the outset to create a game of high tactics. The second dates from 1924 and is quietly positional, with Black inexorably exploiting minor weaknesses in White's position. The modern style is somewhere between these two – controlled aggression coupled with dynamic defence.

GAME 1

	White (Anderssen)	Black (Kieseritzky)
1	e4	e5
2	f4	

The King's Gambit. White sacrifices a pawn for quick development and attacking chances.

2		P×f4
3	Bc4	b5

A counter-sacrifice to divert the bishop.

4	B×b5	Qh4+
5	Kf1	

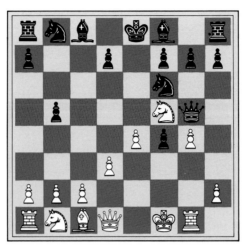

Figure 17
Position after Black's 11th move

Robust tactics like these are rarely seen today.

5		Nf6
6	Nf3	Qh6
7	d3	Nh5

Black threatens: 8 ... Ng3+; 9 P×g3, Q×h1+. If now 8 Kf2, Qb6+ and takes the bishop next move.

8	Nh4	c6
9	Nf5	Qg5
10	g4	Nf6

If Black had taken the pawn *en passant* he would have lost his queen.

11	Rg1	P×b5

See figure 17.

12	h4	Qg6
13	h5	Qg5
14	Qf3	

Threatening to trap the queen with B×f4.

14		Ng8
15	B×f4	Qf6
16	Nc3	

White has almost all his pieces in play plus control of the centre in exchange for a bishop.

16		Bc5
17	Nd5	Q×b2
18	Bd6	

Another sacrifice.

18		Q×a1+
19	Ke2	

... and another.

19		B×g1
20	e5	

Threatening mate in two: 21 N×g7+, Kd8; 22 Bc7.

20		Na6
21	N×g7+	Kd8
22	Qf6+!	Nxf6
23	Be7 mate	

See figure 18.

See figure 18.

Figure 18
Game 1: final position

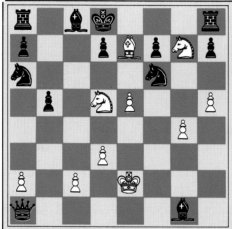

GAME 2

	White (Bogolyubov)	Black (Capablanca)
1	d4	Nf6
2	Nf3	d5
3	e3	e6
4	Bd3	c5
5	b3	Nc6
6	0—0	Bd6
7	Bb2	0—0
8	Nbd2	Qe7
9	Ne5	P×d4
10	P×d4	Ba3

This move, by exchanging off the black-squared bishops, creates small potential weaknesses in White's defences. See figure 19.

11	B×a3	Q×a3
12	Ndf3	Bd7
13	N×c6	B×c6
14	Qd2	Rac8
15	c3	a6
16	Ne5	Bb5

White can now exchange bishops, so doubling the black pawns, but this would be insufficient compensation for the pressure that Black could then exert against White's queen's side pawns.

17	f3	B×d3
18	N×d3	Rc7
19	Rac1	Rfc8
20	Rc2	Ne8

The knight must be redeployed to a more active square.

21	Rfc1	Nd6
22	Ne5	Qa5
23	a4	Qb6

White must now lose a pawn however he plays.

24	Nd3	Q×b3
25	Nc5	Qb6
26	Rb2	Qa7

The queen is driven away temporarily. She now stands on the same diagonal as the white king, which often means danger.

27	Qe1	b6
28	Nd3	Rc4
29	a5	P×a5
30	Nc5	Nb5
31	Re2	

White is now threatening 32 R×e6

Figure 19
Game 2: position after Black's 10th move

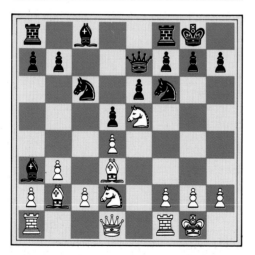

Figure 20
Game 2: final position

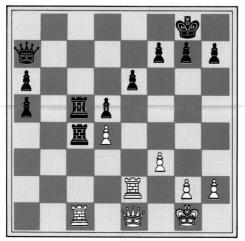

when if 32 ... P×e6; 33 Q×e6+ followed by Q×c8+ would turn the game round. Black is alert to this.

| 31 | N×d4+ |

A crushing sacrifice!

| 32 | P×d4 | R8×c5 |

White resigns, for if 33 P×c5, Q×c5+ will get the rook back and also win the queen, whilst 33 R×c4 would allow Black to continue ... R×c4; White's d-file pawn would be lost and the subsequent ending would be hopeless (see figure 20).

Notice that the entire game was played out on the queen's side and that at no time was either king under direct attack.

Chess problems

Chess problems should not be confused with the game. Problems are composed positions in which the solver is required to find the unique move that will allow White (it is a convention that White wins) to give checkmate in the stipulated number of moves. Chess problems follow the laws of chess.

RELATED GAMES

Chess variants are collectively known as Fairy Chess (Fairy Chess problems are another rich field). They are virtually uncountable: probably a new variant is invented every few days. Most are worthless but a few have become established games in their own right, such as Progressive (or Scotch) Chess, Kriegspiel, Losing Chess and Hexagonal Chess.

GLOSSARY

Chess has a rich jargon, and terms that you are likely to come across are given below:

Combination	A series of moves, often forcing, to secure an advantage.
Develop	To activate pieces, hence 'development'.
En prise	Literally 'in a position to be taken'.
Exchange	(verb) To surrender a man for a like man or one of equal value. (noun) To win the exchange is to capture a rook for a bishop or knight.
Fianchetto	To develop a bishop on the long diagonal, i.e. at b2, g2, b7 or g7.
Fork	A simultaneous attack on two or more men, particularly by a knight.
Gambit	The sacrifice of a pawn or piece in the opening.
J'adoube	Literally 'I adjust'; a warning given before adjusting men on the board.
Pin	The partial or total immobilization of a man because of a latent threat to a man beyond it.
Skewer	A double attack on a line such that if the first man escapes, the second man is captured.
Skittles	Quick, non-serious play. Also called Blitz Chess.
Tempo	Time, as represented by a single move.
Touch and move	Except in friendly games, it is mandatory to move the man you touch or to capture an opposing man touched. If this is not legal, there is no penalty.
Zugzwang	Literally 'forced move'; the situation of being obliged to move when one would prefer not to because it will result in the worsening of one's position.

51

XIANGQI

Xiangqi, or Chinese Chess, is a highly tactical board game for two players. It is very old, and is almost certainly derived from the ancient Indian game of Shatranj, the two-player version of Chaturanga, the ancestor of Western Chess, though the board now used is of indigenous design.

Xiangqi is the game of the ordinary people of China, but the game is little played outside Chinese communities partly because its appearance, like that of Shogi, frightens people off. This is sad, especially considering that a thousand years ago figurines, the universal language of the games-player, were used in Xiangqi.

EQUIPMENT

Cheap sets of wooden or plastic pieces and paper boards can be purchased at almost any oriental emporium. The board (figure 1) is a symmetrical grid of 90 points (intersections) divided into two territories by a central band known as the river. Centrally placed at each end of the board is a nine-point palace denoted by a cross. In addition, there are seven points marked on each side, which are the stations for certain pieces at the start of the game.

Each side has an army of 16 men, which are shown, with their Western equivalents, in figure 2. The men are round and flat, like draughtsmen, and their ranks are indicated by ideograms, which are usually embossed on the pieces. The two armies are commonly red and black, but sometimes red and blue or red and green.

PLAY

The object of the game is to capture (checkmate) the enemy General or immobilize (stalemate) the enemy army. The starting position is shown in figure 3. Play is on the intersections and it is a convention that Black moves first, although outside tournament play the

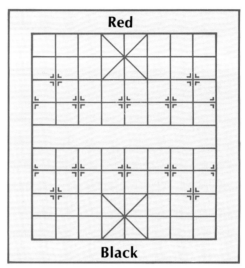

Red

Black

Figure 1 The board

player to move first is usually decided by agreement, without regard to colour. Play alternates, each player taking it in turn to move one of his men.

Moves

The men fall into two groups, those whose movements are circumscribed and those who may move freely anywhere on the board including through or within the palaces. The restricted pieces are the general and the mandarins, both of which may not leave the palace, and the elephants, which may not cross the river. Much of the board is also closed to the soldiers on account of their move.

The general moves one point at a time, orthogonally only, and always within the palace. The two generals may not face each other down an empty file: there must be at least one piece of either colour between them. If a piece is moved off a file to leave the two generals alone on it, it is tantamount to moving into check.

The mandarin moves one point at a time, diagonally only, and always within the palace.

The elephant moves two points diagonally, forward or back, provided the intermediate point is vacant; it cannot cross the river.

2 Elephants or Ministers

1 General or Governor

2 Chariots

5 Soldiers

*Figure 2
The men for each side, showing the ideograms and their Western equivalents*

2 Horses

2 Ballistas or Cannons

2 Mandarins or Counsellors

The *soldier* moves one point at a time straight forward, but when a soldier crosses the river (which counts as a move) it may move sideways as well as forward, though still only one point at a time. Once it reaches the end rank it can only move sideways.

The *chariot* moves exactly like the rook in Chess or Shogi, orthogonally over any number of vacant points.

The *horse* moves like the knight in Chess but in two steps, first orthogonally and then diagonally. The intermediate point must be vacant, and the horse therefore cannot jump like the knight in Chess or Shogi.

All the above pieces capture by displacement – moving on to the point occupied by the enemy piece, which is removed from play.

The *ballista* moves identically to the chariot but it alone of the pieces captures in a different manner to which it moves. It must leap over a man to reach its prey; this man, known as the screen, may be of any rank and of either colour. There can be any number of empty points between the ballista and the screen, and between the screen and the victim. The first man on an orthogonal line from a ballista is therefore a screen, and the next man beyond the screen is, if hostile, the man under attack. If, therefore, there are less than two men on the line, or the second man is friendly, then the ballista has no capture along that line.

Powers of the pieces

The chariots remain the strongest pieces at all stages of the game, while ballistas can threaten the enemy from the security of a friendly screen.

Soldiers have little defence value because they cannot retreat and cannot defend one another but in attack they can prove very dangerous since soldiers cannot be blocked. They also make useful screens for the ballistas.

The elephants have access only to seven points between them but they readily defend each other and can guard effectively against attacks down the centre or from the side. The mandarins have access to even fewer points – only five – but they too can shut out attackers by mutual defence and form a second buffer within the palace.

Horses tend to increase in value as the number of men in play is reduced because they are not so easily blocked. Conversely, the power of the ballistas is reduced when there are less men about to act as screens.

As a rough guide, the relative values of the men are: chariot (C) 10, ballista (B) 7, horse (H) 6, elephant (E) and general (G) 4, mandarin (M) 3, soldier (S) 2.

Figure 3
The starting position

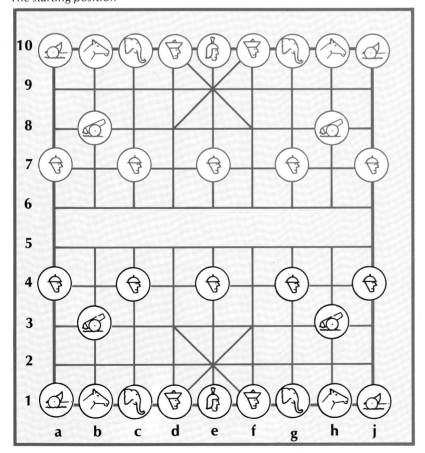

Figure 4
Example of ballistas in action

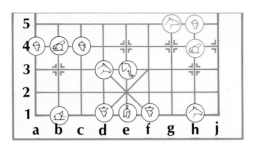

Figure 5
Example of check

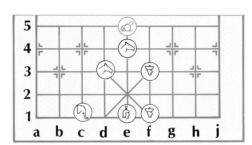

Check and checkmate

A general is in check when it is attacked. If a player cannot at once remove the threat, either by capturing or blocking the attacker or by moving the general out of check, then it is checkmate and the player has lost the game. Stalemate occurs where a player whose general is not in check is unable to make a legal move, and is a loss for that player.

Perpetual check is not tolerated: if both players repeat their moves twice in succession the first player must make a different move on penalty of losing the game. Draws by agreement are not unusual in Xiangqi, though they are less common than in Chess.

Figure 5 shows an example of check. Black can take the attacker with the horse on the left, or he can move the screen (the second horse) away, or he can move the general to the left. Alternatively, he can interpose either of the mandarins or the elephant. If he sacrifices the elephant – 1 Ee3, B×e3; 2 Ge2 – the ballista, unable to move, can be captured next turn.

Figures 6 and 7 show examples of checkmate. In figure 6, although the general stands next to the unguarded chariot, the chariot cannot be taken because the general may not leave the palace. The ballista covers the general's only escape point. In figure 7 the two ballistas on the centre file are very strong. Capture of the ballista e7 by the horse would still leave the general in check, while the interposition of the mandarin would put the general in check from the second ballista. The general cannot move out of check since he would then be facing the rival general on an open file.

STRATEGY

Strategy would be fairly straightforward if it were not for the horses and ballistas. Creating scope for the horses demands considerable skill. In figure 8 a black horse attacks an undefended red horse

Figure 4 demonstrates the peculiar powers and weaknesses of the ballista. The two ballistas here attack each other. The red ballista is protected by a soldier (which also defends the horse) while the black ballista is twice guarded, by the chariot and by the horse in the palace. Red could here play the horse to h3, where it would serve as a screen for the ballista which would then be threatening the black horse. A move by the red horse to e4 would break the mutual attack of the ballistas but would allow Black to capture (B×e4) and Red could only take the soldier c4 in compensation.

Red could play Bh3, attacking the horse in the palace, or he could, for example, play Be4+, when Black could get out of check by exchanging ballistas (the red one is protected by the horse), by moving the elephant back, thus destroying the screen, or by playing either mandarin in front of the general, where it would be twice defended. If it were Black's move in the position, an advance of soldier c would lose him soldier a to the ballista.

that has crossed the river but is blocked by its own soldier. However, Red can move the soldier sideways to face the black horse. Now the situation is reversed: both the red horse and soldier attack the black horse. Further, the soldier blocks the advance of the black horse.

A ballista's power to pin two pieces against the general is shown in figure 9. Neither the mandarin nor the elephant can move without exposing the general to check.

Openings

The starting position (refer back to figure 3) is symmetrical, so every series of opening moves has its twin, thus halving the number of variations possible. Even so, the choice is daunting. The open lines offer early penetration to the major pieces – the chariots and ballistas. The horses are immediately under attack from the ballistas, but are defended by the chariots, which are usually brought into play along their adjacent files or via the second rank. Notice that no diagonal-moving piece can cross the river; apart from the major pieces, only the horses and the soldiers can be employed in attack.

Openings fall into three main groups called the ballista, horse and soldier openings, according to which man is moved first. In the ballista openings, the most popular, one of the pieces is moved to the central file, immediately attacking the opposing soldier and posing a latent threat to the general. The horse openings are more cautious, while the soldier openings, usually an advance of one of the soldiers on files c, e or g, are designed to facilitate the march of one or both horses to the centre.

One of the sharpest and most popular of the ballista openings is Tang-t'ou Pao against Ping-feng Ma (Cannon at the head against Screening Horses) which has a half-dozen main variations and a host of sub-variations. The following is a modern example of this key opening.

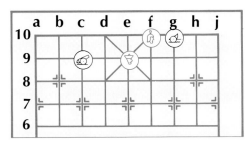

Figure 6
Example of checkmate

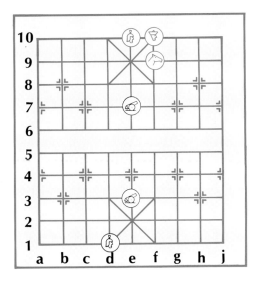

Figure 7
Example of checkmate

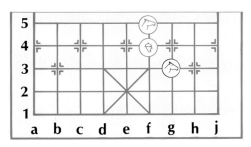

Figure 8
Attack by a black horse

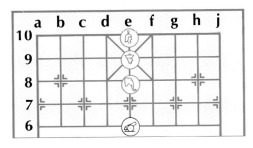

Figure 9
A ballista pinning two enemy pieces

	Black	Red
1	Bbe3	Hc8
2	Hc3	Cb10
3	Cb1	Hg8

The second 'screening horse' takes up post.

	Black	Red
4	Sg5	Sc6
5	Hg3	Ege8
6	Bh5	Bh9

A move to gain mobility. Red expects an attack on his right.

| 7 | Sc5 | |

Protected by the ballista on h5.

| 7 | | Bc9 |
| 8 | Hd5 | Sg6 |

Red gains no advantage by S×c5 here.

9	S×c6	S×g5
10	Sc7	B×c7
11	H×c7	Bb3
12	Bh9	

If Black rescues his horse, Red plays S×h5 (remember that a soldier over the river can also move sideways).

12		Ch10
13	Ch1	B×g3
14	C×b10	H×b10

Black exchanges chariots to free the advance of his horse.

| 15 | Hb9 | |

Black immobilizes the red horse.

| 15 | | Mfe9 |

Necessary, otherwise a horse check at d8 would force the general forward, effectively destroying the defence value of the mandarins. (See figure 10.) Black eventually won.

Play in Xiangqi is focused on the centre because the generals are confined to the palaces there, but flank attacks are common. The major pieces penetrate down the files but operate mainly along the ranks. The following short game illustrates many of these points.

	Black	Red
1	Bhe3	Hg8
2	Hg3	Hc8
3	Se5	Mde9
4	Hc3	Ch10
5	Se6	S×e6
6	Hce4	

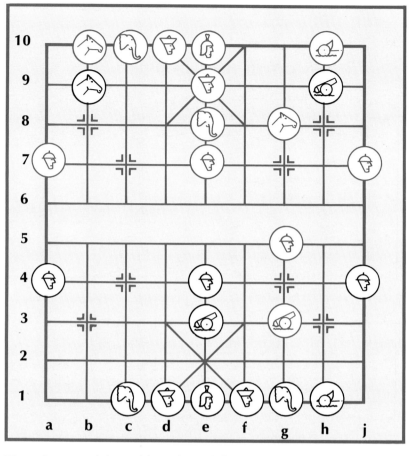

The advance of the soldier cleared the way for the horses to march to the centre. Now the horse makes a screen for the ballista.

	Black	Red
6		Bh4
7	B×e6+	Ece8
8	Be3	B×e4+
9	H×e4	Ch6
10	Cj2	Cd10
11	Cb1	

Now the chariots are all developed.

| 11 | | Ba8 |
| 12 | Cf2 | |

A common station for chariots.

| 12 | | B×a4 |
| 13 | Hf6 | Ch8 |

The red horse is attacked.

| 14 | H×e8 | Cd8 |

The horse was threatening checkmate at both c9 and g9. If 14 ... E×e8; 15 B×e8 mate.

| 15 | Hd6+ | |

The ballista e6 is attacking the general.

15		He7
16	B×e7+	Gd10
17	H×c8+	C×c8
18	Cd2+	Chd8
19	Bd7+	Ce8

Figure 10
Position after Red's 15th move

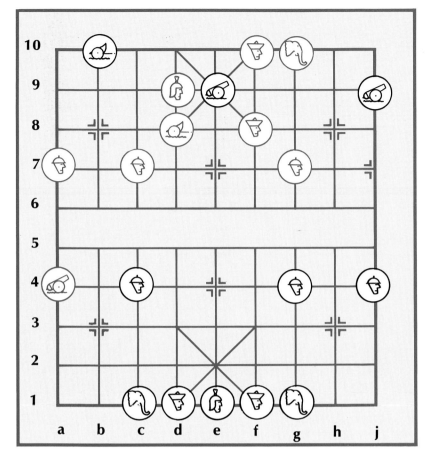

Figure 11
Final position

The ballista cannot be taken because it is defended by the general.

This violent game demonstrates the strength of the ballistas working in concert and also the strength of the chariots. The relative impotence of the soldiers is evident. Notice that Black did not have to move a defender.

End game
A win can often be secured with surprisingly light forces because generals cannot share an empty file and because stalemate is decisive. Here is an example, with a lone ballista forcing the win against a general defended by its two mandarins. Observe the parts played by the black general and mandarin (figure 12).

	Black	White
1	Be1+	M10e9

If instead M8e9, then Black has stalemate with Gf1 or Gf3.

| 2 | Gf3 | Gd10 |
| 3 | Md3 | |

Stopping the general moving back in the centre.

3		Mf8
4	Bd1	Mfe9
5	Ge3	

Zugzwang! If now 5 ... Gd9; 6 Me2 mate.

| 5 | | Ge10 |
| 6 | B×d8 | |

Black will now capture the other mandarin in the same manner, and the ballista will then give mate using the black mandarin as screen and with the black general holding the centre file.

RELATED GAMES

One of the enlarged forms of Xiangqi played in China is the Game of the Three Kingdoms. This uses three board halves joined so that each player (Banner, Fire and Wind) shares a bifurcated river frontage equally with his two rivals. The game was intended to represent the War of the Three Kingdoms (AD 221–264).

20 B×j7+   Ccd8
21 Cb10+
Now Red's moves are forced.
21   Gd9
22 Bj9+   Mf8
23 C×d8+   C×d8
Or 23 ... G×d8; 24 Cd10 mate.
24 Bee9 mate
The end position is shown in figure 11.

Figure 12
An end game

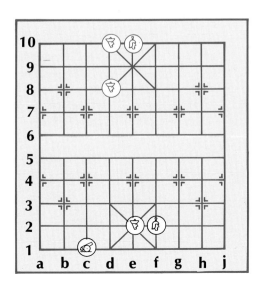

SHOGI

Shogi, or Japanese Chess as it is some-times called, is an ancient and complex board game for two players with the same aim as Chess: to checkmate the opponent's king. It possesses, however, a feature that is unique in the chess family – captured pieces can re-enter the play. This creates situations rich in tactics which class Shogi amongst the world's best strategy games.

Shogi is the national game of Japan. Millions play it there and many make their livings as professionals, but sadly Shogi has made little impact outside Japan. In part this is due to its presentation; in part because the game starts slowly – there are no 'scholar's mates', as in Chess, to catch the interest of the beginner.

EQUIPMENT

Shogi sets can be bought at specialist games shops, though the markings on the pieces may differ slightly from those shown here. The game is played on an uncoloured board called a shogi-ban which is marked with 81 rectangles or squares in a 9 × 9 array (figure 1). Four of the intersections are accentuated to indicate promotion zones (explained below).

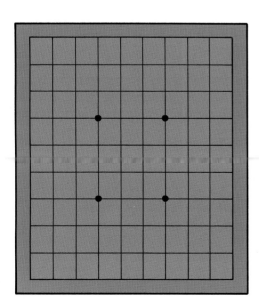

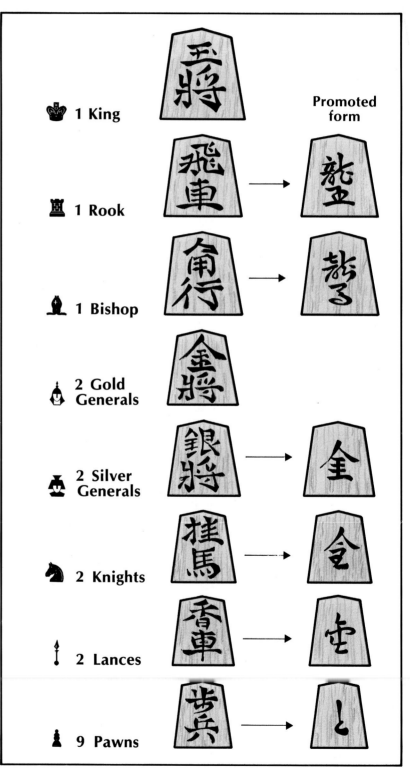

Figure 1
The shogi-ban

Figure 2
The men for each side

Figure 3
The starting position

Black

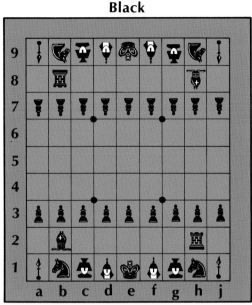

White

Each side starts with an army of 20 men. The ranks of the men are denoted by Japanese inscriptions (in Westernized sets, Chess symbols are used), and the major pieces are slightly larger than the others. The two sides are not differentiated by colour and the flat, wedge-shaped pieces are always placed on the board so that they point towards the opponent and thus show the side to which they belong. Most of the men also have inscriptions on the reverse; these show the new ranks of pieces if they are

promoted (explained below) so that pieces promoted during a game can simply be turned over.

Figure 2 shows the men and their distribution for each side, together with their Western equivalents.

PLAY

The object is to capture – checkmate – the opponent's king. The starting position is shown in figure 3. Play is on the squares and players move alternately. Although Shogi pieces are not distinguished by colour, the players are frequently referred to as Black and White, as in Chess. Black moves first.

Moves

The moves of the various pieces are illustrated in figure 4. Notice that the moves of the king, rook and bishop are identical to those of Chess. The knight in Shogi moves only forward and is therefore much less powerful than his Western relative, while the pawn does not have the option of an initial two-square advance. The lance, and the gold and silver generals have no counterparts in Chess.

Capture is by displacement. All the pieces, including the pawn, capture in the same manner in which they move.

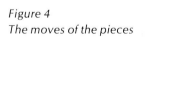

Figure 4
The moves of the pieces

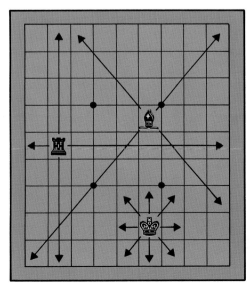

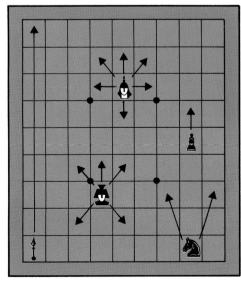

Promotion

All pieces except the king and the gold generals (which are blank on the reverse) can be promoted to a higher rank. Promotion is achieved at the end of a move in which the piece enters, leaves, or is wholly within the promotion zone. This zone is made up of the three ranks of squares farthest from the player – the ranks on which the opponent's men stand at the start of the game.

An unpromoted man must be promoted if it is played to a square from which it could not legally move again in its unpromoted role. This means that a lance or a pawn which reaches the ninth rank or a knight which reaches the eighth or ninth rank must be promoted since these pieces move only forward. Otherwise promotion of all men is optional.

A promoted rook or bishop commands all adjacent squares in addition to its usual lines (see figure 5; in diagrams, promotion is sometimes shown by putting the symbol of the piece within a circle). The pawn, lance, knight and silver all share a common rank on promotion – they become gold generals. There is usually little profit in not promoting a rook, bishop or pawn since promotion adds to their powers. This is not the case with the remaining pieces

whose powers, though enhanced, are also changed by promotion.

A piece that is not promoted at the first opportunity can still be promoted on a subsequent move provided that part at least of its move is made within the zone. Promoted pieces retain their powers until captured. Typical promotion moves are demonstrated in figure 6.

Captured pieces

When a player makes a capture he puts the piece beside him into his 'Reserve Base'. If the piece was promoted in the course of play, it is turned over to show its original rank. This piece now belongs to the capturer and is said to be 'in hand'. A piece in hand may, on a player's turn, be placed – 'dropped' – on any vacant square on the board, subject to certain restrictions. A 'drop' counts as a move and play passes to the opponent.

The following restrictions apply to pieces played from hand:

1 All dropped pieces are unpromoted. A piece may be dropped within the promotion zone but it cannot be promoted until it has moved.

2 A piece may not be dropped where it cannot again be moved in its unpromoted form (ninth rank for lance and pawn; eighth or ninth rank for knight).

3 A pawn may not be dropped on a file on which the player already has an unpromoted pawn.

4 A pawn may not be dropped so as to checkmate the king.

These are the only restrictions; a piece can otherwise be dropped anywhere. Thus a pawn could be dropped on the first rank or a knight on the central square, which neither could reach from the starting position. Note also that any man, including the pawn, can be dropped to give check and any man except a pawn can be dropped to give checkmate.

It is common in the later stages of a game for both players to have a number of men in hand and checkmate is often achieved by a succession of drops.

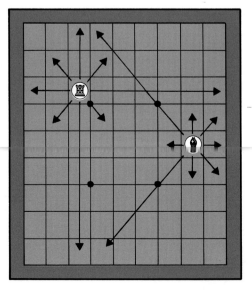

Figure 5
The moves of a promoted
rook and bishop

Powers of the pieces

As most pieces can be in any of three states – unpromoted, promoted or in hand – it is difficult to ascribe relative values to them. Roughly, a rook is equal to three generals, a bishop a little less. Gold and silver generals are approximately the same value: one is equal to about two knights or lances.

The rook is essentially an attacking piece with the bishop at its best in the earlier part of the game (notice that the bishops share the same diagonal at the start). The golds, because they have only one line of retreat, are usually best employed in defence, while the silvers are useful both in attack and defence. Lances and knights are attacking pieces – they have little value as defenders. Pawns are not to be despised. In defence they can shut out the major pieces, while a promoted pawn is fearless in attack since it is an unattractive prize. Do not take more pawns into hand than needed.

Check and checkmate

Check and checkmate are exactly the same as in Chess. A king is in check when it is under attack by an enemy man. A player whose king is in check must immediately do one of three things:

1 Capture the attacking piece. This will not be possible if the king is attacked by two pieces simultaneously.

2 Interpose a piece between the king and his attacker. This could be achieved by moving a piece in play or by dropping a piece from hand. This will not be possible if the attacker stands next to the king.

3 Move the king out of the line of attack.

If none of these moves is possible then the king is checkmated and the player delivering the checkmate has won. It follows that a player may never make a move that places his king in check. Figure 7 shows some examples of check and checkmate.

Draws are rare in Shogi. In a match, games that are unresolved through both sides repeating the same moves are declared 'no contest' and are replayed.

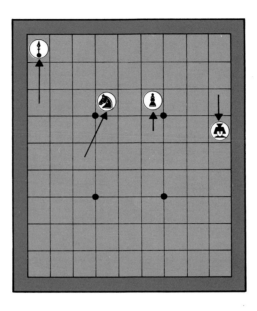

Figure 6
Typical promotion moves

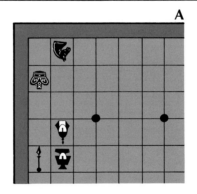

A

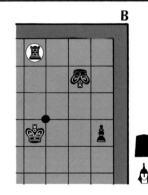

B

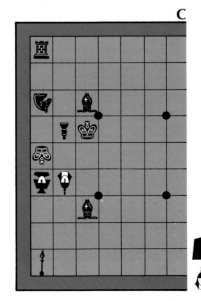

C

Figure 7
Examples of check and checkmate. In diagram A, the king is in check. White must now either capture the lance with the gold; interpose the gold, silver or knight; drop a man between the king and lance; or move the king away.

In diagram B, Black drops his gold in front of the pawn to give checkmate. In diagram C, Black drops his gold on b5. Gold is then attacked by all of White's men but none can take it without exposing the king to check. It is checkmate. (Black can also mate by B×b6*.)

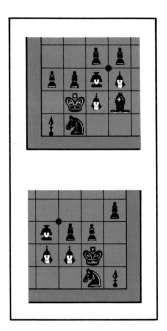

Figure 8
Examples of castle positions

Handicapping

In Japan, Shogi players are classified as in Go into kyu (amateur) and dan (master) grades, and there is an elaborate handicapping system. In family games a balance can always be struck by the stronger player removing a piece or two before play starts.

STRATEGY

The first move confers little advantage in Shogi. A normal game will follow a regular sequence similar to the opening, middle game and end game of Chess. The first dozen or so moves (the opening) are used to secure the king within a castle and prepare to attack. (Unlike in Chess, there is no castling move.)

The middle game often starts with a pawn sacrifice with the immediate aim of getting a major piece (rook or bishop) promoted. The two armies become locked in conflict with one or both sides breaking through into the enemy camp. In Shogi, the flanks assume a greater importance than in Chess, the centre less so. Since most of the men cannot retreat (the lances, knights and pawns), while others advance more easily than they go back (the generals), a common strategy is to entice the opponent's men forward with the idea of exposing the king to attack from the rear.

The end game in Shogi is the final attack. A piece or two in the vicinity of the king is usually needed in addition to men in hand.

Openings

Opening play is characterized by the need to find room for the rook and bishop to operate. Because most of the pieces take only short steps, development is normally slow. This has a two-fold advantage for the beginner: he does not have to worry unduly about what his opponent is doing since it is unlikely that an early attack can be mounted, and the order of moves, critical in Chess, is, for this reason, often of little account.

That does not mean that haphazard play will go unpunished. An important feature of any opening is the protection of the king. It is usual to move him into a castle at the side of the board. A castle is simply an arrangement of defending pieces, which commonly includes three generals, surrounding the king. The reason for this close defence is that vacant squares in the vicinity of the king are open to enemy drops: an exposed king is at least as vulnerable as his Western counterpart. Two typical castle positions are shown in figure 8.

Shogi openings are classified into two main branches: the Static Rook and the Ranging Rook openings. In the Static Rook openings the rook remains on the right side of the board and the king usually finds sanctuary on the left, while in the Ranging Rook openings the rook joins the bishop and the king's castle is on the right; in both cases the king and rook are on opposite sides of the board. This is putting things simply (the king is sometimes kept in the centre, for example) but is true of the mainstream of openings.

The drop

Shogi strategy is largely conditioned by the drop. In Chess, a position can be simplified by captures; in Shogi, captures result in more pieces being taken into hand, thereby increasing the number of potential plays.

When pieces are exchanged, remember that promoted men revert to their original ranks. Thus a gold for a gold may be a poor exchange if your opponent's started life as a pawn and yours as a silver.

A piece may be much more powerful in hand than in play. A knight for example has only two moves at most on the board but in hand it can be dropped at an appropriate moment to attack almost any square. Quite often play is directed towards the capture of a piece that is required to be dropped elsewhere.

Drops, as shown in the following end game, can be used defensively as well as

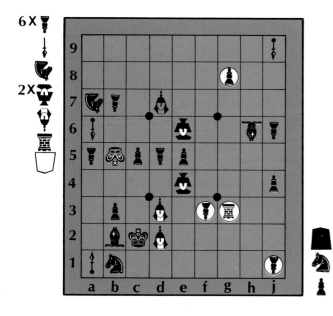

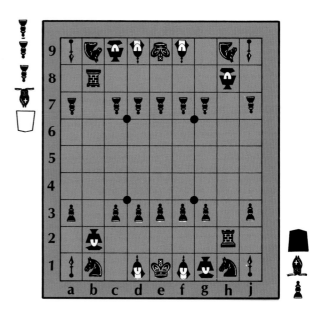

offensively. A dropped piece may block a line of attack or, more subtly, occupy a square of value to the enemy.

End Game

An end game is shown in figure 9; notice the defended gold behind the White king. The moves from this position are given below. (Japanese notation uses arabic numerals right to left for the files and Japanese numerals top to bottom for the ranks, with abbreviated titles for the men in diagrams. The symbol > = drop and * = promotes.)

Black	White
1 Nc3+	Kb6

Taking the pawn equally leads to mate.

2 N>c4+	

If 2 P>b5, N×b5.

2	K×c5
3 Ba3+	Kc6
4 Gd6 mate	

Remember, P>c5 mate would be illegal! The interesting point in this ending is that at the end White had no less than 13 men in hand whereas Black had a solitary pawn. If Black's attack, which started previously to the position, had not succeeded he would have been smothered. Once you start giving up men in an assault it is often a case of mate or succumb.

Example of play

Here is the score of a short game – most games last about 50 moves.

Black	White
1 Ph4	Pb6
2 Ph5	Pb5
3 Ph6	

The cautious Gc2 to protect the weak pawn b3 is usual here.

3	P×h6
4 R×h6	

Now both sides have a pawn in hand, but the defender gets his first, which can be crucial in an exchange.

4	Pb4
5 P>h7	

If Black had played P×b4, White would have dropped his pawn at b3 to win the bishop. It is a common Shogi tactic to entice a man off a square so that a drop can be made.

5	P×b3*
6 P×h8*	S×h8
7 Rh2	

White can always force the rook back by P>h7.

7	PP×b2
8 S×b2	

The position is symmetrical but White has two extra pawns in hand – a commanding lead. (Figure 10 shows how the board now looks.)

Figure 9 (above left)
An end game position

Figure 10 (above)
Position after White's 8th move

Figure 11
Final position

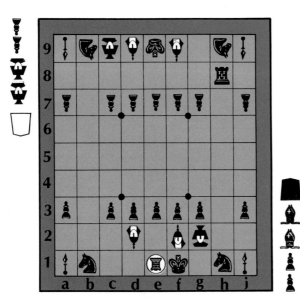

8   P>h3

Taking immediate advantage of his superiority.

9   R×h3

Moving the rook away would give White too strong a hold.

9		R×b2*
10	R×h8*	B>b3
11	S>c2	B×c2*
12	G×c2	PR×c2

White threatens G>d1 mate.

| 13 | Gf2 | S>g2 |

Closing Black's escape.

14	S×g2	G>d2+
15	Kf1	PRd1+
16	S>e1	PR×e1 mate

The final position is shown in figure 11.

Shogi problems

Three Shogi problems are shown in figure 12. Black, whose king is never present, mates by a series of checks. White is assumed to have in hand every piece not shown. Mate must be executed in the minimum number of moves against best play by White. This may sound rather formalized but in fact it reflects a common situation. The attacker draws heavily on his reserve base in the closing stages of a game. If he pauses to make a non-checking move his opponent, who has been accumulating men in hand, is ready to strike back.

The solutions to the problems shown are:

A: 1 PBe8+, Sd×e8;
   2 S>d8 mate.
or 1 ..., Sf×e8;
   2 S>f8 mate.
B: 1 B>a8+, K×a8 (if K×c9; R>b9
    mate);
   2 R>a7+, Kb9;
   3 P>b8+, K×c9;
   4 Ra9+, any >b9;
   5 PR×b9 mate.
C: 1 S>j7+, Kh9;
   2 Sg9*+, K×g9;
   3 B>h8+, Kh9;
   4 Sj8*+, K×j8;
   5 Rj7*+, Kh9;
   6 PRj9 mate.

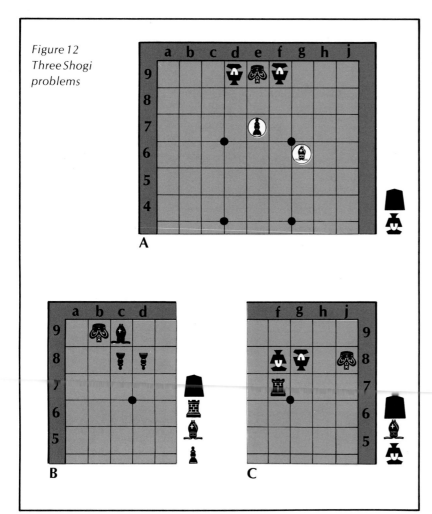

Figure 12
Three Shogi
problems

A

B

C

HASAMI-SHOGI

Hasami-Shogi is a name commonly given to two quite distinct board games, the first of which is very popular with Japanese children. Both are for two players and have simple rules, although they involve considerable strategy.

Game 1

The game is played on a Shogi board and each side has nine men – one player using pawns and the other promoted (reversed) pawns, although counters of different colours can be used instead. The starting position is shown in figure 1.

Play takes place on the squares and the object is to trap all but one of the opponent's men. The men move exactly like the rook in Chess or Shogi – straight forwards, backwards or sideways over any number of vacant squares.

Capture is by the escort method: the victim is trapped, either vertically or horizontally, between two men of the other side (figure 2A). Some players allow the corner capture shown in figure 2B. More than one man can be trapped on a move, as in figure 2C where Black's move captures three men. The white man at top centre is not captured because there is a vacant square next to him. A man can, however, move safely between two enemy men (figure 3). Captured men are removed from play.

Pieces are more vulnerable to attack in the centre of the board than at the edges. The following moves, using Chess notation explained on pp.46–7, show a typical game in progress (Black moves first):
1 e8, a7 (threatening the black man);
2 f7 (Black has prepared a counter), e7×;
3 d7×, e7! (and one of the two black men will fall).

Black might have tried:
1 e8, a7;
2 d7 when White could renew the threat with j7. Play might now continue:
3 e7, f6 (threatening e6);
4 f8, e8! (etc.); or
4 f7?, e7×;
5 f5×, (either man) g7×.

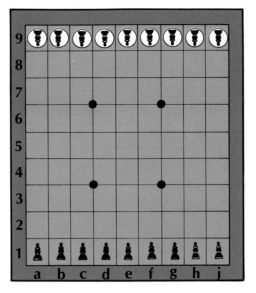

Figure 1 The starting position

Game 2

A Shogi board or part of a Go board is commonly used. Each side has 18 men, which can be counters of any convenient design (Go stones are ideal). They are arranged at the start in the first two ranks of each side of the board (figure 4).

The object of the game is to be the first player to form a line, either horizontally or vertically, of five of his own men. No man in the line may be in the player's first two ranks, and diagonal lines are not permitted.

The men move orthogonally, as in game 1, over any number of vacant squares, but they may also jump over an adjacent man of either colour to a vacant square immediately beyond. Diagonal and multiple jumps are not allowed, and jumps do not constitute captures. Capture is by the same method as in game 1, shown in figure 2.

In one variant of Hasami-Shogi, the men are allowed to move only one square at a time (except when jumping) with the aim of capturing all the opponent's men. In another variant, there is the same restriction and the aim is to form five men in a row, orthogonally or diagonally. These variants, however, make for a slower game.

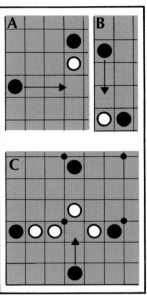

Figure 2 Methods of capture

Figure 3
Moving without capture

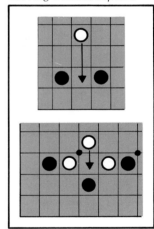

Figure 4

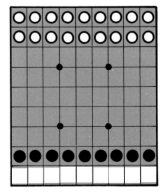

GO

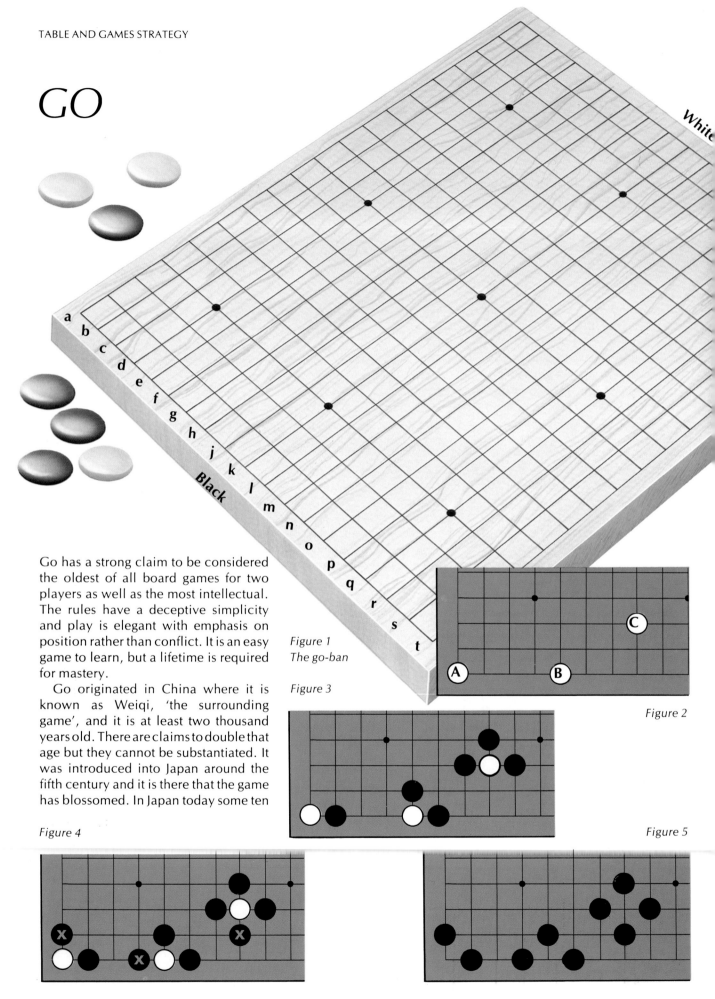

White

a b c d e f g h j k l m n o p q r s t

Black

Go has a strong claim to be considered the oldest of all board games for two players as well as the most intellectual. The rules have a deceptive simplicity and play is elegant with emphasis on position rather than conflict. It is an easy game to learn, but a lifetime is required for mastery.

Go originated in China where it is known as Weiqi, 'the surrounding game', and it is at least two thousand years old. There are claims to double that age but they cannot be substantiated. It was introduced into Japan around the fifth century and it is there that the game has blossomed. In Japan today some ten

Figure 1
The go-ban

Figure 3

Figure 2

Figure 4

Figure 5

66

million players support many hundreds of professionals. As yet, Go has made no great impact outside the East although there are an increasing number of publications about the game in European languages.

The board has changed in size over the centuries and may change again, but the simplicity of the rules strongly suggests that the game itself has altered little. A curious feature of Go is that sometimes situations arise that are not covered by the rules. Guidance is given by Nihon Kiin, the ruling body for the game in Japan, and terminology is largely Japanese.

EQUIPMENT

The board, known as the go-ban, is shown in figure 1. Ideally it is made of wood. It is marked with a regular, slightly elongated grid of 19 × 19 lines. Nine intersections, known as star points, are accentuated: these are used in handicap games. For ease of reference the vertical lines of the board are lettered a–t (omitting i) and the horizontal lines are numbered 1–19, both starting from Black's left-hand corner.

The men are lentil-shaped counters, called stones, of two colours – 181 black and 180 white, totalling the number of intersections (points) on the go-ban, a traditional relationship that has little bearing on the game. Properly, the white stones are of shell and the black of slate, but today all but the most expensive are made of plastic.

PLAY

The object of Go is to enclose territory. Play starts with the empty board between the players. Black begins by placing a stone on any point, and White then places a stone on any vacant point. The game proceeds in this manner, players occupying vacant points in turn. Once placed, stones are never moved but they may be captured.

Territory is secured by surrounding vacant points with stones of one colour. The game ends when both players are satisfied that there is no more territory to be gained or prisoners to be taken. The winner is the player with the higher score: points of territory owned less the number of stones taken prisoner.

A stone is captured by depriving it of liberties. A liberty is any vacant point adjacent to the stone along a line. In figure 2, stones A, B and C have respectively two, three and four liberties. Notice that adjacent diagonal points do not come within the definition. In figure 3, the three stones each have one liberty remaining. In figure 4, the last liberty of each stone has been taken by Black's play. Captured stones are at once removed from the board (figure 5) and are retained by the capturing player until the end of the game.

Two or more stones occupying adjacent points form a group (figure 6). A group is captured in the same way as a single stone. In figure 7, Black deprives the white group of its last liberty, and removes the captured stones (figure 8).

Figure 6

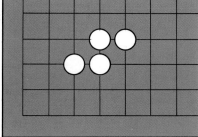

Figure 7

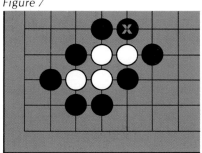

Figure 8

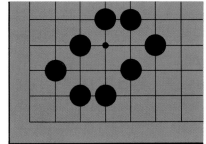

Liberties may be inside as well as outside a group. The group in figure 9 has a total of nine liberties, three inside and six outside. The outside liberties are filled in figure 10 and only the inside ones remain.

Whether a group is alive (cannot be captured) or whether it is dead (doomed) is the basis of Go. In figure 10, Black to play must place a stone on b1 to secure his group (figure 11). Now he has reduced his liberties to two separate points, known as eyes. White cannot play into either eye without committing suicide – which is forbidden. Therefore Black's group is safe. The precept is that any group with two or more eyes is safe from capture, but note that an eye is always within a group, never outside it.

If Black had made the mistake of playing at c1 (or a1) his group would have been dead since White could then have played on either of the remaining points – say b1 (figure 12). White's stone has a liberty, so the play is legal. Now White threatens to play at a1, depriving the black group of its last liberty and so capturing it. This would not be suicide, since the black stones would at once be removed from the board, leaving the two-stone white group with three liberties. Black could now play at a1 himself to capture the white stone on b1, but then his group would have only one liberty – on b1 – which White would occupy next move.

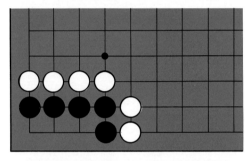

Figure 9

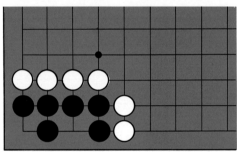

Figure 10

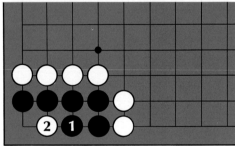

Figure 11

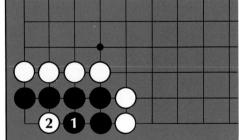

Figure 12

Figure 13
Ko position

Figure 14
Seki position

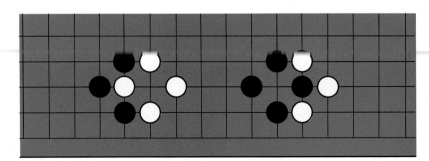

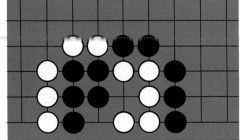

If White had the move in figure 10, he would play at b1 and the black group would then be dead.

This example is in part theoretical. In practice, both players would abandon the position once the outcome was determined. At the end of the game, Black, if he had played at b1, would count two points for territory owned. If White had played first at c1, he would have taken the five black stones prisoner and counted seven points of territory for a total swing of 14 points – assuming, that is, the surrounding white stones were not themselves surrounded and captured, which is what Go is all about.

Rule of ko There is a tactical situation governed by a special rule known as the rule of ko ('almost eternity'). This rule forbids a player to make a move that leaves the position identical to what it was after his last move. Consider the sequence in figure 13. Black, to play, could capture the white stone on the left by playing in the centre of the white group. But now White could play back on the point to recapture, so returning to the first position. This sequence could continue indefinitely but the rule of ko means that White must first make at least one move elsewhere before he can retake. (A ko can also occur in the corner or at the edge of the board.)

Seki Sometimes a position is reached where neither side can move without loss. Look at figure 14. If either side plays on one of the two enclosed points, the other will occupy the remaining point to capture the opponent's group. This situation is called seki. Seki positions, if any, are neutralized at the end of a game, and the territory is not counted for either one side or the other.

Game phases

A game is divided into three phases, the opening, middle game and end game. In the opening, players sketch out territory by placing stones in the corners and along the sides of the board because fewer stones are needed to secure territory here as the board edges act as boundaries. A typical opening (fuseki) is shown in figure 15. Notice how embryo groups are already forming. Opening play in a corner is known as joseki.

Now the middle game starts. In this phase a series of battles develop as groups are formed and joined, with both sides building walls to fence off territory and to prevent incursions.

The end game is the tidying up of loose points when all main issues have been decided. After both players pass in turn, the counting starts. The first step is to fill any neutral points (dame) with stones of either colour. Now prisoners are put back on the board to fill points in the opponent's territory. Lastly, the territories are adjusted into more or less

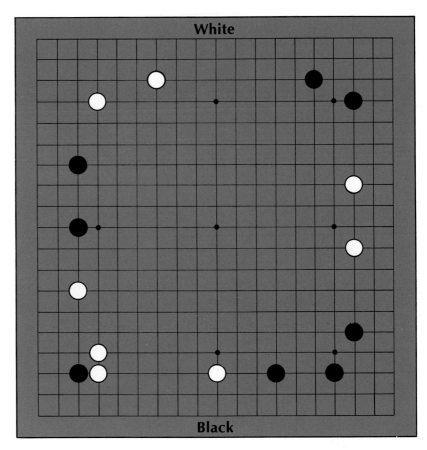

Figure 15
Example of an opening

regular shapes. All these actions are to facilitate counting. A final, adjusted position is shown in figure 16. Black has won by three points.

Handicapping

Go has an excellent handicapping system. The weaker player places up to nine stones on the star points before play begins, as follows:

2-stone handicap	d4, q16
3-stone handicap	d4, q4, q16
4-stone handicap	d4, d16, q4, q16
5-stone handicap	as 4-stone plus k10
6-stone handicap	d4, d10, d16, q4, q10, q16
7-stone handicap	as 6-stone plus k10
8-stone handicap	all star points except k10
9-stone handicap	all star points

White then starts. Larger handicaps are sometimes given.

STRATEGY

Economy is the key to strategy. Stones should only be connected to meet a direct threat. In figure 15, the three black stones at bottom right lay claim to about 16 points in the corner. Black need not play here again until White approaches. Only when he is direly threatened will Black find it necessary to make two eyes.

Weak positions are best abandoned or a counter prepared. A common tactical threat is the *shicho* (ladder) shown in figure 17. If Black tries to escape he is driven towards the board edge (figure 18) where his whole group will be captured. Black has three choices: he can surrender the position totally; he can plan to attack the white stones; or he can prepare an escape route for his trapped men, for example by playing at d4. Now Black threatens to continue as in figure 18, when his group will join with the stone d4 (figure 19) and he will be in a position to counter-attack with d7 or f4, in each case simultaneously attacking two white

stones. If White takes the two black stones, Black can add a second stone to make territory in the corner (figure 20).

Another common theme is the *snapback* (figure 21). White has several threats but Black gets there first with a neat sacrifice. He plays d4 (figure 22); if

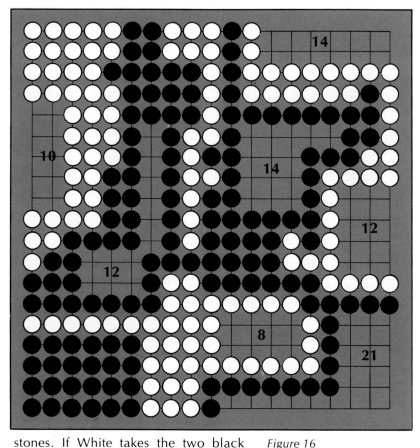

Figure 16
A final position adjusted for counting

Figure 17

Figure 18

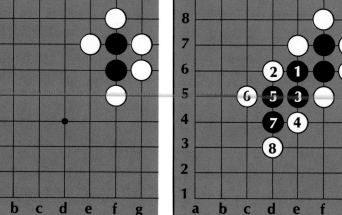

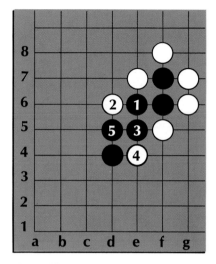

Figure 19

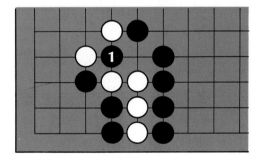

Figure 20

Figure 21

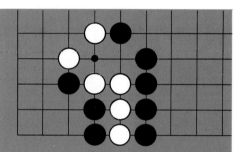

Figure 22

Figure 23

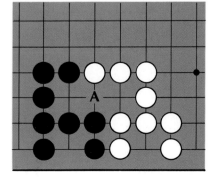

Figure 24

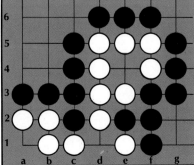

White now captures with e4, Black returns to d4 to take the five white stones.

It often happens that the same point is vital to both sides. Figure 23 is a simple example. Whoever plays first at A secures a live group.

An important concept in Go is *sente*. To have sente is to have the move and so to dictate, to a large degree, the course of play. A player retains sente by maintaining a series of threats. Eventually, he will be obliged to make a defensive move or his opponent will find a larger threat, when sente will change hands. It is usually worth giving up a few stones to retain sente.

The most interesting and most critical clash in a Go game is a *ko-fight*. There may be several ko-fights in a game – or none. These fights arise from the rule of ko which denies the second player the right to an immediate recapture. Consider figure 24. If White is to play, he will occupy d1 to create a live group with two eyes, one at a1 and one at e4. But if Black is to play, he will go to d1 to capture e1. Now the two white groups each have one eye, and Black threatens next to play at either e4 or a1 to capture one of them, when the other will also fall.

But the black stone d1 is itself vulnerable. White cannot play at e1 at once as this is a ko, so he must play elsewhere. The ko is worth nearly 30 points so White must find a play that is worth more, bearing in mind that if Black then captures, White will be able to add a second stone to the first. This is called a ko threat. If Black replies to it, White will be able to recapture in the ko and will then threaten to fill in at d1, so it will be Black's turn to find a ko threat somewhere that is larger than the points at stake. Play can thus see-saw for some moves before the ko is resolved. The player who has the most ko threats wins the ko, so it is often wise to conserve threats against the possibility of a ko arising.

A final piece of advice. Be content with small profits: striving after large gains can lead to large losses.

71

GO-MOKU and RENJU

Go-moku and Renju – a refinement of Go-moku – are games of alignment which work best for two players although four can play. Go-moku has been marketed under a variety of names, and despite similarities to Go and the fact that Go-moku is widely played in Japan, there is no link between the two games. Between experts, the first player in Go-moku will always win, and because of this, Renju has been developed. Renju is Go-moku with a number of restrictions, so that unlike Go-moku it confers no advantage on either player.

GO-MOKU

The Go-moku board is a regular lattice of 19 × 19 lines though smaller or larger boards can be used. A Go board and stones are commonly used, but the game can be played with pencil and paper. According to convention one side is Black, the other White.

The empty board is placed between the players. Play is on the intersections (though it could alternatively be in the squares) and the players take turns to put a stone on the board on any vacant point, Black starting. Once placed, stones are never moved until the end of the game and there is no capturing.

The object is to get five of one's own stones next to one another in a line, orthogonally or diagonally. Clearly, the first player to get four stones in a row with a vacant point at either end (called an 'open four') will win, since his opponent can stop only one end on his next turn. It follows that an 'open three' (three stones in a row with vacant points at both ends) must be stopped if it can be extended into an open four next move.

Often one player forms two open threes simultaneously early in the game. White can do this in figure 1 by playing at A. Black will now lose since he cannot prevent White extending one of his open threes into an open four on his next move. Experienced players ban open threes.

RENJU

Renju ('row of gems') is played on a 15 × 15 board. Black plays on the centre point to start. He is under three restrictions:

1 He cannot simultaneously form two or more open threes.

2 He cannot simultaneously form two or more fours, open at one or both ends

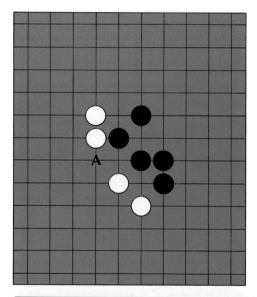

Figure 1
Two open threes formed by White in a game of Go-moku

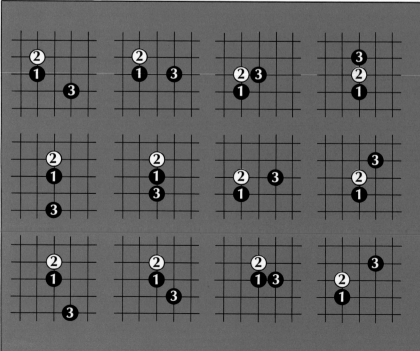

Figure 2
Renju: the standard opening patterns – Hogetsu (left) and Kagetsu (right)

or in the middle.

3 He cannot form an overline (six or more stones in a line).

In addition, Black may suffer a restriction on where he places his second stone. There are normally no restrictions on White.

The only way in which Black can force a win in Renju is to form simultaneously an open three and a four.

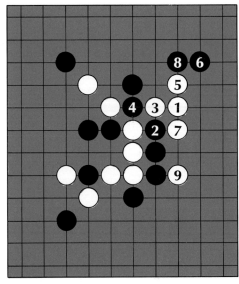

Figure 4
White wins

Figure 3
A game of Renju in progress

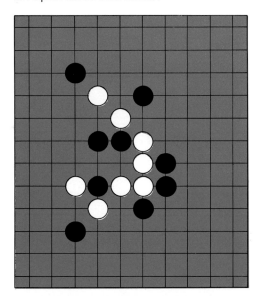

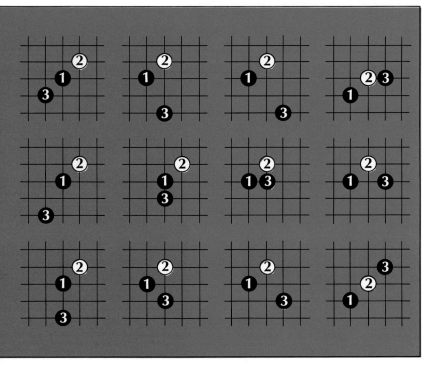

STRATEGY

In both Go-moku and Renju, Black must try to retain the initiative from the outset and aim to concentrate his forces so that they can be expanded in several directions. White is usually forced to counter Black's threats for a while, during which his stones are liable to be scattered and uncoordinated.

The first White play should be adjacent orthogonally to the black stone (the kagetsu openings) or diagonally (the hogetsu openings). To play at a distance from Black is to invite disaster. There are 24 opening patterns, shown in figure 2.

The position in figure 3 is from a game of Renju. Black has allowed his stones to be separated. White, with the move, now wins. In figure 4, each White move is a threat. White 9 is unanswerable since Black can only stop the line of five by himself forming a double three, which is illegal. This is a curious feature of Renju: White's usual strategy is to force Black into a position where his only response is an illegal move. If this had been a game of Go-moku, White 7 would have to have been played one point lower to block Black's threat.

WORD, PAPER AND PENCIL GAMES

Word games and pencil and paper games have long been a popular amusement for spare moments. The materials, if needed at all, are cheap and readily to hand, little preparation is needed, and the games are easy to learn and quick to play. However, the games included here are much more than trivial time-fillers. The simple ideas behind them, translated into equally simple rules, can be surprisingly challenging as well as entertaining. Some of the games are in fact distinctly difficult and call for quite a lot of thought. Several are likely to be new to you, and others – such as the familiar Noughts and Crosses – are presented in a more demanding form.

For those who like a creative challenge, there are games such as Crystals and Sprouts, while an old favourite like Battleships – even the name sounds archaic – responds well to innovations.

Generally it is wise to play the games here intermittently and not at one long sitting, so that they retain their appeal. Like many good things, they are best enjoyed when fresh.

WORD GAMES

SPOOF WORDS

This excellent game, the basis of a popular television show, requires a number of players and a large dictionary. It is sometimes known as the Dictionary Game.

One player, the selector, chooses an obscure word from the dictionary and announces it without giving its meaning. He then copies down the definition. Everyone else writes down a plausible meaning for the word. The selector collects the entries, adds in the true definition, and numbers them. He then reads them out in a level voice so as to give no indication of the validity or otherwise of a definition or of its source. Players then vote in turn on the true definition. They earn 2 points if correct and 1 point for every vote their own definition received. A game is to any agreed number of points.

Be careful to compose your definition in the style of the dictionary.

BOTTICELLI

This oral word game calls for some general knowledge and is best for several players.

One player assumes the role of a well-known personality, living, dead or fictional, but announces only the first letter of his or her name. The other players, not necessarily in turn, try to identify the celebrity by asking indirect questions.

The game goes like this. Supposing the first player says 'H' with Lady Hamilton in mind, then the sort of questions that might be posed, with valid answers, are:
Q. Did you write *For Whom the Bell Tolls*?
A. No, I'm not Hemingway.
Q. Did you cross the Pacific on a raft?
A. No, I'm not Thor Heyerdahl.
Q. Are you a Roman emperor?
A. No, I'm not Hadrian.
And so on until the quizzed player is stumped or gives the wrong answer, when the interrogator is allowed to put one direct question calling for a yes/no answer. For example:
Q. Are you fictional?
A. No.
Indirect questioning is then resumed. The player who correctly guesses the personality starts a new game.

Questions and answers can be informal if you are in familiar company:
Q. Did you import tuskers into Tuscany?
A. No, I'm not Hannibal.

GHOSTS

You need a good vocabulary for this game, which is best with three or four players.

Players take it in turns to call out a letter of the alphabet. Each player is trying to contribute to the spelling of a word that he has in mind (the players may be thinking of different words) but not to complete one – if he does, he loses a life and when a player has lost three he is out of the game (he becomes a ghost!). The last player in wins. In selecting a word a player naturally tries to avoid one whose last letter ends with him.

For example, the first two players might call respectively 'S' and 'T'. There are of course hundreds of words that start 'ST'. Suppose you are the third player and have STYLE or perhaps STYPTIC in mind: you call 'Y'. Disaster: you have completed a word – STY – and forfeit a life; you could have called any vowel with comparative safety.

Anyone may challenge a player who announces a letter to state the word he has in mind (bluffing is permitted). If the player can name a legitimate word, the challenger loses a life, otherwise the player does.

Another version of the game allows players to add letters in front of the sequence as well as behind, and perhaps the best variant, Anaghosts, permits letters to be given in any order – for example, TCHY could be expanded into YACHT, HATCHERY, CARTOGRAPHY, etc.

BOXES

This two-player game has become a classroom classic. Its skill can be enhanced with a slight modification.

A grid of dots of convenient size (8 × 8 or 10 × 10 are suitable) is drawn on a piece of paper. Players take turns to join any two dots that are adjacent either vertically or horizontally. You cannot join the same pair of dots more than once, nor can you pass your turn. The aim is to complete cells (boxes) by adding the fourth side to cells that are already enclosed on three sides. On completing a box, the player marks it with his initial and takes another turn. The game ends when every cell has been enclosed. The winner is the player who has scored the most boxes. A game in progress is shown in figure 1.

Boxes tends to be a little tedious to begin with since the game lacks strategical signposts. It is only in the late stages in the scramble to complete boxes that it becomes interesting.

BOX CLEVER

This version of the game gives more scope for strategy. One player adopts rows, the other columns. The first player marks any row of dots with a token, and the second player does the same with a column. The row and column intersect at a point which the second player now joins to an adjacent point in the usual way. The first player must now move his marker to another row and similarly joins the point of intersection to an adjacent point (see figure 2).

Play continues in this way, with boxes being formed as in the basic game and a player completing a box earning another turn. If a player is unable to draw in a line because all the points along the opponent's row or column are full, then he misses a turn but he must move his token to permit the opponent to play on the next turn.

As in Boxes, the winner is the player who has completed the most number of boxes.

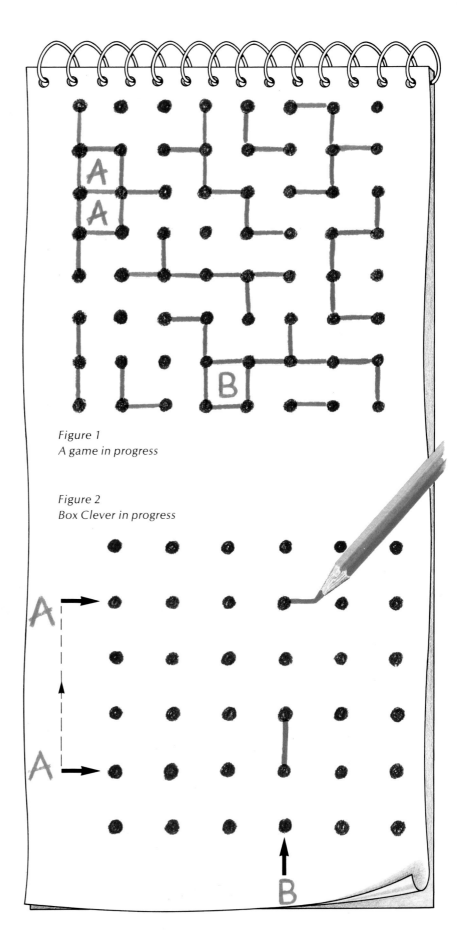

Figure 1
A game in progress

Figure 2
Box Clever in progress

FOOTSTEPS

This little psychological game is deeper than is at first apparent. Two players take part and the better they know each other, the better the game.

A sheet of paper is drawn up as shown in the figure and a coin or token is placed in the centre. The object is to get the token to the opponent's base line.

Each player has an agreed allocation of points – 50 is a good number – and keeps a record of these on a slip of paper. Both players start by writing down the number of points they wish to invest (minimum 1) and then comparing them. The higher bid wins and that player moves the token one place towards the opponent. If bids are the same, the token is not moved. The number of points bid by each of the players is then deducted

from their total allocation. Subsequent rounds are played in the same manner, the number of points allotted being deducted after each round. If a player uses up his 50 points, the opponent can advance with impunity by investing one point at a time.

The ideal is to win each round by a single point. A good mind-reader can often achieve this, which is why the game plays well when close friends or relatives compete. If players are of unequal strength, reduce the stronger player's allocation by 5 or 10 points.

3-D NOUGHTS AND CROSSES

The familiar two-player game of Noughts and Crosses, played on a 3 × 3 grid, is very simple and the three dimensional version of it (3 × 3 × 3 grid) is not much more difficult; both can be won easily by whoever first occupies the centre cell. This variant is more challenging.

Draw four grids, each 4 × 4, one below the other. The players take it in turns to mark any vacant cell using contrasting colours or symbols. The first player to achieve a line of four of his own colour or symbol wins. The lines must be straight, but can otherwise travel in any direction including diagonally, either in one plane or all four (it is not possible to create a line of four using two or three planes). In figure 1, Red has won.

The game can be made more difficult by requiring the play to be visualized. Using a suitable notation, like that in figure 2, players call out and record their moves (e.g. 'B12') but do not mark the grids. An incorrect claim loses the game.

Figure 1
Red wins

Figure 2
Suggested notation

A
1	2	3	4
5	6	7	8
9	10	11	12
13	14	15	16

B
1	2	3	4
5	6	7	8
9	10	11	12
13	14	15	16

C
1	2	3	4
5	6	7	8
9	10	11	12
13	14	15	16

D
1	2	3	4
5	6	7	8
9	10	11	12
13	14	15	16

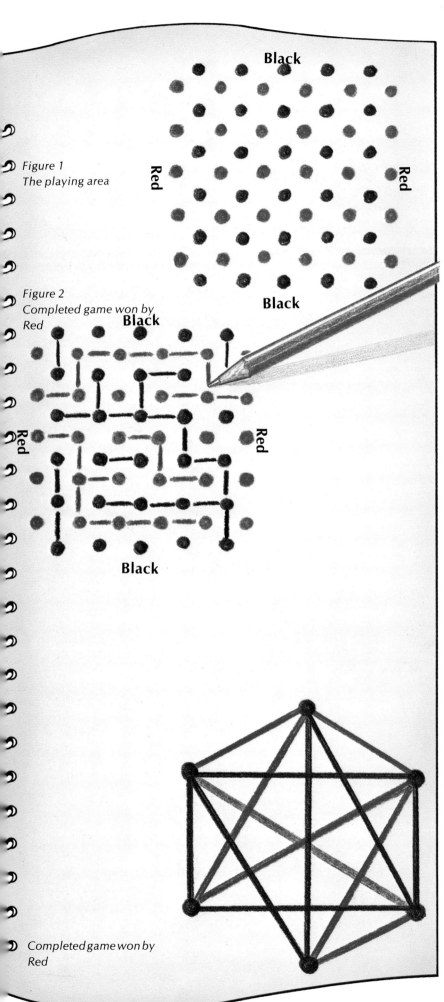

Figure 1
The playing area

Figure 2
Completed game won by
Red

Completed game won by
Red

GALE

This two-player game looks like Boxes but is related to Hex.

Draw two interspaced networks of dots, each 6 × 5, in contrasting colours. This is the playing area (figure 1).

Players choose colours. A turn consists of linking a pair of adjacent dots with a vertical or horizontal line, each player keeping to dots of his own colour. No line may cross another line. The aim is to establish a continuous connection lengthways across the field from one side to the other. The first player to do so wins. A completed game is shown in figure 2. Red has won.

In Gale, the first player has the advantage but there is no known winning strategy. Larger playing areas can be used if a more complex game is wanted.

SIM

Sim is a simple and quick game for two people. Surprisingly, nobody has established whether it is an advantage to start.

Six dots are drawn in the shape of a regular hexagon. A player on his turn must draw a straight line between any pair of dots not previously joined. Contrasting colours can be used, or one player can draw dotted lines.

The first player to form a triangle joining three dots and with all sides in his colour is the loser. Triangles formed by crossing lines are not considered. A completed game, won by Red, is shown in the figure. The maximum number of lines possible, and hence turns, is 15, and there must be a winner – there are no draws.

Strategy in Sim is unclear but it is better to complete a triangle of which two sides are yours rather than one which includes two of your opponent's since this reduces his choice of plays.

79

SPROUTS

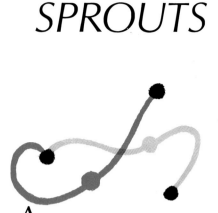

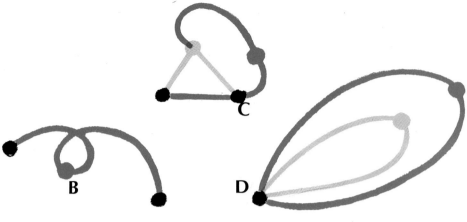

Figure 1
Illegal play by Brown

Figure 2
Reducing connections

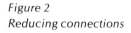

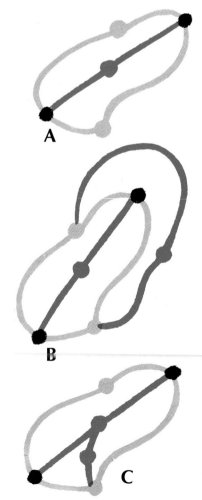

A pencil and paper game for two players or four in partnerships, Sprouts pleases the eye, with a strong appeal to the creative, and is quick to learn and to play. It has its origin in that branch of geometry known as topology which is concerned with those properties of a figure that remain unchanged when the figure is distorted by extension or bending. A completed game looks rather like a large, half-opened Brussels sprout.

This curious little game was invented at Cambridge some 20 years ago. Now familiar to most serious games players, it deserves a much wider audience both for its originality and its ingenuity.

PLAY

A fairly large sheet of paper is used, a number of points being marked on it at random. Five is a good number to begin with but experienced players favour seven or more. The number of game turns cannot exceed three times the number of points chosen, less one; thus a five-point game cannot take more than 14 turns.

The first player draws a continuous line starting and finishing at one of the points. Two points may be joined or the line can start and end at the same point. The line may be as straight or convoluted as the player wishes but it cannot pass through a point, since this would amount to drawing two lines, not one. The player then marks a new point anywhere along the line he has drawn, when his turn ends.

The players alternate in this fashion. There are only two rules:
1 No line may cross itself or any other line;

2 No point may have more than three lines joined to it.
The winner is the player who draws the last legal line.

Figure 1 shows illegal plays for the Brown player. In examples A and B he has crossed a line; in example C he has joined three existing points, while in example D he has joined his line to a point already linked to three lines.

STRATEGY

Sprouts depends on forward planning. The maximum number of game turns is known before play begins. On each turn, the number of available connections is reduced by at least one.

It sometimes happens that a play reduces by two the number of available connections by isolating a point. Consider figure 2A. Three plays have been made, each joining the same two original points. Brown is free on his next play to join any two of the three points available. If he joins the two outside points (figure 2B) the one in the centre cannot be used. If he joins an outside point to the centre point (figure 2C) then the new point he creates is equally barren.

Herein lies the basis of strategy. From the start, one player is striving to finish on an odd number of game turns, the other on an even number. Thus at any given time one player will be trying to change the sequence by achieving a two-connection reduction (as in figure 2), while the other will be trying to maintain the regular single-connection reduction.

Sprouts shares with Boxes a concealed initial strategy. It is not certain whether, in an eight-point game for example, it is an advantage to start or not.

HEX

Hex was invented by the Danish poet, Piet Hein, and is a mathematical game of pure skill for two players. It requires no equipment other than a piece of paper or card on which to draw the board.

PLAY

Hex is best played on a lozenge-shaped board composed of interlocking hexagons, 11 to each side. A pair of opposite sides is designated White and the other pair Black. The game can also be played on larger or smaller boards and, if hexagons prove difficult to construct, equilateral triangles can be used. They achieve the same end, which is six directions of contact in the case of an inside cell, four in the case of an outer cell and two each for the four corners. Both boards are illustrated in figure 1.

Players can use contrasting counters (Go stones are ideal) or coloured pencils. The board starts empty. Each player in turn occupies an empty cell (or intersection if the second board is used). The object is to make an unbroken chain linking one's two sides. The corners are common property.

STRATEGY

Theoretically the first player wins. The central cell is the key and some players do not permit this to be occupied on the first move. However the strategy of Hex is so subtle and the alternatives so vast that the first move is only an advantage to an expert. There are marked similarities to the strategy of Go (p. 66), in particular the need to throw up a defence line at a distance from an advancing enemy: a breakthrough is hard to contain when forces are in close contact.

A game position is illustrated in figure 2. White cannot prevent Black from winning. Draws are unknown in Hex; also, a winning line by one player, however constructed, precludes a winning line by the opponent since the first line effectively cuts the board in two.

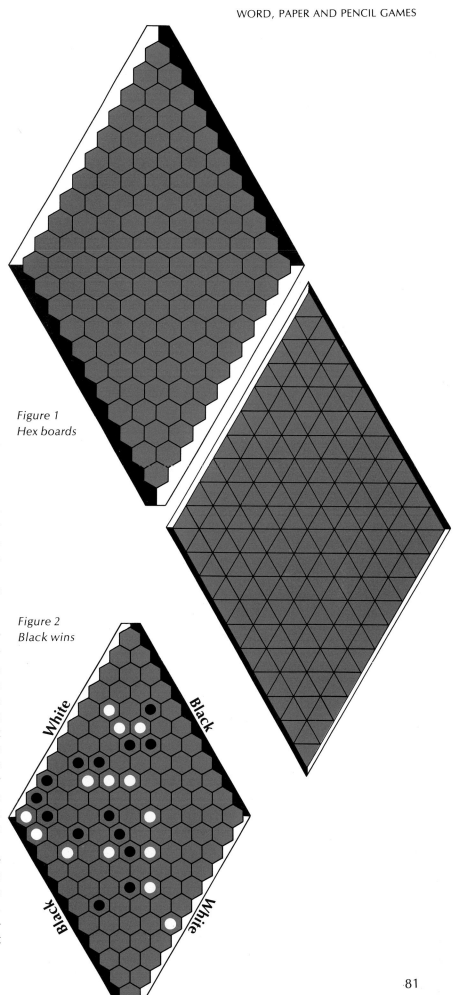

Figure 1
Hex boards

Figure 2
Black wins

81

AGGRESSION

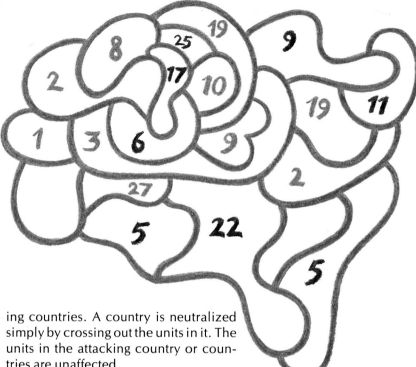

Aggression is an abstract conflict game for two that offers scope for careful planning.

PLAY

The game is played in three stages, preparation, deployment and conflict. A large sheet of paper is required and preferably two pens in contrasting colours.

One player starts by enclosing a small area of any shape to represent a country. The area should be large enough to write inside, but not too large since 20 shapes (or some other agreed number) must be drawn. The second player, using the same pen, does likewise except that his shape must border the first. The first player now adds a third country which in turn must border at least one of those already drawn, and so on until the required number of countries is reached.

Now the second stage begins. Each player has an allocation of units – five for each country in the game is a good ratio – which he distributes as he pleases. The first player (who starts first in each phase) marks the number of units he wants in a country of his choice. The second player, using a different-coloured pen, does likewise, and so on in turn. Deployment may only take place in unoccupied countries and one may not later add units to a country one has occupied. Deployment continues until all countries are occupied or until both players have exhausted their entitlements, thus it is possible for one player to continue his deployment after the other has finished. It often happens that a few countries remain unoccupied. A typical deployment is shown in figure 1.

Now comes the conflict stage. The first player neutralizes any one of his opponent's countries which borders at least one of his own. A country can be neutralized if its deployed units are less than the total of those in all hostile countries that border it. Notice that the defender cannot combine his forces in neighbour-

ing countries. A country is neutralized simply by crossing out the units in it. The units in the attacking country or countries are unaffected.

The second player in turn neutralizes one of his opponent's countries and play continues like this until no more conflicts are possible. The winner is the player with the most countries remaining, regardless of unit strengths.

STRATEGY

The main skill of Aggression lies in the second stage. Wise deployment is more than half the battle.

Since your aim is survival combined with economy of deployment, try to create buffer countries which, though certain to be neutralized, shield weak countries from attack. Key countries are those which can combine in a number of attacks. A concentration of units in these may be desirable. Conversely these are the countries, when held by your opponent, you will wish to neutralize first.

A local situation with Black to play is shown in figure 2. The best move is for 11 and 8 to combine to neutralize 17. Now Red will eliminate one of the four countries bordering his 21, but Black will then combine the other three to attack Red 21, leaving the situation 3–0 in Black's favour. If Black first neutralized 21, Red 17 would strike at 11 and 8 in turn, reducing the local situation to 2–1 to Black.

Figure 1
Deployment of units

Figure 2
A local situation, with Black to play

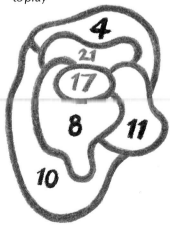

CRYSTALS

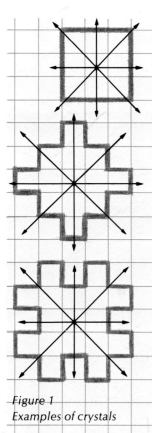

Figure 1
Examples of crystals

This is a game for the creative although it is also competitive. It has an unusual aim — to form symmetrical patterns, two-dimensional representations of the visual harmony one usually associates with crystals.

Any number can play but it is best for two or three.

PLAY

Squared paper is necessary. Any size playing area can be used, but as a guide a grid of 19 × 19 gives a good game. For a shorter game, use a smaller grid. Each player has a crayon of distinctive colour. Symbols can be used instead of colours but are not as aesthetically pleasing.

Players in turn fill in any blank cell. The filled cell is called an atom and the process of filling it is called seeding. The object is to form crystals; the bigger a crystal, the more points it scores.

A crystal is defined as a shape which is symmetrical about its four major axes: the vertical, the horizontal and the two diagonals. Examples of crystals are shown in figure 1. A crystal must be solid: it cannot include a hole nor can it include atoms that are only joined at the corners. The three shapes in figure 2 are not crystals. Finally, a crystal must contain at least four atoms of one colour but none of any other colour.

A player announces a crystal on his turn and outlines the area. He scores one point for every cell in the crystal and so will encompass the largest possible area, limited only by the proximity of a rival atom or the edge of the grid. Thereafter no player may seed an atom within the crystal. The game ends when players agree that no more crystals can be formed. Figure 3 shows a three-player game in progress.

STRATEGY

It is an advantage to start but it is not necessarily an advantage to form the first crystal, particularly if it is a small one, since this will take your four seeded atoms out of play. Do not overlook defensive possibilities: a strategically placed atom can deprive your opponent of a high-scoring crystal.

Figure 2
Invalid crystals
A: hole occupied by a rival atom
B: not symmetrical about diagonal axes
C: joined at corners

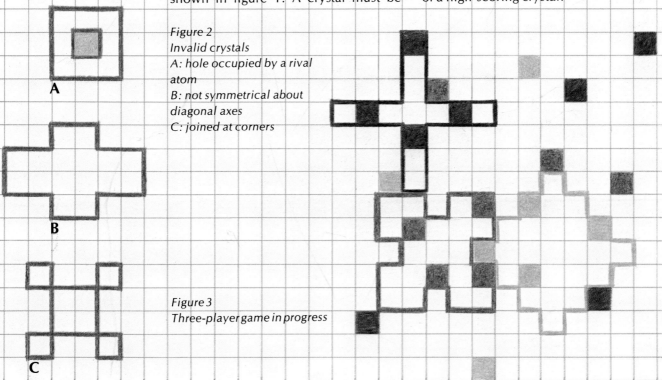

Figure 3
Three-player game in progress

BATTLESHIPS

This is an old favourite two-player game that can be enriched with a little imagination. Marketed versions are available that eliminate the rather tedious preparation and even add visual and sound effects but they are less flexible than the pencil and paper game.

PLAY

Each player starts by drawing two identical grids of convenient size – 10 × 10 is recommended – and marking them with an agreed reference system (say 1 to 10 and A to J). These grids represent sea areas.

Each player is now required to deploy secretly a fleet of ships within his sea area. Each ship occupies a certain number of squares according to type, and a typical fleet is:

   1 battleship (4 squares)
   2 cruisers (3 squares each)
   4 destroyers (2 squares each)
   2 submarines (1 square each)

The ships must be deployed horizontally or vertically and may not touch one another, not even diagonally. Players enter their ships on one of their grids by

outlining or shading in the squares. A typical deployment is shown in figure 1.

Players take it in turns to fire into the other's sea area, the object being to sink the opponent's fleet before he sinks yours. Single shots or salvoes can be fired, as prearranged. The second (blank) grid is used to record these shots and register hits. A shot is fired by simply nominating a square, say 'D6'. The second player refers to his deployment grid and must answer truthfully: 'No' (meaning a miss) or 'Hit on a . . .' (naming the ship type – if a submarine it is sunk).

A salvo is treated in the same way except that squares on which damage occurs are not identified. Suppose it was agreed to fire salvoes of three shots: the attacker might announce, 'F6, G4, H6', to which, using figure 1, the reply would be: 'Two misses; one hit on cruiser.'

A ship is only sunk when all its squares have been hit. Figure 2 illustrates a recording grid marked with the results of 12 shots against the disposition given in figure 1. The attacker has had the good fortune to register five hits, including a submarine sunk; this is much better than the average hit ratio of about 1 in 5.

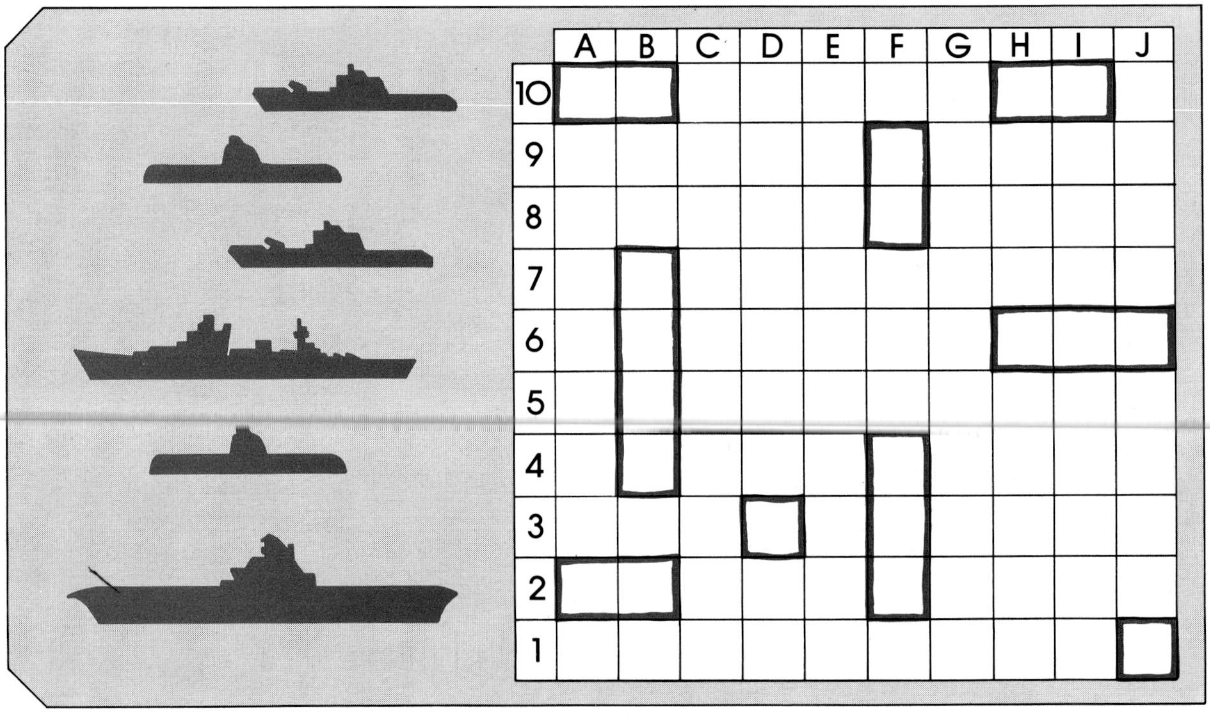

Figure 1
Typical deployment

STRATEGY

The basic game offers little scope for skill. Freak deployment – like putting your ships round the edge or grouped in one area – is liable to recoil, since suspicions may soon be aroused. Random deployment is best.

The battleship, paradoxically, is the easiest target: after the first hit its location can be quickly established. Submarines are of course the hardest to find, but do not forget the rule forbidding diagonal deployment: if you record a hit on a square you can eliminate the squares diagonally adjacent to it.

The example in figure 2 is a 'single shot' game. If you are playing salvoes, there will be uncertainties as to where a hit occurs and the grid must be annotated accordingly.

RELATED GAMES

These are as broad as your imagination. So many versions of the game have been invented that it is impossible, and in any case undesirable, to record them all. It is better for players to create their own games and modify them with experience; there can be as much entertainment in doing this as in actual playing. Here are a few possibilities that can be tried out:

1 Increase the size of the grid and vary the fleets.

2 Allow diagonal deployment.

3 Relate the number of shots in a salvo (some versions use 20 or 25) to firepower, which in turn is related to the number and type of ships: as your fleet is depleted so is your firepower.

4 Let each player start with an agreed number of points which he then allocates secretly, subject to certain limits, between ships and salvoes. The player with most surviving ship squares (half a battleship would count two for example) is the winner.

5 Introduce new elements – reconnaissance planes, mines, searchlights – there need be no restrictions.

You can, of course, reshape Battleships completely by turning it into a space game or a safari or some other theme involving conflict. The game is infinitely adaptable to suit your moods and tastes.

Figure 2
Recording grid

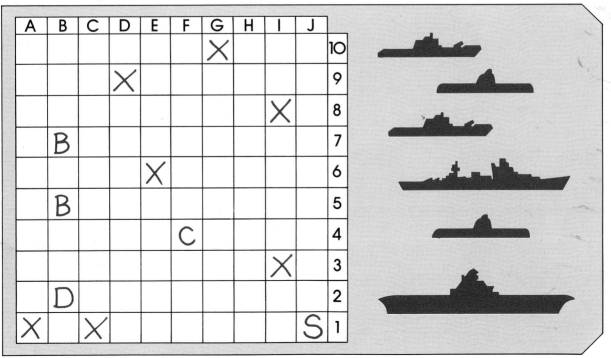

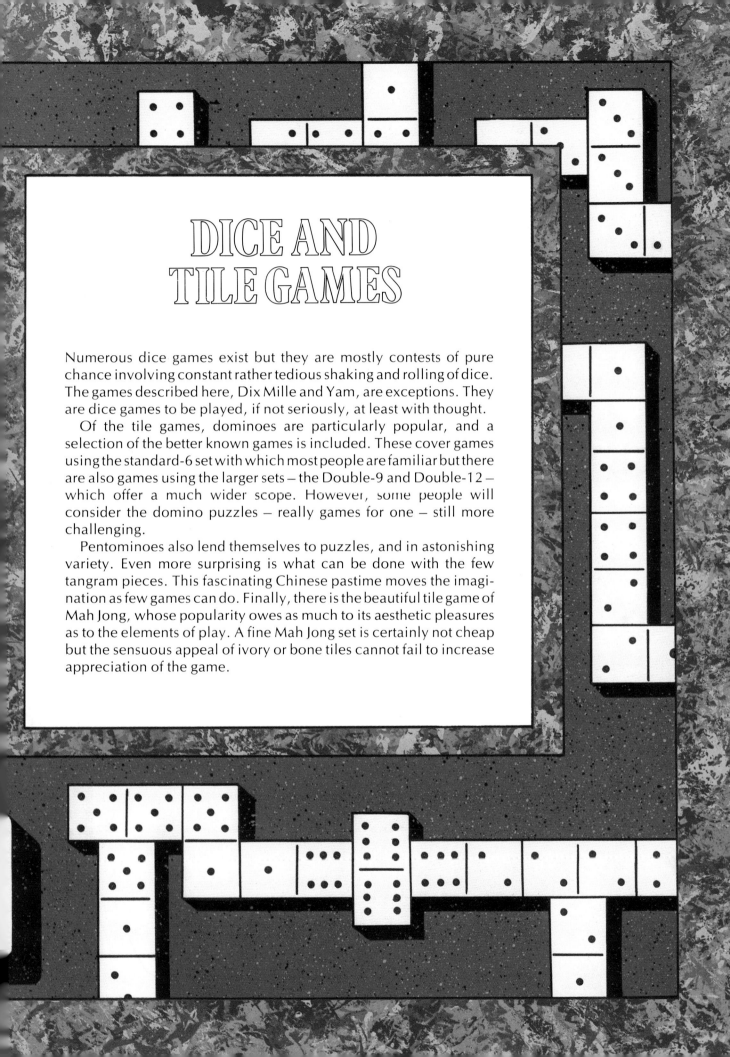

DICE AND TILE GAMES

Numerous dice games exist but they are mostly contests of pure chance involving constant rather tedious shaking and rolling of dice. The games described here, Dix Mille and Yam, are exceptions. They are dice games to be played, if not seriously, at least with thought.

Of the tile games, dominoes are particularly popular, and a selection of the better known games is included. These cover games using the standard-6 set with which most people are familiar but there are also games using the larger sets – the Double-9 and Double-12 – which offer a much wider scope. However, some people will consider the domino puzzles – really games for one – still more challenging.

Pentominoes also lend themselves to puzzles, and in astonishing variety. Even more surprising is what can be done with the few tangram pieces. This fascinating Chinese pastime moves the imagination as few games can do. Finally, there is the beautiful tile game of Mah Jong, whose popularity owes as much to its aesthetic pleasures as to the elements of play. A fine Mah Jong set is certainly not cheap but the sensuous appeal of ivory or bone tiles cannot fail to increase appreciation of the game.

YAM

Yam is a dice game popular in bistros in parts of France. Five dice, a shaker and some paper to keep the score is the only equipment necessary. Any number can play.

PLAY

Draw up a score sheet similar to that shown in figure 1 with a column for each player (here called A, B and C).

Players take it in turns to throw the dice. On each turn, a player may have up to three throws. On the first roll, all five dice are thrown. If he likes the five numbers, the player may stop here. If not, he may take out those that please him and throw the remaining dice again, when he will have a similar option: to

Figure 1
Completed score sheet

	A	B	C	
1	4	0	0	
2	0	0	6	
3	9	12	6	
4	12	0	16	
5	20	15	15	
6	18	24	18	
Total	63	51	61	
Bonus	30	—	30	
Minimum	21	18	26	
Maximum	0	23	27	
Full House	0	0	42	
Straight	45	50	0	
Yam	0	70	0	
Total	159	212	186	

accept his new 'hand' or to throw part or all of it a third time. He may elect to throw dice he held back on the second throw.

After the third roll at the latest, the player must enter a score in any unfilled box of his choice. He cannot choose not to do so, even though it may mean scoring zero. Since there are 11 scoring boxes to be filled, a game will consist of 11 rounds. The winner is the player with the highest score.

The scoring combinations are:
1 *Single numbers* (1–6 on score sheet) when the score entered is the number shown multiplied by the number of dice showing that number. For example, if after three throws the dice show 6:2:2:2:2, and the player elected to score 2s, he would enter 8 (4 × 2) in the appropriate box.
2 *Minimum* – any combination of five dice when the face value is scored. The minimum total must be lower than the maximum.
3 *Maximum* – any combination of five dice when the face value is scored. The maximum total must exceed the minimum total.
4 *Full House* – three of a kind and two of a kind – scores the total of the dice plus 20; thus 3:3:3:5:5 scores 39.
5 *Straight* or *Run* – five numbers in sequence – scores the total of the dice plus 30. Only two scores are possible: 45 (1 to 5 plus 30) or 50 (2 to 6 plus 30).
6 *Yam* – five of a kind – scores the total of the dice plus 40.
In addition, there is a bonus of 30 points for totalling 60 or more in the number boxes. Typical scores have been filled in on the score sheet in figure 1.

STRATEGY

The game is more skilful than may appear. It is a combination of chance and calculation with a dash of common sense. There are few problems in the early stages – it is near the end that it gets exciting.

There are two types of situation in marked contrast to each other that occur in every game and which call for judgment. On the one hand there is a luxury of choice, particularly in the early stages. Suppose you threw 4:4:4:4:4. This is a Yam, and because of the high bonus you would probably enter it in the Yam box. But suppose that was filled? You could enter the combination in your number box (score 20) to put you on the way to the 30-point bonus, or in the Full House box (the fact that the triple and the pair are the same number does not matter), or the Minimum box, though that would be something of a waste, or even the Maximum box, though that would be also a waste because you should be able to score more than 20. It depends largely on which boxes are available.

Later in the game, on the other hand, you will be squeezed and your decision will be where to put your zero. Since this situation is almost certain to arise, it is well to keep one or two boxes in reserve for this purpose. The 1-box is a good dustbin as the most you can score in this box anyway is 5, and the 2-box is almost as good. The Minimum box can obviously accept almost any hand, but better is the Yam box. The chances of throwing a Yam are not good and if you are squeezed it probably means that you have only a few rolls left anyway.

Taking a decision when your throw is complete is one thing: it can be much harder after the first roll. Consider the position in figure 2. Here you have to decide firstly whether to accept the roll for your Minimum box and if not, what combination you will go for and hence what dice you will save before you roll again.

To accept the throw for a score of 19 for Minimum would not be wise. The decision lies between going for a Straight by rolling one of the 5s, or keeping these and rolling the 4:3:2. Rolling a 5 would give you an excellent chance of a Straight as the sequence 5:4:3:2 is open

at either end, so a 1 or a 6 will do – and you have two rolls. Against that, if you fail you will end with a miserable score, perhaps for the Minimum box. The stakes are high, but a Straight is not a hard combination to get and there is a big bonus.

With two 5s in hand, you are odds-on to get one more at least, when you would need only two 6s to get the number bonus and there are alternative chances for a Full House or a good Maximum.

Figure 2
A game in progress

RELATED GAMES

A more varied game is had by allowing three scoring columns for each player. The first column must be filled in sequence from top to bottom, the second likewise from bottom to top and the third in any order, as in the basic game. For example, if a player scored 1s on the first round, on the second round he would have the choice of scoring 2s in the first column, a Yam in the second (starting at the bottom) or any combination in the third. Another variant has four columns for each player, three scored as above and the fourth for single rolls only, entered in any order.

You may meet this game in many forms and under many names – Yacht, Cheerio, Crag, Double Cameroon. In Puerto Rico, where it is a favourite gambling game, it is known as Generale (General). A popular proprietary version is marketed as Yahtzee.

	YOU	
1	4	
2	6	
3	12	
4	12	
5		
6		
Total		
Bonus		
Minimum		
Maximum		
Full House		
Straight		
Yam	0	
Total		

DIX MILLE

Dix Mille is a simple French dice game for any number of players. As its name suggests, the object is to be the first player to reach a score of 10,000 points.

PLAY

Six dice are used. On his turn, a player rolls all the dice at once. At least one scoring die or combination must now be removed; if there is none, there is no score and the turn passes to the next player. (Scoring numbers and combinations are given in the table.) The remaining dice are rolled again, and once more at least one scoring die or combination must be removed. A player may continue to roll the remaining dice as long as each time he removes at least one scoring die or combination. It is customary to announce the progressive score for the turn after each roll. If on any roll a player fails to score, his accumulated score on that turn is cancelled and the dice pass to the next player. A player may opt to end his turn after any scoring roll, adding his accumulated total to his existing score.

If a player is reduced to one die (because he has previously removed five scoring dice) he is allowed *two* throws in which to score with it. If he succeeds, then he gets a 500-point bonus and continues his turn by rolling all six dice and then proceeding as before. If he is reduced to one die again in that same turn, and succeeds in scoring, then the bonus is increased to 1,000 and is further increased by 500 points for each subsequent time on that same turn, so it is even possible to reach 10,000 on one's first turn!

If a player has rolled more than one die and they all score, he can elect to score all of them and continue with six dice again, or he can elect to score all but one and try for the bonus.

When a player passes 10,000 he may choose to continue his turn at the risk of cancelling his score in that round, since any player who began after him is entitled to one more turn.

STRATEGY

The key is to stop at the right moment. Fate usually decides when that is, but be influenced by the scores of the other players. Be cautious when ahead, bold when behind – and gamble everything when another player passes 10,000.

Since there are two scoring numbers as well as combinations, the only rolls that are odds against scoring are those with two dice or a single die – but with the latter you roll twice and have a good chance of a big bonus. Thus if you threw 2:3:3:3:5:6 it may prove best to save the three 3s but not the 5 so that you have three rather than two dice to roll. Notice that combinations only count if made in a single roll; thus if you throw 2:3:4:6 having removed a 1 and a 5, you score zero, not for a straight.

SCORING TABLE

Single die
1 – 100 points
5 – 50 points

Three-of-a-kind
1 × 3 – 1000 points
Any other number × 3 – number × 100 (thus three 4s score 400)

Three Pairs
(including six of one number or four of one and two of another) – 1500 points (but see Disaster)

Straight
1:2:3:4:5:6 – 3000 points
With Three Pairs or a Straight, all dice *must* be rolled again. However, if three pairs are all the same number, these can be scored as Three-of-a-kind × 2 when the turn can be ended.

Disaster
Four or more 2s wipe out the player's entire score

DOMINOES

The origin of dominoes, like that of so many traditional games, is obscure although it is the Chinese who have the best claim. The modern Double-6 set however is only about 250 years old, having spread north and west from Italy and France. There are many games played with dominoes only some of which are given here. They are often for two or three players or four in partnerships.

EQUIPMENT

Dominoes, commonly called bones, are rectangular tiles, twice as long as they are wide and twice as wide as they are thick. Each domino is divided into two squares by a central division. Each half-tile is either blank or contains a number of incised dots, known as pips.

There are many different domino sets in use of which the Double-6 set (figure 1) is the most widely distributed in the West. This pack comprises 28 tiles, one each of every possible combination of pips from zero (blank) to 6. Double-9 and Double-12 packs are extensions of the Double-6 and are also common. These larger sets permit more players and also more difficult games. Chinese dominoes, widely used in the East, have

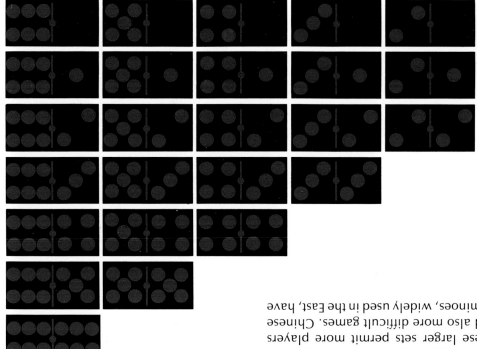

Figure 1
Double-6 set

only 21 tiles, the blanks being omitted. The Chinese set corresponds to all possible permutations of two ordinary dice.

In most domino games each tile after the first is placed contiguous to a tile already played so that adjacent half-tiles match. Combinations may seem limited, yet there are eight billion ways in which a chain can be formed with a Double-6 pack.

A Double-6 set contains seven suits. A suit is all those dominoes bearing a single number like 3 or zero (blank), so there are seven tiles to a suit. The suits naturally overlap; thus the 5:2 belongs to both the five and the two suit. Tiles with a repeated number, for example the 2:2, are known as doubles or doublets. In many games a double is played at right angles to the chain, in forming the chain, or leg as it is properly called, common to so many domino games, direction can be changed to adjust to the space available. Only the ends of the leg are 'open'—that is, may be played against. Consider the rest of the leg like the discard pile in a card game. Figure 2 shows a typical leg in the making.

PLAY

The dominoes are shuffled face down on the table and become the stock or bone-yard. A player's dominoes may be stood up on their sides in front of him or they may be held in the hand. In games for two or three players, each plays for himself. In four-player games partnerships are usual, with the partners sitting opposite each other. Play is clockwise.

Block

This is the basic and most widespread domino game. Two, three or four can play.

Each player draws his hand from the boneyard. There is no consensus on the number of tiles drawn. Seven tiles each is common practice if two are playing; otherwise five each is common. How-ever, six or seven dominoes each regard-less of the number of players is not unusual, while some authorities rec-ommend eight tiles less the number of players, hence four each in a four-handed game.

The player with the highest double starts by placing it face up in the centre of the table. This is known as the set or starter. The second player puts a tile at right angles to it so that the touching half-tile matches. Thereafter each player puts down one tile in turn at either end of the leg. A player unable to play passes (knocks) and the game ends when a player goes out ('domino') or all players knock in turn.

The player who goes out scores the sum of the pips on the tiles held by his opponent(s). If he is in partnership, the side scores the sum of the opponents' pips less the pips of the partner left in. If all pass, then the player with the lowest count scores the sum of the other play-er(s) spots less his own (if partnerships), the difference between the two sides is

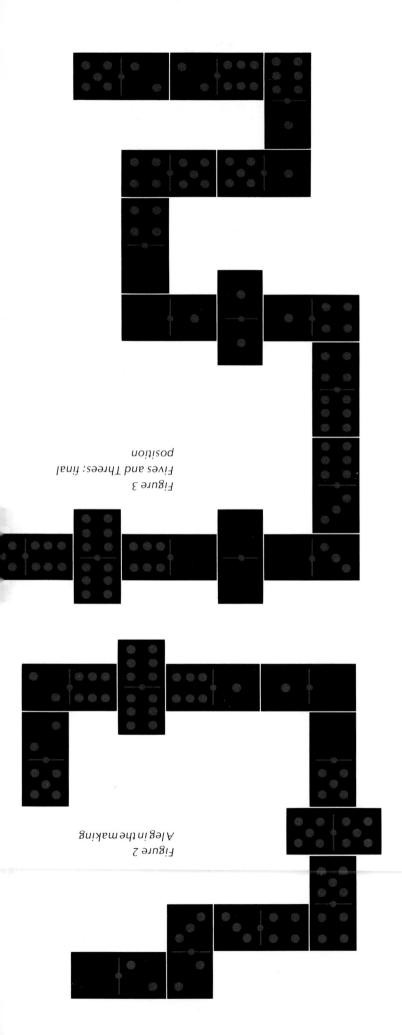

Figure 2
A leg in the making

Figure 3
Fives and Threes: final position

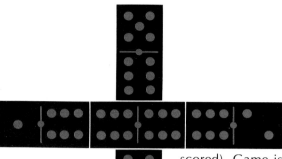

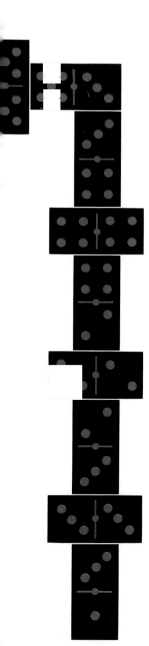

*Figure 4
Sebastopol: initial
arrangement*

scored). Game is to an agreed total. A Cribbage board (see p. 128) is often used to keep score.

Muggins

This game, also called Fives or All Fives, is similar to Block except that in addition to going out first a player strives to make the ends of the leg sum to a multiple of five. He scores 1 point for each five. Thus if the starter is a double-5, the player scores 2; and if the leg has a 4:4 at one end and :6 at the other, play of a double-6 would earn 4 points for 20. A running score is kept.

At the end, multiples of 5 spots score 1 point against the holder. Numbers are rounded up. For example, A goes out and his partner C holds the 6:3 while B and D together hold 5:4, 4:1, 3:2 and 2:1. C's pips are deducted from the total held by B and D = 13; so A and C score 3 points. Play is usually to 61.

If at any time a player cannot add to the leg he must draw from the boneyard until able to do so. When the boneyard is exhausted, players must pass but as in most domino games, you cannot pass if you are able to play.

If a player fails to claim a score to which he is entitled, an opponent may do so by saying 'Muggins!'. (Compare Cribbage.)

Draw

This is also very similar to Block. The only significant differences are that the starter may be any tile and a player on his turn may draw any number of tiles from the boneyard even if he is able to play to the leg. However, the last two tiles in the boneyard are never used.

Thus if A puts up the starter, B may play to the table, draw a tile from stock and then play to the table, or he may continue to draw tiles from stock even though he holds a tile of the starter suit. His turn ends only when he plays a tile to the table. When the boneyard is exhausted (that is, when two tiles remain), a player passes if he cannot play to the table.

In the partnership game, players draw six tiles each, leaving only two available in the stock.

Fives and Threes

This game is similar to Muggins except players score for multiples of 3 as well as 5. Each player (up to four) draws seven tiles. The lowest double is the starter. A play that results in the sum of the two ends of the leg being a multiple of 3 or 5 scores 1 point for each such multiple. Thus 15, the highest-scoring total, earns 8 points (5×3 and 3×5). The player or side that goes out scores an additional point. There are no penalties and the first side to reach 31 is the winner. In the partnership game, score only the difference between the two totals.

Here is a game of Fives and Threes:

A 0:0	
B 0:3 (score 1)	C 2:2 (score 2)
C 0:6 (score 3)	D 2:3 (score 1)
D 6:6 (score 8)	A 3:3
A 3:6 (score 6)	B 1:0 (score 2)
B 6:4	C 0:4 (score 2)
C 6:5 (score 3)	D 4:5
D 4:1 (score 2)	A 5:1
A 1:1	B 1:6 (score 4)
B 5:5 (score 4)	C 6:2
C 5:3 (score 1)	D 2:5
D 3:4 (score 2)	A Pass
A 4:4 (score 2)	B Pass
B 4:2	C 3:1 (score 2)
	– out.

Remaining tiles: A 2:1; B 2:0; D 5:0.

The final position is shown in figure 3. A and C score 21 + 1 for going out, and B and D score 24, so B and D get 2 points.

Sebastopol

This game is for four players. After the deal – seven tiles each – the holder of the double-6 plays it to the table. The next four tiles played must be adjacent to it (see figure 4). Thereafter tiles may be added to any of the four arms. Doubles, other than the 6:6, can only be extended one way. Score as in Block.

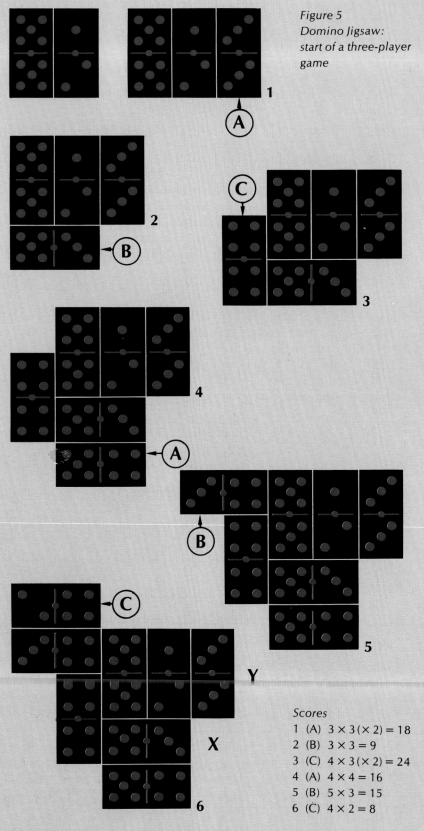

Figure 5
Domino Jigsaw:
start of a three-player
game

Scores
1 (A) $3 \times 3 (\times 2) = 18$
2 (B) $3 \times 3 = 9$
3 (C) $4 \times 3 (\times 2) = 24$
4 (A) $4 \times 4 = 16$
5 (B) $5 \times 3 = 15$
6 (C) $4 \times 2 = 8$

Domino Jigsaw

One of the most fascinating, different and difficult of all domino games is this invention of Sid Sackson's. It can be played by two, three or four players, and requires two Double-6 sets. The 0 and 6 suits are removed, leaving 30 tiles in all.

Two players draw 14 tiles from the stock, three draw nine tiles each and four, playing as individuals, seven tiles each. In the three-player game, the odd domino is discarded unseen. The two remaining tiles are exposed side by side to form a square. (If two identical doubles are turned up, there is a re-deal.) These are the starters.

The table array expands as a single group, each player in turn being obliged to place a tile from hand so as to extend two or more lines of half-tiles vertically or horizontally. The player scores the number of half-tiles, including those he has just placed, in each line, the lines being multiplied together. If the tile played is a double, the score is doubled. Each line, vertical and horizontal, must display a regular pattern of pips, the pattern being established as soon as a half-tile in the line is repeated. Observe that pips are only used to establish patterns; they do not affect the scoring. There is one prohibition: no more than three tiles, adjacent to one another, may stand lengthwise in line.

A player who cannot go passes. When one player puts down his last tile the game ends except that any player who started after that player is entitled to one more turn. The game may also end through no-one being able to play. At the finish, players are penalized 5 points for every double and 25 points for every other tile held. The player with the highest overall score is the winner.

Do not be put off by the apparent complexity of this excellent game: it is worth the learning. Figure 5 shows the start of a three-player game: after two rounds, A has scored 34, B 24 and C 32. Notice that no piece can ever occupy the space marked 'X' in diagram 6 since the vertical row requires a 3 whereas the horizontal row can accept neither a 3 nor a 5. Observe also that a tile placed vertically at 'Y' would be an illegal play.

Solitaire Games

There exists a wealth of domino puzzles which make attractive games for the solo player. In the matching puzzle, a regular array of tiles is assembled so that all touching half-tiles are married, as in most domino games. Figure 6A shows a well-known example using the Double-6 pack. Three other designs, all using the Double-6 set, are given in figures 6B–D. In the pentacle, the half-tiles forming each of the five squares must total 36; while the pyramid requires that the half-tiles in each vertical column sum to three times their number. Thus the end tiles at the bottom must be 3s, and the two central columns must each total 21.

Figures 6E and 6F are matching puzzles using a Double-7 pack (or use a Double-9 pack minus the last two suits).

STRATEGY

Domino games have a deceptive simplicity and it is a revelation to witness the skill of the experts who can often 'read' a player's hand after a couple of rounds.

In most games it pays to go out first and a good principle therefore is to play from your longest suit to maintain maximum flexibility. If you control a suit (hold the remaining tiles of it) you can often 'stitch up' one end of the leg. For example, you control the 3 suit and hold 5:3, 3:3 and 3:1. If an end tile opens a 5 or a 1, you play the appropriate 3 tile which 'stitches up' that end. You later play the double, then the remaining tile.

Be careful not to be left with a 'widow' – a double that is unplayable because the remaining six tiles of the suit have been matched. Play it as soon as the fifth tile of the suit appears.

A caution valid for all domino games is that you should always conceal whether your play is from choice or necessity.

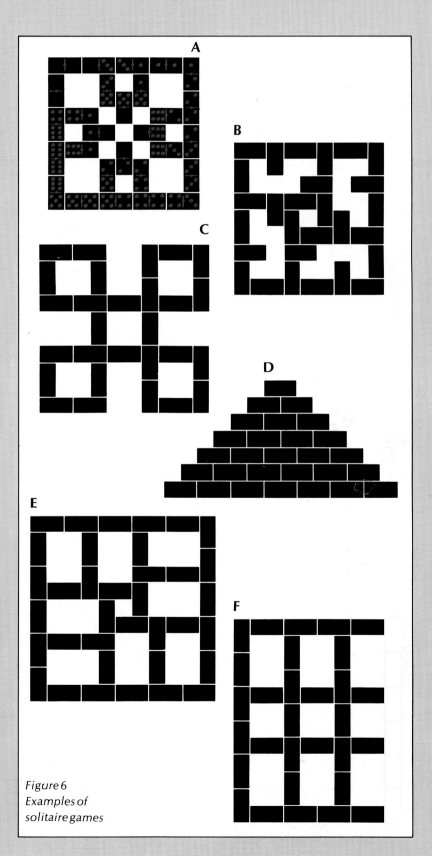

Figure 6
Examples of
solitaire games

TANGRAM

Tangram, or Wisdom Puzzle, is an ancient Chinese creative game, ideal for one player, though competitive play is possible. It is said to have been the favourite pastime of Napoleon in exile.

PLAY

Tangram is a set of seven two-dimensional pieces cut from a square (right). Marketed sets are available cheaply but it is easy to make Tangram from any durable material.

The pieces are put together to make shapes (silhouettes) of everyday objects. Basically there are two ways to use Tangram; to create designs of one's own or to solve, in competition if desired, the creations of others by putting together the pieces to match the outline shapes. Incredibly, more than 2,000 designs have been published and countless thousands more must have gone unrecorded. It is permissible, though unusual, to have a piece or pieces in isolation from the others providing they form part of the same creation.

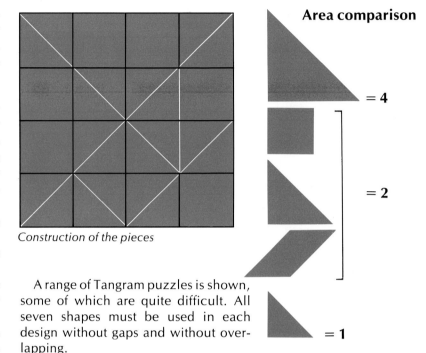

Construction of the pieces

Area comparison

A range of Tangram puzzles is shown, some of which are quite difficult. All seven shapes must be used in each design without gaps and without overlapping.

Many attempts have been made to popularize similar sets of shapes, sometimes patterned or coloured. None has matched the elegance or simplicity of Tangram.

Arrow

Candle

Skater

Urn

Fish

Sailboat

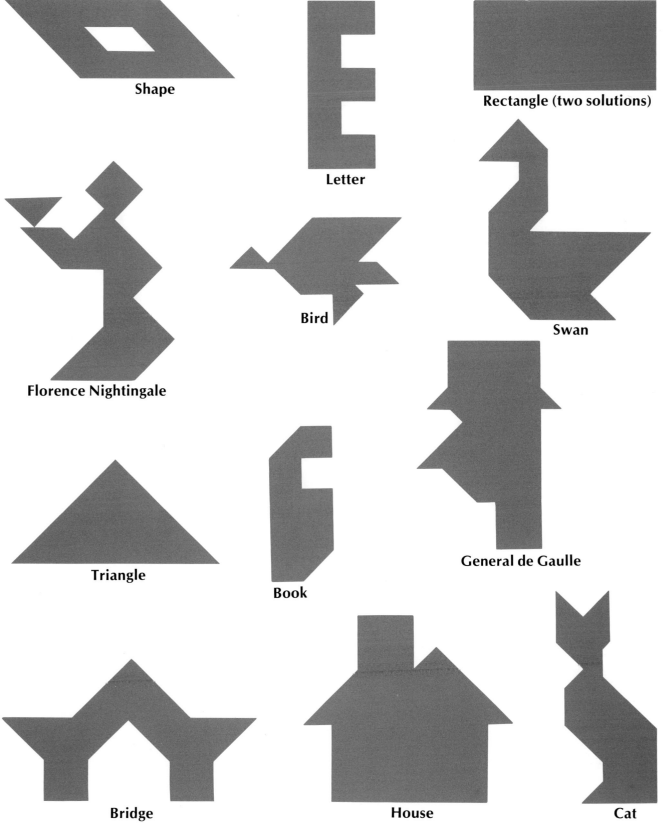

Shape

Letter

Rectangle (two solutions)

Florence Nightingale

Bird

Swan

Triangle

Book

General de Gaulle

Bridge

House

Cat

MAH JONG

Mah Jong's main appeal lies in the elegance of its play and procedures. The game itself, which requires four players, is similar to Rummy. Many myths surround its origins but it is almost certainly little more than a hundred years old. It is derived from a Chinese card game or' games, the symbols (suits) of the cards being imitations of early paper money.

More than any other game, Mah Jong has suffered from innovations and it is not possible to identify a definitive version. There are three mainstreams: the Chinese, both classical and modern, the Japanese and the American (the most elaborate) but within these, and particularly in the Western game, there are almost infinite variations mostly relating to the admissibility of 'special hands'. The game described here approximates to that played universally prior to 1920 – the 'classic' Chinese game which has simpler rules and deeper strategy.

EQUIPMENT

Mah Jong is played on a table with a set of 144 rectangular tiles identified on one side and blank on the other. They are made of plastic, bamboo, bone or ivory and are often backed. The game can also be played with Mah Jong cards.

Each player has a rack to accommodate his hand, although this prop is scorned in the East where players hold their tiles in the hand. Also used are dice, tallies for scoring and sometimes a wind indicator disc.

A Mah Jong set has three suits, Bamboos, Characters and Circles, each suit numbered 1 to 9. There are four winds, East, South, West and North and three dragons, Red, Green and White. There are four each of all the above tiles making a total of 136. In addition there are eight bonus tiles that have no part in the actual play: one each of four flowers and the four seasons, both groups numbered 1 to 4 and corresponding respectively to East, South, West and North. A complete set of tiles is shown in figure 1.

Figure 1
Set of tiles

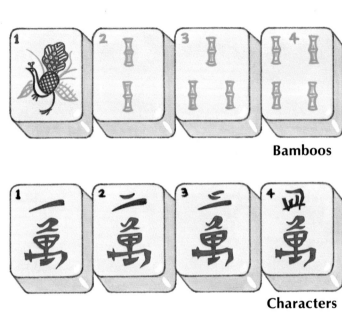

Bamboos

Characters

Circles

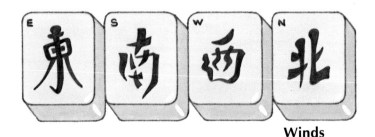

Winds

Flowers

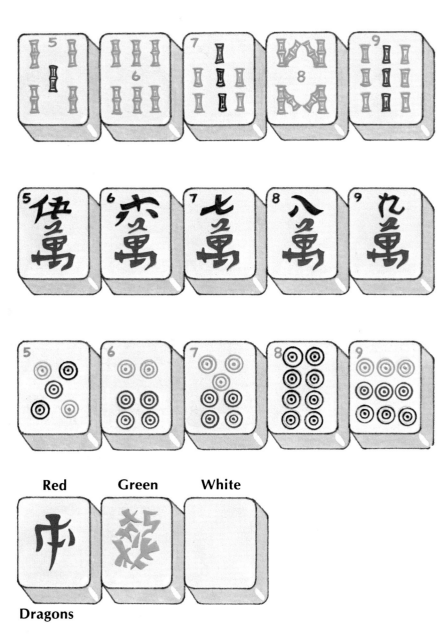

Dragons

Red　　Green　　White

Seasons

PLAY

At the start of a round each player assumes the name of a wind. North sits on the left of East and South on the right—notice that this differs from the arrangement of the compass points. All procedures and play are anticlockwise and East is always the dominant wind. In each game there is a 'prevailing wind' which is displayed on the wind indicator, if used. The prevailing wind rotates anticlockwise from East and only affects the scoring. Each player plays for himself. The tiles are shuffled face down and stacked, two high, in the form of an enclosed wall (see figure 2).

East rolls two dice and counts the total round the players, starting with himself as 1. This is to determine who breaks the wall. If a total of 9 were thrown, for example, East would break the wall. The player concerned rolls the dice again and counts the total of both his and East's initial roll (four dice) along the tiles in front of him, starting at the right and moving round on to the next wall on his left if the dice sum to more than 18. He removes the two tiles where his count ends and puts them separately on the wall just to the right of the break. Each player in turn, starting with East, takes two stacks (4 tiles) from the wall to the left of the breach until he has 12. East now takes one stack (2 tiles) and the other players one tile each in turn so that each player has 13 tiles except East who has

Figure 2
The wall: tiles arranged for play

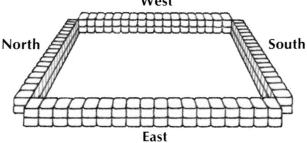

North　　　　　　　South

West

East

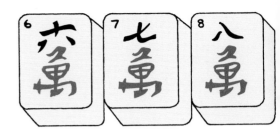

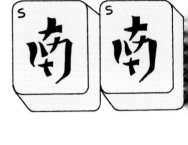

14. Figure 3 shows how the deal works in practice.

Tiles are now examined and sorted on the racks. The object is to form combinations of tiles of which there are three kinds:

Chow – a run (sequence) of three tiles in the same suit;

Pung – a set of three identical tiles;

Kong – a set of four identical tiles.

A player can go out ('Mah Jong') when he has four combinations plus an identical pair. Figure 4 shows a Mah Jong hand.

Before play starts, players holding bonus tiles declare them face up on the table and draw replacement tiles from the Kong box. The Kong box (shown in figure 3) consists of the 16 tiles immediately to the right of the break. If now, or at any time later, a player picks up a bonus tile from the wall, he puts it on the table face up and draws a replacement from the Kong box.

Now play starts with East discarding a tile, which is placed face up at random within the wall. At the same time he announces the discard, for example '2 Circles', 'West wind'. Any player may claim a discard to complete a Pung, a Kong or to go Mah Jong (which takes precedence). If there are no takers, the player whose turn it is next may claim it to complete a Chow. Combinations can be exposed (face up on the table in front of the player) or concealed (kept in hand). If a combination includes a discard, it must be exposed. On claiming a tile from the table, the player must discard a tile from hand when play passes to the player on his right.

A player on his turn, provided the previous player's discard is not claimed, takes the next tile from the wall (to the left of the break), declares any combination he wishes, and then discards to the centre. Only the last discard may be claimed: all others are 'dead'.

If a player picks up a discard to complete a Kong, or adds a fourth tile to an exposed Pung, or on his turn, and after drawing from the wall, declares a concealed Kong, he takes a tile from the Kong box before discarding. This is done to keep the balance of the hand correct; for example, a player could go Mah Jong with four Kongs and the obligatory pair (18 tiles) plus bonus tiles against his original holding of 13 tiles. Concealed Pungs and Kongs that are declared are identified by turning one or two of the tiles respectively face down.

A player who needs only one tile to go Mah Jong is said to be 'fishing' and must announce this. A player who is fishing may 'rob the Kong' to go Mah Jong if a player adds to an exposed Pung. If a player discards a tile that permits another player to go Mah Jong, the first player is said to have 'let off a cannon' and is subject to penalty.

The game ends when one player has gone Mah Jong or the tiles have been exhausted ('wash-out'), in which case there is a re-deal. Notice that any tiles remaining in the Kong box are not available for play.

As well as the normal Mah Jong hand explained above, there are a number of special hands which enable a player to go out and also to earn extra points. The most important of these are shown in the table opposite.

Scoring

At the end of a game players expose and score their hands. Detailed scores are shown in the table opposite. Scoring is

Figure 3
The deal: letters indicate allocation of tiles from the wall

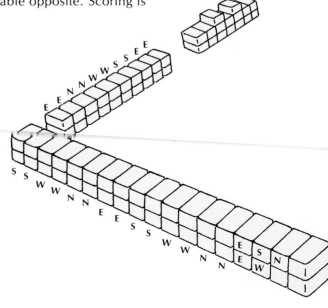

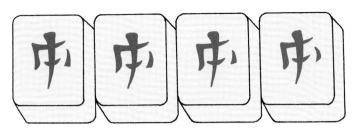

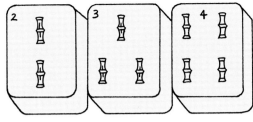

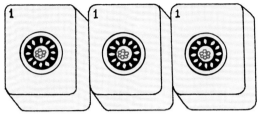

Figure 4
A 'Mah Jong' hand

SPECIAL HANDS

Heaven's Blessing
East picks up a complete Mah Jong hand after any extra tiles have been drawn for bonus tiles or Kongs

Earth's Blessing
Any other player goes Mah Jong by claiming East's first discard

Gathering the Plum Blossom from the Roof
Going out with the 5 Circle drawn from the Kong box

Catching the Moon from the Bottom of the Sea
Going out with the 1 Circle if it is the last tile of the wall

Fourfold Plenty
A hand containing four Kongs and a pair

Three Great Scholars
A set of each of the Dragons, another Pung or Kong and any pair

Four Blossoms over the Door
A hand containing a set of each of the Winds plus any pair

All Symbols
A hand entirely of honour tiles (i.e. Winds and Dragons)

Heads and Tails
A hand composed entirely of 1s and 9s

Imperial Jade
A hand composed entirely of all-green tiles. The all-green tiles are the 2, 3, 4, 6 and 8 of Bamboos and the Green Dragons

Thirteen Grades of Imperial Treasure
A hand composed of one each of all the major tiles (1s and 9s of suits, the Winds and Dragons) with one paired

SCORING

A player's total score is made up of his basic score multiplied by the number of doubles he has earned.

Basic score

Bonus tiles (flower or season) – 4 points

Sets   Chow – nil
        Pung (exposed):
           Minor tiles – 2 points
           Major tiles – 4 points
        Kong (exposed)
           Minor tiles – 8 points
           Major tiles – 16 points
        Pung and Kong (concealed)
               – double above totals

Pairs   Any pair of:
       Dragons
       Player's Wind   } 2 points
       Prevailing Wind

(If player's Wind is Prevailing Wind – 4 points)

Player going Mah Jong only
Going Mah Jong – 10 points
Final tile from wall – 2 points
Only place (going Mah Jong with the only possible tile) – 2 points

Doubling

Each of the following qualifies for one double of the basic score:

  No-score hand (all Chows)
  No Chows
  Concealed hand (no sets exposed)
  One suit hand (one suit and honour tiles only)
  Robbing the Kong
  Pung or Kong of following:
    Player's Wind
    Prevailing Wind
    Dragons
    Player's flower and season (pair)
    All four flowers
    All four seasons

Limit score

All Special Hands

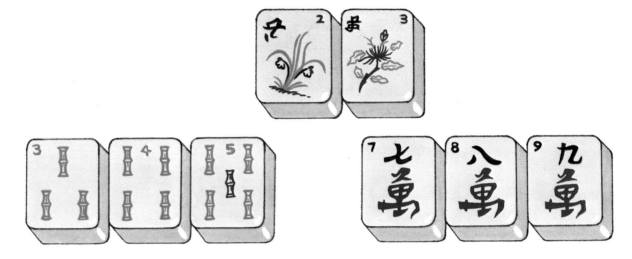

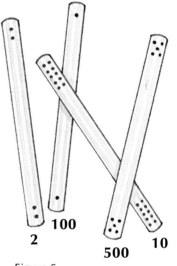

the least attractive part of Mah Jong because of its complexity and unhealthy doubling system. It can be seen that the point value of a hand that carries a number of doubles can reach a phenomenal total, so an upper limit is imposed – 1,000 points is usual. Many of the special hands are limit hands.

Scoring can be done on paper but tallies are more commonly used. Each player starts the game with 2,000 points in tallies or some other agreed amount. There are four different types of tally, illustrated in figure 5.

All players pay the player who went Mah Jong the total score of his hand, East paying double, or receiving double from the others if he was the player who went Mah Jong. The rest of the players then settle between themselves according to the differences of their respective scores, East again giving or receiving double. Notice that the player who went Mah Jong pays no-one.

If East wins, or there is a wash-out, the players retain their winds for the next game, otherwise South becomes East Wind and the other players are redesignated accordingly. The prevailing wind is always changed after every game.

STRATEGY

Despite the strong chance element, Mah Jong is a skilful game. As in most 'imperfect information' games – those that have a hidden factor – the laws of probability must be put to work.

In Mah Jong, unlike in most card games, discards are always visible; as the game progresses, therefore, more and more information becomes available.

Scoring reflects one's chances. If you hold two green dragons and one has already been discarded, you have but a single chance to complete the Pung. If none has been discarded, it is possible that another player has the other pair so both of you may wait indefinitely.

Chows are the easiest of all combinations to achieve, which is why they do not score. If you hold, say, the 4 and 5

100

2

500   **10**

Figure 5
Tallies

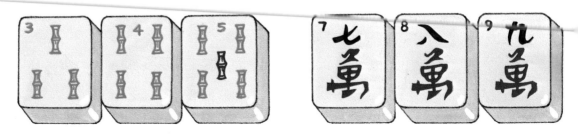

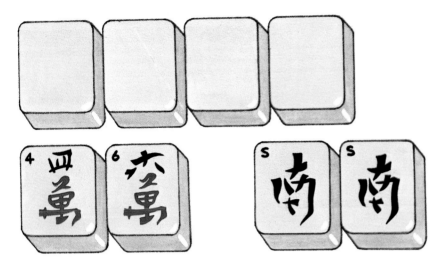

Figure 6
A 'fishing' hand

Figure 7
A 'Mah Jong' hand

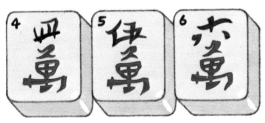

the game comes in. At some point you decide that one player is well ahead in putting his hand together. At this stage, you should try to go out as quickly as possible if you are near to doing so, even if it means abandoning hoped-for doubles. If Mah Jong seems remote you should abandon it and play instead to thwart the leader by holding up tiles you suspect he wants even at the expense of breaking your own combinations, and by forming an unspoken alliance with other players, perhaps to help a low-scorer to go out.

The player who goes Mah Jong often does so in response to a perceived threat, so it is common for one of the other players to score much higher than the winner of the hand. If at the end chance determines the outcome, you can seek solace in the Chinese conviction that this is the mandate of heaven, to be esteemed above skill!

A sample hand may clarify the scoring process. You are South, which is the prevailing wind, and have announced that you are fishing (figure 6). The Kong and bonus tiles are exposed but the other tiles are concealed. You now draw Summer (2 of Seasons) from the wall. Your replacement tile must be from the Kong box and this is 5 Characters, which allows you to go Mah Jong (figure 7).

Your basic score is 12 for bonus tiles, 16 for the exposed Kong, 4 for a pair of Winds (own and prevailing), 10 for Mah Jong and 2 for only place – total 44. The Kong earns 1 double and the pair of player's flower and season another. So you get 176 from North and West, and 352 (double) from East – 704 in all.

Circles there are eight tiles (four each of the 3 and 6) that could complete your set. The hand you pick up should determine your strategy. With bad tiles, strive for an early Mah Jong by forming Chows. You will need at least eight or nine towards a limit hand to make that your aim – and that will be a rare occurrence. Aim for flexibility: retain embryo combinations that offer the most alternatives but always bear in mind the scoring potential of doubles and be prepared to revalue your objectives as the game progresses.

It is natural to concentrate on going Mah Jong with the best possible hand but experts put more emphasis on defensive play. Every discard carries a message – put the messages together and you have a picture of the other players' hands. Experts can deduce fairly accurately the holdings of the other players after about 10 rounds. It is here that the real skill of

PENTOMINOES

Pentominoes are geometrical shapes which are used for a variety of solo or two-player games and puzzles. Their popularity lies partly in their flexibility and partly in their manageable number — there are only four tetronimoes (shapes made up of four squares) while hexominoes (shapes made up of six squares), which number 35, are much more complex.

EQUIPMENT

A set of pentominoes can be bought cheaply or is easily made from card or some durable material. A pentomino is a shape made up of five identical squares arranged so that every square is adjacent along at least one of its sides to another square. There are 12 distinct pentominoes which represent the different ways in which the five squares can be put together without overlapping. Pentominoes can be turned round or over and are sometimes identified by letters that correspond roughly to their shapes. They are illustrated in figure 1.

Golomb's game

What may be described as the basic pentomino game is named after its inventor, Solomon Golomb. In Golomb's game, a board of 8 × 8 cells, which need not be chequered, is used. The board must be married with the pieces: a pentomino should cover five cells exactly.

The 12 pentominoes are placed adjacent to the board between the players who take it in turns to select one and place it on the board so as to cover five vacant cells. The last player to place a pentomino is the winner. This can be achieved after five plays, though if the first player is very lax (as well as highly ingenious!) it is possible for all 12 pentominoes to be placed, giving the second player the win.

A completed game is given in figure 2. The pieces are numbered in the order that they were played. The second player wins — all the other 30-odd possibilities

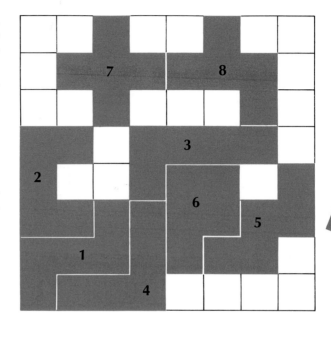

for his eighth move lose. One advantage of Golomb's game is that there will always be a winner — a draw is not possible.

Mating game

A 12 × 9 board is used for this game. One player takes the X, the other the U and these pieces are positioned centrally at opposite ends of the board, which is set lengthwise. The U is placed with its long side bordering the edge. The remaining pieces are now added to the board one at a time in rotation. Thereafter a turn consists of moving a piece to a new position. Pieces X and U may only be moved by the respective players; other pieces may be moved by either player.

The object is to mate the X and U by interlocking them. The first player to do this wins. There are two restrictions: the U may not face the nearest edge, and no piece may be moved twice consecutively. If the game is slow, a further restriction can be added: each move must be to a new part of the board, so a piece cannot be moved where it still occupies any square it occupied before the move.

Figure 2
A completed game

Figure 1
The 12 pentominoes

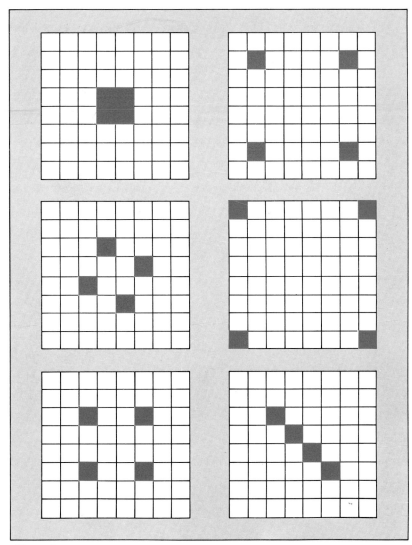

Figure 3
Construction problems

Randolph's game

This game, invented by Alex Randolph, uses an 11 × 11 board with the central cell blanked off. Each player has a set of pentominoes and, again, the last player to place a piece wins. This game has the advantage that the players have more control over the pieces.

Solo games

Pentominoes lend themselves to construction problems and the astonishing interrelationships between the various pieces are not always apparent until a few puzzles have been attempted.

The 12 pentominoes total 60 cells. They can be assembled into rectangles measuring 3 × 20 (two solutions), 4 × 15, 5 × 12 and 6 × 10 cells – the last-named has over 2,000 different solutions not counting reflections and rotations. Every pentomino can be reproduced at exactly three times the size using nine of the remaining pentominoes, for example, assemble a V using nine pentominoes other than the V.

The 12 pieces can be arranged on the 8 × 8 board to leave four blank cells symmetrically positioned. All the examples in figure 3 are possible. The square of four blank cells can be positioned anywhere.

The problems are for practical purposes endless. In the rectangle constructions, for instance, you can consider faultlines (straight lines from one side to another, separating the assembly into parts) and crossroads (points at which four pieces meet). Experiment will suggest other games.

Figure 4 demonstrates a solution of a difficult one: place eight of the pieces on the 8 × 8 board so that they touch only at the corners.

Related games

A game with an added dimension – literally – is space pentominoes or Quintillions, in which the pieces are one cell thick. They open a range of three-dimensional games and puzzles.

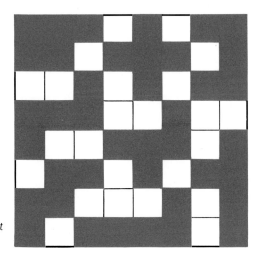

Figure 4
Eight pentominoes on the 8 × 8 board touching only at the corners

CARD GAMES

Playing cards have been known in Europe for at least six centuries but whoever designed the first pack was almost certainly inspired by early Chinese money-derived cards. Whatever their origin, in terms of benefit against outlay there can be little in this world cheaper than a pack of cards.

The selection of card games here has been drawn from many nations and some of the games may well be strange to you. Where a game is familiar, you may find that the version given here is not what you are used to playing. Few card games have codified rules, and variants of the popular ones are beyond counting. There is nothing absolute about any of the rules; if you find that a game plays better your way or with a modification or two to the rules here, then make the change – that is how games evolve.

To those unfamiliar with or new to card games, terms used in the following pages are explained below:

Standard pack This has 52 cards, plus two Jokers. The cards are divided into four suits, two red and two black, of 13 cards each.

Suits These are spades (♠), hearts (♡), diamonds (♢) and clubs (♣).

Ranks In each suit, cards normally rank in the following descending order: Ace (A), King (K), Queen (Q), Jack (J), 10, 9, 8, 7, 6, 5, 4, 3, 2 (sometimes referred to as the deuce). The picture cards – K, Q, J – are known as court cards.

Wild card A wild card is a card that may represent any card at the holder's choice.

Trump card A card of a suit that takes precedence over any card of any other suit; hence trump suit, to trump.

Trick A packet of cards to which each player has contributed one, the player with the best card winning the trick.

Discard In a trick-taking game, any card played that is not of the suit led or a trump.

Seating Elder is on the left of dealer, followed by Younger. Play is normally clockwise.

BLACK MARIA

This is the best of the Hearts family of card games in which the object is to avoid taking penalty cards in tricks. Black Maria, also known as Black Lady, is for three to seven players. It is often treated as a fun game but in fact, despite the vagaries of the deal, it calls for a lot of skill, particularly if a small number play.

PLAY

The pack is dealt out face down and singly, so first equalize for number of players by taking out deuces as necessary. For example, with five players remove two deuces.

Players examine their hands, then each passes three cards (two if five or more are playing) to the player on his right. Do this simultaneously because a player may not look at the cards passed to him until he has selected his discards.

The player on the dealer's left leads and others must follow suit if possible. The highest card of the suit led takes the trick. Ace ranks high and there are no trumps. The winner of a trick leads to the next trick.

The object is to avoid taking tricks with hearts in them (each heart card carries a 1-point penalty), or with ♠Q, the Black Maria (which carries a 13-point penalty or in some schools a 5-point penalty: the latter is preferable). No points are gained for taking tricks.

The game ends when one player amasses 50 penalty points or some other agreed total, when the lowest scorer is the winner.

STRATEGY

Choosing which cards to exchange calls for more reflection than may appear. Examine the four hands given in figure 1. North has a good hand. The high clubs are well protected by the low cards. Pass on ♦10 9 8 to void a suit. East's hand is good despite the array of penalty cards. The hearts look safe: East will hope always to be able to play under a heart lead. No doubt here: pass ♠A K Q — East will have the advantage of knowing where the Queen is.

South also does not have a bad hand — a few low cards with good spade protection if he is passed the Queen by East. Exchange ♦Q ♥9 7. West would like to get rid of half his hand — all his suits are vulnerable — but it is probably best to discard ♥A Q ♣K. The hands now appear as in figure 2.

No-one has been punished. North now has a small worry in hearts but will hope to discard at least ♥A on a diamond. He would be advised to play high on the first club lead.

East feels comfortable. The only danger is ♣10 — a good lead to open. South looks safe, being void in hearts, but in fact is vulnerable to discards in spades and diamonds on the first round and clubs in the second — Black Maria is about discards! West's worry is the high diamonds. In particular, it is dangerous to be left with trick-taking cards late in the play because it may be difficult to lose the lead. Play as high as possible if you feel a round is safe from penalties — provided you can lead low to the next trick. The 2s, 3s and 4s are your friends in Black Maria.

Figure 1
Hands before exchanging

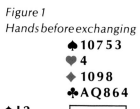

```
              ♠ 10753
              ♥ 4
              ♦ 1098
              ♣ AQ864
♠ J2        ┌─────────┐   ♠ AKQ
♥ AQ63      │    N    │   ♥ KJ10852
♦ AKJ42     │ W     E │   ♦ 63
♣ K5        │    S    │   ♣ 102
            └─────────┘
              ♠ 9864
              ♥ 97
              ♦ Q75
              ♣ J973
```

Figure 2
Hands after exchanging

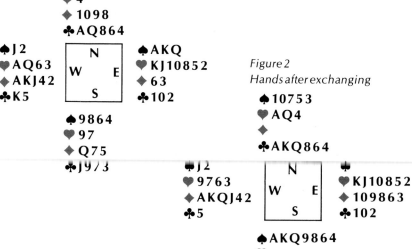

```
              ♠ 10753
              ♥ AQ4
              ♦
              ♣ AKQ864
♠ J2        ┌─────────┐   ♠
♥ 9763      │    N    │   ♥ KJ10852
♦ AKQJ42    │ W     E │   ♦ 109863
♣ 5         │    S    │   ♣ 102
            └─────────┘
              ♠ AKQ9864
              ♥
              ♦ 75
              ♣ J973
```

GOPS

Gops is a quick and entertaining game for three which is more about memory than card skills.

PLAY

Divide a standard pack, minus Jokers, into suits, then shuffle one of these well and place it face down in a pile in the centre of the table. Players each take one of the remaining suits, the ranks representing auction values from 1 (Ace) up to 13 (King), a total of 91 points. The cards in the middle have the same ranking sequence and corresponding values.

The object is to bid for the centre cards, one at a time, and to win cards worth on aggregate the most points when all have been auctioned.

The first card is turned over beside the pack, after which each player selects a card from his hand to represent his bid for the point card and places it face down in front of him. The three cards are exposed simultaneously. The highest bidder takes the point card and the bid cards are put to one side or they may be kept face up in piles in front of the players. If two (or all three) put in the same top bid (i.e. cards of the same rank), then the point card is withdrawn and the total point count is correspondingly reduced. Alternatively, the card can be left on the table and another turned over, the two cards then being sold in a single auction. If there is a tie for the last card or cards, these are withdrawn.

STRATEGY

Everyone starts with the same auction values, equal to the point cards at stake, so the average bid should be of about the same value (rank) as the card being auctioned, though it rarely is.

You must decide whether you are going to try to win an auction, when you can afford to bid at least twice as high as the point value of a middle-ranking or low card (remember, your share of the points is theoretically only 30 +), or you

are going to opt out, when you will play your lowest auction value.

Everyone is likely to bid high for the court cards so the risk of a tie is considerable. Memorizing the point cards and your opponents' bids is obviously ideal but try at least to keep running totals in your head – they will help you gauge your bids, particularly towards the end.

Consider the hands in the figure, showing a game in progress. Player A, who has a mere 10 auction points remaining, recalls that player B has spent 69 points and C 67 points. The two cards remaining in the auction he believes, correctly, to be the 8 and 7. He decides to pitch low for the 5 and bids the 2. B and C both think that their 7s may be lost in the bids for the two remaining cards, so they play them out: auction cancelled.

A knows B now has 15 points left and C 17. He also thinks, again correctly, that they both have a court card, so his 5 could prove valuable. Both B and C know that the 8 is to come but A doubts that they know each other's hands. So he plays the 5. B and C oblige by ducking, both confident that they will take the last trick. A has come out of the play handsomely considering he started with a mere 10 auction points.

SKITGUBBE

This is something unusual: a skilful card game for three players. Skitgubbe ('Grubby Old Man') is a traditional Swedish game. There are no winners, only a loser – the Grubby Old Man. A round takes barely 10 minutes.

PLAY

The standard pack is used, without Jokers. The dealer distributes three cards face down (all three together) to each player and the remaining cards are placed face down in the centre to form the stock. Ace ranks high.

There are two phases to the game. The first phase is trick-taking. The suits are disregarded; only the ranks count. The elder hand leads a card and replenishes his hand from the stock. The second player and then the dealer do likewise. The highest card takes the trick and the winner stacks the trick face down in front of him. If two or three cards match in rank, they are left on the table and the contenders only play again, repeating if necessary, the winner taking up all the cards played to the trick. See figure 1 for example.

The winner leads to the next trick and

play proceeds until there is only one card left in the stock. This card determines the trump suit for the second phase. If at this last stage every player has at least one card left, the final trick is played in the usual way; the winner picks up the last card in the stock and exposes it, then adds it to his tricks. If there is deadlock on the last trick, or if any player is without cards, the player with the lead takes and exposes the one card left in the stock – the trump, and players add to their tricks any unplayed cards.

All players now pick up their tricks and sort them into suits. These constitute their hands for the second phase. The object now is to get rid of cards as quickly as possible. Once a player does so, he drops out. The last player left in is the Grubby Old Man.

The elder hand starts by putting down a card, or two or more in sequence of the same suit. The next player must choose between playing a higher card (or cards, if in sequence) of the suit led; or playing a trump, or trumps in sequence, if void in the suit led; or taking up the cards on the table and adding them to his hand. If he cannot play higher, he must pick up the card(s).

Figure 1
Player C wins the trick at the third attempt and takes all the cards

*Figure 2
An end play*

If he beats the card led, the next player must play higher. If the second player trumps, the third player must overtrump, not revert to the suit led. If all the players in turn have played to the table, then the cards are withdrawn from play and the player who led last time leads again. If the second or third player picks up the cards, either by choice or compulsion, the next player in rotation leads.

If several rounds are to be played, keep a score by counting the number of cards held by the player left in at the end of each round; the player with the highest total is the Grubby Old Man; or alternatively agree a point limit and whoever passes it first is the Grubby Old Man.

STRATEGY

In the first phase, the aim should be to take tricks with high cards in them – but not too many. Tricks with sequences are useful. The ideal is to be left with a balanced hand for the second phase; voids in a suit are dangerous – the suit may turn out to be trumps. The last trick is worth winning: it gives you a trump and it may be a good one.

Figure 2 gives an example of hands before end play. Hearts are trumps and player A leads ♠Q. Player B can now put up the King or take the Queen into hand. If he puts up the ♠K, C trumps and the table cards are removed. Now player A leads ♢3, B plays the ♢Q and C the ♢AK, so C goes out. A is now to play and he puts down his trump pair, leaving B the Grubby Old Man.

If instead B ducks the lead by picking up the ♠Q, C will lead ♢AK and A will be obliged to pick up – he cannot trump because he has a low card of the suit led. B is to lead and plays ♢Q, C trumps and goes out, and A must pick up since he cannot beat ♡K. Now B goes out by playing his spade sequence and it is A who is Grubby Old Man.

WHIST

Not many years ago Whist was one of the most widely played of all card games. A simple trick-taking game, it is still a good family game for four players and makes an ideal training ground for other trick-taking games, for card control generally, and for partnership play.

PLAY

The standard pack is used, without Jokers. Ace ranks high.

Players cut for or agree partners, who sit facing each other. The dealer distributes singly 13 cards face down to each player and turns over the last card, leaving it exposed on the table. This card determines the trump suit. (Alternatively, the trump suit can be determined beforehand.)

The aim of each team is to win the majority of tricks – the more the better. The player on the left of the dealer leads, after which the dealer takes the exposed trump card into his hand. The second and subsequent players must play a card of the suit led if they are able; otherwise they may trump or discard. The player of the highest card in the suit led, or of the highest trump if any trumps were played, takes up the four cards as a packet – the trick.

The winner leads to the next trick. When all 13 tricks have been resolved, the winning team scores 1 point for every trick taken above six. A game is 5 points (in the USA, 7 points). The best of three games is a 'rubber' and earns two extra points. Honours holdings (A K Q J of trumps) are often scored but this is not recommended because it puts a premium on chance.

STRATEGY

Fundamental to all strategy is the need to plan and play as a team. It is all too easy, in the heat of a game, to concentrate on promoting tricks from one's own cards and to forget the partner's hand. If you never lose sight of the fact that you are playing two hands, not one, you are already a useful Whist player.

Memory plays an important part: to be able to recall all cards played is the ideal, but few can manage this. Try at least to remember trumps, the honours in other suits and the number of cards played in each. You learn about partner's hand from his play, as much by his discards as the tricks he wins.

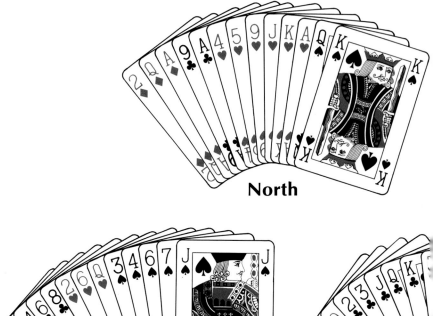

North

West

South

The hands after a typical deal

The order of play to a trick is of paramount importance. The first player controls the suit and should have a good idea of who will win it and therefore where the lead will lie for the next trick. The second player usually plays low unless he is strong in the suit led (he has the comfort of knowing that his partner plays after the third player). If the lead was a low card, the third player will play high, and the fourth player has little to worry about.

The figure shows a typical deal. Clubs are trumps. North has an attacking hand (high cards with a long suit), East has fine trumps and useful spades. South is dismal but may hope for a trump trick: his diamonds offer little prospect. West has a defensive hand – guards in three suits.

North to lead would come out with ♡A. East follows with ♡10 – a high-low discard that signals to his partner that he has a doubleton (a two card suit) – and South signals likewise with ♡8. West puts up ♡2 and North-South take the first trick. The next trick goes ♡K, ♡3, ♡7, ♡6, and North-South win again. It is now clear to North that ♡Q must lie with West since both East and South have signalled voids. So he leads another heart. East deduces North has read his play and so now also places ♡Q with West. That means if he plays a low trump, South is likely to over-trump and if he puts up an honour he risks establishing the ♣10, so he discards a diamond. North-South should make seven tricks.

East on lead would play out ♣J (a signal that he holds King and Queen) with the aim of drawing trumps before attacking with spades. South on lead would put down ◇6 (the fourth highest card of his longest suit – another 'message to partner'), putting West in an awkward position. If he puts up ◇K it will be overtaken with ◇A and North will lead out the Queen. On the other hand, if he plays ◇3 (better) North should 'finesse' – play ◇Q in the hope that the King is on his right. Either way North-

South make two tricks in diamonds.

West on the lead would open ♠4 (again, the fourth highest of his longest suit) – good news for East who would now know that he and his partner command spades. This is a common occurrence: a suit that looks only promising, or even weak, may when married with partner's holding add up to a lot of tricks.

RELATED GAMES

German Whist (which is not regional) is a good game for two. Pack, ranking and playing rules are as for Whist. Deal 13 cards each and place the next card face up by the pile of remaining cards, the stock; the exposed card determines the trump suit. The winner of the first trick takes the exposed card, and the loser takes the top card from the stockpile, exposes it and adds it to his hand. The next card in the stockpile is then turned up and the winner leads to the new trick. When the pack is exhausted, the winner is the player with most tricks, and he scores the difference between the two players' tricks (e.g. 17−9 scores 8 points). Game is 50 points. Interest lies in the up card: if it is good, you try to win the trick; if not, you may deliberately lose it.

Chinese Whist for four players (partnerships) is skilful. Deal six cards face down in a line to each player, then six face up on top of the down cards, and lastly one down. The playing hand comprises this card with the six up cards. The dealer now selects the trump suit. Usual Whist rules apply except that the six concealed cards may not be examined.

When an exposed card is played, the one below it is turned over and becomes available. Score 1 point for every trick over six. Game is 7 points. A two-player version calls for a deal of 12 packets to each player and two in hand. Three can also play: discard ♣2, then deal eight packets to each. Players score 1 point for every trick above five. The first to reach 10 points wins.

East

SOLO WHIST

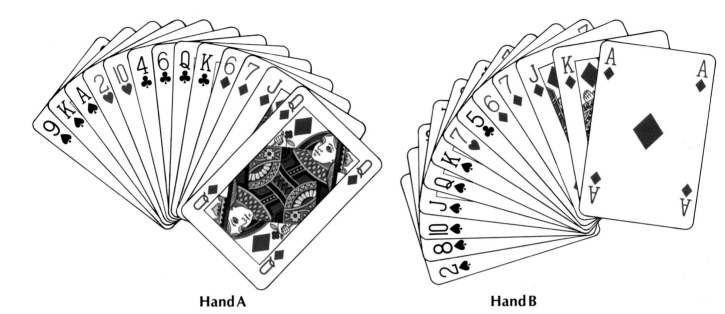

Hand A   **Hand B**

Long one of Britain's most popular card games, particularly in works and social clubs, Solo is also good family entertainment for four. The game can be adapted for three but is not as satisfactory. Solo has features in common with both Whist and Nap, and has a pleasing variety of play. It is usually played for small stakes and these add to, but are not essential for, the game's enjoyment.

PLAY

The standard pack is used, without Jokers. Ace ranks high. Players bid and score as individuals but may combine or form partnerships during play.

Cards are dealt round face down three at a time, the final cards singly. The dealer turns over the last card, which defines trumps, and does not take it into his hand until the first card is led. The players examine their hands, then the bidding begins (see below). Each player calls in turn. As in Bridge, each bid must be higher than the previous one, the highest bid determining the play. A player who passes may not then bid with the exception noted below but a player who bids may bid again if he is overcalled. Here are the calls in ascending order:

Pass (i.e. no bid).

Prop and Cop. A bid of 'I prop' means that the caller proposes a partnership with any other player to make 8 of the 13 tricks. A subsequent bid of cop ('I cop') establishes partnerships.

Solo. A bid for five tricks. This and the following calls are for play against the combined opposition.

Misere. A bid to lose all tricks in no trumps.

Abundance. A bid for nine tricks but with the privilege of nominating the trump suit.

Royal Abundance. An abundance in the existing trump suit. This call is only used as an overcall of abundance.

Open Misere. As misere, but the bidder plays the whole hand face up on the table after the first lead.

Abundance declared. A bid for all 13 tricks in no trumps, the bidder, exceptionally for this call, leading first.

Eldest, and no other player, may raise his prop to solo if he is not copped and may cop a proposal after passing.

If all players pass, there is a re-deal. The player to the left of the dealer leads, other than in abundance declared, and the hand ends when the contract is made or defeated, except if the game is being played for stakes and there are bonuses

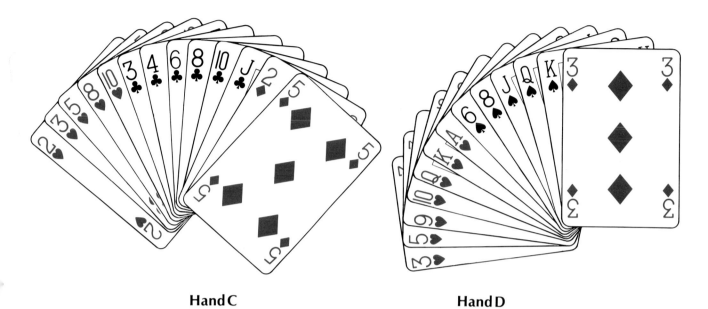

Hand C

Hand D

and penalties for overtricks and under-tricks. Where the game is played for stakes, the losers pay the winners in prop and cop while in other contracts one player pays to or receives from the rest. Stakes are agreed beforehand.

The rules of play are as for Whist, the winner leading to the next trick.

STRATEGY

This depends largely on the contract. In prop and cop each partner should hold about four tricks (a safe five would prompt a solo call). Where partners sit opposite each other the play becomes identical to Whist except for the need to make or spoil a fixed number of tricks.

Solo is the commonest contract and usually the least interesting, if only because it is often unbeatable – if the probable trick count falls short of nine, the declarer must settle for five. For solo and higher contracts you cannot gamble on support from a partner – you have not got one. This calls for cautious bidding: apparently solid bids can get defeated.

A misere call is unwise if you are short of deuces, particularly if you have a long suit without the 2. As declarer, you will have little choice in the play. Defence against a misere is based on the theory

that it can probably be defeated, other-wise the caller would have elected for open misere. A short suit is usually a safe lead since it is unlikely declarer will be void. If you share a long suit with the declarer, play it out so that your partners can discard freely.

Abundance is commonly formed round a long suit (trumps) where by playing these out first it is possible to squeeze the defence into making com-promising discards. Position at the table is important. If it is your turn to lead, you are much better placed to attack – and hence to bid – than if you are the second player.

The figure illustrates four hands. Hand A is a good cop (and fair prop) hand if diamonds are trumps but not otherwise. Hand B should be an easy solo in spades but is vulnerable with diamonds as trumps. Hand C looks a reasonable gamble for a misere since there is a good chance of throwing ◇5 on a spade lead – but it is not: two rounds of clubs followed by the ♣2 could spell ruin. Hand D, a two-suiter, promises an abundance but the lead will be important. Declarer would not welcome a spade lead with the danger of four quick tricks to the opposition, spades still not safe and the ♡J unaccounted for.

NAP

A

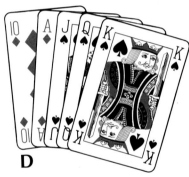

B

C

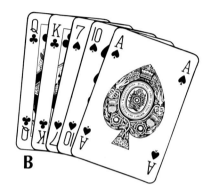

D

E

Biddable hands in a five-player game

This is a fast card game for any number, best played for small stakes (or a token prize for best scorer). Nap or Napoleon is of French origin as its name suggests. However, it is most popular in England where Nap schools can be found everywhere. Local rules are frequent but these hardly disturb the play.

PLAY

The standard pack is used, without Jokers. Ace ranks high. Five cards are dealt singly face down to each player. The stock is put to one side and may not be examined.

Players now bid for the number of tricks they think they can make against the other players combined. The successful bidder leads and the first card out is trumps – so the bidder chooses the trump suit. The winner of the trick leads to the next.

The lowest call is 2, the highest 5 (Nap), but Nap is beaten by Wellington (also 5, but the stakes are doubled) which in turn is beaten by Blucher (again 5, but the stakes are redoubled). A Blucher call implies that there are three players who believe that they can make every trick, which is not so surprising when you realize that each may be planning to nominate a different trump suit.

A Misere call can be made, which contracts to make no tricks and is rated between a call of 3 and 4. In Misere there are no trumps.

Only the contract is paid for: under-tricks or overtricks do not count. If the bidder wins his contract, the other players each pay him the equivalent of the number of tricks he bid, Misere counting as 3, but Nap counting as double (10). If the bidder fails, he pays all the other players a like amount, except for an abortive Nap, when he only pays out 5. Similarly Wellington counts as 20 (10) and Blucher 40 (20).

The five-player round shown in the figure should clarify the bidding. A bids 2 since he would hope to make two diamond tricks (with half the cards in stock, the odds are that Ace and King will not both be against him). B bids 3 – two spades and a club look possible; as a general rule it pays to be aggressive at Nap. C goes Misere – a risky call but he is banking on a club lead to get rid of his spade. D bids 4 – he is gambling on either the ♠A missing or making the ♦10. E goes Nap, which he makes effortlessly.

A would have succeeded with his call but Misere should fail on any lead. Suppose C leads ♦4. The play would go ♦A, ♡9, ♦Q, ♣K. D now leads ♦10 (a spade lead also defeats the contract) and there follows ♣A, ♦J, ♣Q, ♠9. A then leads a heart which E overtakes and finally comes out with ♡2 which C will have to cover with ♡3. The other two bids (B and D) would also fail but there is an abnormal number of high cards in circulation.

BRIDGE

Contract Bridge, invariably shortened to Bridge nowadays, is probably the world's most popular card game. Millions would argue it is also the best. It is the only card game to enjoy a set of rules that is internationally accepted. There are two-player and three-player versions but none compares with the four-player partnership game now universally played.

Contract Bridge is a little over 50 years old. It is a direct descendant of Auction Bridge which in turn was derived from Whist, and card-play in all three games has much in common. What is different about Bridge is the scoring system, which heavily influences the bidding, a feature of the game, and to a lesser extent the subsequent play.

Some would say Bridge is not a family game, but Bridge learnt and played in the family, without acrimony, is good preparation for social play.

PLAY

The standard card pack is used, without the Jokers. It is usual for two packs, with contrasting backs, to be used alternately in deals.

Cards rank, A, K . . . 2 (low). In the bidding only, the suits rank, in descending order, spades, hearts, diamonds, clubs, but a call in no trumps has precedence over spades. Spades and hearts are called the major suits, diamonds and clubs the minor suits.

Partners are agreed and face each other across the table. Each partnership works as a team but the bids of each partner are binding on both. The aim is to win the most points in play, especially by succeeding in contractual bids and so earning a bonus for winning games and for winning the rubber (the best of three games). A slightly different system is used in tournament play.

Deal all the cards out singly, 13 to each player, ending with the dealer. Players study their cards and then call in turn, the dealer starting. Calling goes clockwise and each player on his turn may either bid or pass. A player who passes may bid in a later round.

Each bid must exceed the previous bid in value. The purpose of the bidding is to establish the trump suit, if any, and the number of tricks the declarer must make. This is known as the contract. A contract is reached when the bid of one player is followed by passes from the other three players in succession. (On the first round, if all players pass the hand is thrown in.)

The declarer is the partner who first bid the trump suit of the contract (or first bid no trumps if the hand is to be played in no trumps) – even though the final call may have been made by his partner. The player to the left of the declarer leads, and declarer's partner, who is referred to as dummy, then puts his hand face-up on the table in front of him, with the trump suit on his right if the hand is being played in trumps, and takes no further part in the play. One player in each partnership collects his side's tricks.

The lowest bid is 'One club'. This is a contract for the partnership to make seven tricks (that is, one more than the basic six tricks), with clubs as trumps. An overcall is either for the same number of tricks but in a higher-ranking suit (or in no trumps), or a call that is numerically higher, which takes precedence. Thus 'One no trump' beats 'One diamond', and 'Three clubs' beats 'Two spades'. A call of 'Four hearts' would mean that declarer is contracting to make 10 of the 13 tricks with hearts as trumps.

Instead of passing, or calling a suit or no trumps, a player on his turn may double the opponents' call. This does not alter the bid but increases the penalties for the losing side. Either of the opponents may in turn redouble. Penalty calls are automatically cancelled by a subsequent bid. Here is an example of a typical bidding sequence. North dealt and opened the auction.

North: One diamond
East: No bid (or 'Pass')

South: One no trump
West: Two spades
North: Three hearts
East: No bid
South: Three spades
West: Double
North: Five diamonds
East: No bid
South: No bid
West: No bid

North is the declarer and the contract is five diamonds. To succeed he must get 11 of the 13 tricks. Diamonds are trumps and East leads. Dummy (South) then puts his hand face-up on the table. North now plays a card from the exposed hand and must follow suit (play a card of the same suit as that led) if possible, otherwise he may play any card. Similarly, East and finally North play a card of the suit led or another card if they are void in that suit, the four cards making a trick which belongs to the side that contributed the highest card of the suit led, or the highest trump if any were played. The winner of the trick leads to the next.

Supposing these cards had been played to the trick:

East: ♣2
South: ♣A
West: ♣3
North: ♣7

South (dummy) has won the trick so North would pick it up (South is playing no part in the hand, remember) and then select a card from the table to lead to the next trick.

SCORING

Scoring is not the easiest part of Bridge and some people never trouble to learn it but it is impossible to bid intelligently without knowing how many points are at stake. It is usual for one player in each partnership to keep the score.

A Bridge score sheet (see figure 1) is printed with twin columns headed WE, for the points earned by the scorer's partnership, and THEY for the opponents' points. Roughly half-way down is a

horizontal line that cuts the columns in two. 'Below the line' are entered only those scores that count towards game, that is, scores made by fulfilling contracts. All other scores are entered 'above the line' – overtricks, bonuses, penalties. Column totals determine the winners at the end of play.

The big points bonuses are for rubbers. You get 700 for a rubber if your win is by two games to nothing, 500 if your opponents managed to win a game.

Game is reached by scoring 100 points up, which may be earned in a single hand or a number of hands. For every trick of your contract over six you score, according to the trump suit (or no trumps):

No trumps– 40 for the first trick,
             30 for subsequent tricks
Spades   – 30
Hearts   – 30
Diamonds– 20
Clubs   – 20

Thus you would reach game exactly with a successful contract of three no trumps or five of a minor suit (diamonds or clubs) and comfortably with four of a major suit (spades or hearts). Remember that only tricks that you have contracted to make will count towards the game. If, for example, you bid three spades and then win 10 tricks, you will score 120 points but only 90 points go 'below the line'; the other 30 are scored 'above the line'.

When either side achieves a game, a horizontal line is drawn across the score sheet below the score. This is to make clear that each side is now starting a new game with nothing below the line; part scores are not carried forward to count towards the next game. All points are added up at the end of a rubber and the totals of the two sides compared. It is quite possible for the side that loses the rubber to end up with a higher point count amassed from part scores and penalty points.

Consider this short rubber. North/South call three no trumps and make four (i.e. 10 tricks). This earns 100 below

Figure 1
A score sheet

WE	THEY
	+5
30	500
100	
40	120
30	
	100
200	720

the line and 30 above. As this is game, a horizontal line is drawn below the score. North/South now call and make two diamonds (40 points), and subsequently make one heart (30 points). East/West now win a game with four spades bid and made (120 points). Finally, East/West bid and make three no trumps. East/West thus win the rubber and score the 500 bonus. The North/South score sheet would look like that in figure 1. East/West carry forward 520 points to a subsequent rubber. In practice, point totals are usually rounded up or down to the nearest hundred, so East/West's win would be expressed as +5.

When one side wins a game they are said to be vulnerable. In the rubber scored above, North/South were vulnerable after the first game and both sides were vulnerable after the second. Certain bonuses and penalties are increased in these circumstances. The penalties for undertricks are shown in the table, right.

A bid of six of a suit or no trumps is called a small slam and a bid of seven (a contract to win every trick) a grand slam. These, and certain other bonuses, are shown in the table. Honours refer to the top five cards in the trump suit (A K Q J 10) or the four Aces in a call of no trumps. All scores given in the table are 'above the line' and do not count towards game.

STRATEGY

Intelligent bidding is the starting point of good Bridge and many more books are written about this stage of the game than about the card play. It is not much use having good cards if you are in the wrong contract or your opponents are in the right one, so the main aim is to arrive at the right contract or to get the opponents in the wrong one. But there is a secondary aim: bidding should also be directed towards signalling information to your partner and finding out about his hand — always remember that Bridge is a partnership game.

PENALTIES FOR UNDERTRICKS

	Not Vulnerable			Vulnerable		
		Doubled	Redoubled		Doubled	Redoubled
1 undertrick	50	100	200	100	200	400
2 undertricks	100	300	600	200	500	1000
3 undertricks	150	500	1000	300	800	1600

and so on in proportion

BONUS SCORES

	Not Vulnerable			Vulnerable		
		Doubled	Redoubled		Doubled	Redoubled
1 overtrick	trick value	100	200	trick value	200	400

and so on in proportion

Little slam	500	750
Grand slam	1000	1500
For making doubled or redoubled contract	50	50

Bonus for honours in one hand

Four of trump suit—100
Five of trump suit—150
Four aces in no trumps—150

Bonus for unfinished rubber

One game—300
Part-score in unfinished game—50

On picking up the cards, the first step is to sort and evaluate the hand. With an even distribution of cards to all players, a suit will be almost entirely played out in three tricks (the phrase is 'it will go round three times'), and the potential trick-winning cards are obviously A K Q J. (Two honours often fall on the same trick.) Values are given to these cards as a basis of assessment:

Ace — 4 points
King — 3 points
Queen — 2 points
Jack — 1 point

In addition, you may count 3 points for a void suit, 2 points for a singleton (a one-card suit) and 1 point for a doubleton (a two-card suit) since in the right contract this shortage in a suit should enable you to trump the opponents' high cards. However, these counts should be used with discretion — it could be unwise to allow 3 points for a void in the suit your partner has just bid!

Using these rules, it is possible to give a point value to any hand. The hand in figure 2 for example has 14 points in high cards plus 2 points for the singleton.

In addition to high cards, distribution is an important factor. Consider the hand in figure 3. The point count is quite low but the seven-card suit holds promise. Since this means that there are only six diamonds among the other three players, it is quite possible that the Queen will fall on the first two tricks or lie with partner. In that case there are seven quick tricks if diamonds are trumps and possibly also if the hand is played in no trumps. On the other hand, if the Queen is with an opponent and is guarded (that is, is backed by at least two other diamonds), then when the third trick is lost to the Queen there is no way that the

Figure 2
Evaluating a hand

lead can be recovered to capitalize on the five good diamonds remaining unless they are the trump suit. Unequal distribution makes for interesting Bridge – and problems of judgment.

The order of play to a trick is important. The first player has choice of lead (though he may not always want it) whereas the last player usually has the easiest decision. The practice is for the second player to play a low card but to cover an honour (e.g., if a Jack is led, cover it with a higher card if possible) and for the third player to play high. These are guiding principles only but it is wise to follow them unless you have reason not to.

A hand of about 13 points is necessary to open the bidding in a suit, a few more to call no trumps (do not count distribution points here). When bidding, avoid inflections, hesitations and similar ploys

to suggest the nature of your hand. Seating reflects the order of play, which in turn should be reflected in the bidding. For example, if the player on your right opens one spade and you hold ♠K J and two others in the suit, you can reasonably expect to make both your honours. However, if the call is on your left you may make neither.

The first bid is usually at the one level. Remember that you should use the bidding to exchange information with your partner and this can only happen if the bidding goes round a few times, so do not be in a hurry to reach a contract. There are two types of bid: the natural bid which means exactly what it says; and a bid that is part of a system and relays certain information or puts an obligation on partner. Dozens of bidding systems, or conventions as they are commonly called, are in use and the merits and

Figure 3
Uneven distribution

demerits of each are hotly debated. Some are complex, others are simple, but all are designed to arrive at the best contract or defence.

A simple convention, incorporated in many systems, is Blackwood. This is used to find out a partner's high card holding when a slam is in prospect. The convention call is four no trumps, which requires the partner to disclose the number of Aces he holds, which he indicates by bidding thus: five clubs (he has no Aces); five diamonds (one Ace); five hearts (two Aces); five spades (three Aces – though this holding is unlikely). A subsequent call of five no trumps asks for Kings in the same way.

Certain hands are opened above the one level. A very strong hand (say 24 points) warrants an opening call of two provided it contains a suitable trump suit. An 'opening two' usually forces the partner to respond even if he has not a point in his hand, in order to keep the bidding open. A hand with seven or eight cards in a suit headed by honours and perhaps with an Ace or equivalent (e.g., K Q) in another suit can be opened with a call of three. This in fact is a weak call but it makes it very difficult for the opposition to enter the bidding – wherein lies its value. Partner should not respond to a pre-emptive bid, as this three call is known, unless holding very good cards.

In order to respond to your partner's opening call at the one level you need to hold only about 6 points. If you have a powerful hand you should indicate this by 'double jumping'. To your partner's bid of one diamond you might respond two hearts, which is one higher than necessary and shows a hand of perhaps 13 points plus.

A straightforward hand of Bridge is followed through below. The cards held are shown in figure 4.

North dealt and with a point count of 16 and fairly even suit distribution he bids one no trump. East ponders; he has 13 points including his distribution count, a five-card suit suitable for trumps

Figure 4
A sample deal

North

West

South

East

and he is on the right side of the strong hand, but he can only count two or three tricks and so would need a lot of support from partner. He elects to pass.

South has a good supporting hand and shows his strength and length by calling two spades. West passes, and North, pleased with the support in his short suit, continues, after hesitating over his vulnerable clubs, with two no trumps. East passes and South bids three clubs, not because he wants clubs as trumps but to indicate he holds the Ace – this is called a cue-bid. North closes the contract with three no trumps. Because this call allows game to be reached at the three level (9 tricks) rather than the four or five level of a suit call, it is a contract to be aimed for. Generally about 26–27 high-card points are required between the two hands to make a game, except where distribution is uneven.

East is to lead. His best hope is the hearts and he puts down ♡4. It is routine to lead the fourth highest of your longest suit against no trumps; partner can then deduce exactly how many cards of that suit above the rank led are held by the declarer. North plays ♡5 from dummy and West comes up with ♡10 (third hand high: now East knows North holds K Q J) and North wins the trick with ♡J.

North has now to be a little careful. He wants to use the spades but must give dummy the lead to do so and he can only enter the dummy hand through ♣A. So he leads ♧A followed by ♧4. The only tricks East/West will make are East's three high cards. North will in due course play ♢J from the table. If West covers with the Queen, North will put up the King and his remaining diamonds are good. If not, he will play below the Jack (this tactic is called a finesse) and lead the suit again from dummy if East does not put up the Ace, and again North/South lose only one diamond.

North/South have made the contract and the game with an overtrick. They therefore score 100 below the line and 30 above.

GIN RUMMY

Gin Rummy, which swept America in the 1940s and is still very popular there, is a two-player card game that can be adapted for three. It is fast-moving with a good measure of chance but with considerable scope for skill too. There are a number of different versions but there is no significant difference between any of them. A bonus scoring system is used if the game is played for stakes.

PLAY

A standard pack, without Jokers, is used. Cards rank from Ace (low) to King (high) with court cards counting 10 and other cards their pip value. The suits are equal.

Ten cards are dealt singly, face down, to each player. The top card of the pack is then placed face up on the table to start the discard pile and the rest of the pack is put face down next to it. The non-dealer may take the face-up card into his hand and discard. If he does not want the up-card, the option passes to the dealer. From now on play alternates.

A player on his turn may either take the concealed card from the top of the pack and discard; or take the top card from the discard pile and replace it with one from his hand. Once a card is covered in the discard pile it cannot subsequently be brought into play.

The object is to make sets. A set is three or four cards of the same rank (three 7s, four Qs) or three or more cards *of the same suit* in sequence ($\Diamond$A 2 3; $\heartsuit$J 10 9 8 7). Cards which do not make sets are called deadwood. When the deadwood of his hand totals 10 or less, a player may 'knock'. He does this on his turn by picking up a card (top of the pack or discard pile), knocking – it is usual to rap the table – and then discarding. The hand is then spread face up on the table.

The second player may now 'lay off' any cards from his hand that fit the exposed sets. Deadwood totals are then compared. If, as is usual, the declarer has a lower count, he scores the difference between the totals. If the second player has an equal or lower deadwood count, he scores the difference plus a 25-point bonus. If declarer matches all the

Figure 1
A typical hand

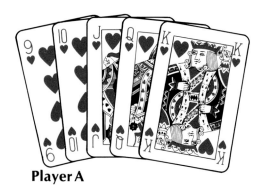

Player A

Player B

A

B

cards in his hand, that is, he has no deadwood after he has discarded, he announces 'Gin' and scores all the opponent's deadwood and a bonus of 25 points. The second player may not lay off on a Gin hand. Notice that sets do not score. The first player to reach 100, or other agreed total, is the winner.

A typical hand is illustrated in figure 1. Player A has knocked with two sets and a deadwood count of 4. Player B is able to lay off two of his cards – 8 6 – on player A's sets and is left with deadwood of 11. Player A scores 7 points. Notice that player A is not allowed to lay off his Ace on player B's sequence.

STRATEGY

Every card taken from the up pile and every discard tells something of the player's hand. Many signals are easy to read: if your opponent picks up a Jack from the discard pile and later a second Jack, he almost certainly has a set; but if he discards a Jack and then picks one up he probably wants it for a sequence. If you have a suspicion of what your opponent is collecting, hold up any card you think he wants. At best you can discard it after you knock, and if he knocks first you are likely to be able to lay it off.

A good memory is indispensable if you want to play Gin well. Try to remember your opponent's discards: these should indicate safe discards for you.

Your hand could have several embryo sets. Which to keep? A pair of high-ranking cards is worth holding for a few rounds in the hope of a match, since players discard their odd high cards early to reduce the penalty count. If you hold two of a rank, the chance of getting a third is about the same as that of completing a sequence.

Generally it is good to knock early – if you can do this in the first few turns you could catch your opponent for a stiff penalty – but sometimes it is better to try for Gin: if your opponent knocks first you are likely to underscore him. As a guide, it is even chances that both players hold a set after picking up.

When no progress can be made towards completing sets, advantage should be taken of reducers – low cards that can be retained while discarding high cards.

When assembling a hand, look for possible alternatives. Keep to the minimum your opponent's chances of laying off. Compare the two hands in figure 2. Both use the same cards but the second hand offers only half the chances of laying off that the first hand does.

Figure 2
Arranging a hand

CANASTA

Much in vogue in the USA about 30 years ago, Canasta is an elaborate Rummy for up to six players. The game works best for two, or four players in partnerships. The rules are not difficult but play can be quite complex.

PLAY

Two standard packs are used, preferably with the same backs, and four Jokers. The Jokers and all deuces are wild, so they can be substituted for any cards. Red 3s are bonus cards and take no part in the play. Ranking and suits in Canasta are irrelevant.

The object is to score points by declaring melds (three or more cards of the same rank grouped together) and to gain bonuses, especially by forming canastas (melds of seven cards or more) which may be mixed (including wild cards) or natural (without wild cards). Wild cards must not exceed natural cards in any meld. A hand ends when one side goes out or the stock is exhausted. Cards in hand at the end of play count against the player. The first side to reach 5000 points wins the game.

The dealer distributes 15 cards face down and singly if there are two players, 13 if three, and 11 if four or more, then places the stock face down in the centre and places the top card face up beside it to start the discard or up-pile. If this card is a red 3 or a wild card, another card is turned over to cover it – and so on if necessary until a natural card is turned.

Play rotates clockwise. Each player on his first turn places any red 3 he holds on to the table in front of him and replenishes his hand from the stock. Thereafter if he picks up a red 3 from stock he does likewise.

A turn consists of drawing a card from stock or taking the up-pile (subject to certain conditions), then – if wished and possible – making any melds and/or adding to existing melds, (own or partner's), and finally discarding. There is a minimum point requirement, depending

A two-player game in progress

on score, for the initial meld(s).

The up-pile is a feature of the game. It may be 'free', in which case the player can take it into hand (the whole pile, never part of it) by melding the top card with at least two of the same rank (one may be a wild card) from his hand, or adding it to an existing meld (own or partner's).

Point values

Joker	50
Aces and 2s	20
8s and above	10
7s and below (except red 3s)	5

Bonuses
(in addition to above)

Red 3	100
All four red 3s	800
Mixed canasta	300
Natural canasta	500
Going out	100
Going out concealed	200

Minimum point requirement for initial meld

Score	
Negative	no minimum
Under 1500	50
1500–2995	90
3000 and over	120

Or the up-pile may be 'frozen'. It is frozen – not available – to a side that has not melded and to all players when there is a wild card or red 3 in it (customarily, the first such card is placed at right angles to the others). An up-pile containing a wild card or red 3 can only be taken by melding the top natural card with two matching cards from hand.

A discarded black 3, known as a stop card, freezes the up-pile to the next player only. Black 3s can never be melded except to go out, and then they must all be natural.

A player goes out by voiding his hand after drawing, either by melding his remaining cards or reducing his hand to one card which he throws away. In the two-player game you may not go out until you have at least two canastas; only one canasta is required where there are more players. The point values of cards, bonuses and minimum point requirement for an initial meld are given above.

STRATEGY

Canastas are the point-spinners. To build these you need to nourish your hand from the up-pile; the more pairs you have in your hand, natural or mixed, the better your chances of winning it. Good players never reduce their holdings below five cards except when going out – the penalties you pay for cards caught in hand are small when compared with the prospective bonuses. Going out earns only a modest bonus and is best used as a defensive measure.

Holding up cards you think the opponent(s) may need is good strategy; so are false discards. Do not be afraid to break up a concealed meld if the position warrants it, or to freeze the pack with a wild card, especially if your hand gives you a good chance of thawing it later – after your opponent has discarded to it generously, of course.

The figure shows a two-player game in progress. Your score is 1950. On the last turn you put down two melds for a count of 100, which meets your minimum requirement (90). It is your turn and you draw from stock because you cannot match the up-card. Fate has bequeathed you a Joker, so that you now have three melds in hand but you cannot put them down to go out because you need two canastas first. The best play is to put none down. Instead, discard a 2 and freeze the up-pile. A 2 does the same work as a Joker and there is no point risking the bonus difference. Now you are well placed, with three natural pairs and a good chance of capturing the discards.

In the two-player game you should hold back where it is safe to do so: you may occasionally get the opportunity to sandbag your opponent by putting down a concealed hand to go out. In the three-player game, however, the best strategy is to go out fast. In the four-player game you ask your partner's permission to go out: his reply has to be followed. In the six-player game you are ill-advised to hold back melds.

CRIBBAGE

This very English pub game, also popular in America, dates back at least 300 years and was built on earlier games. However, there is nothing piecemeal about cribbage. It is a distinctive card game whose devotees – and there is an army of them – are as committed as Bridge fiends. Cribbage calls for quick calculation and is essentially a game for two players or four in partnerships, although it can also be played by three.

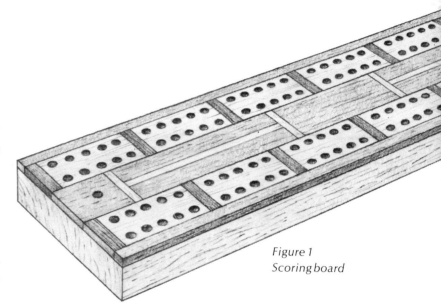

Figure 1
Scoring board

PLAY

Cribbage is a game of scoring combinations. A pegboard (figure 1), a device nearly as old as the game itself, is commonly used for keeping the score, and burnt matchsticks substituted for pegs are equally part of the game's tradition.

A standard pack is used, minus Jokers. Cards count their pip values, with Ace low (1) and all court cards 10. Suits are equal.

In the two-player version, the deal is six cards each distributed singly face down. Players examine their hands and then discard two cards face down to the table. These four cards form the crib and belong to the dealer. The game has two stages: the play-off and the show.

The play-off
The non-dealer cuts the pack. The dealer takes the top card and exposes it. This is the 'starter'. If it is a Jack, the dealer scores 2 points 'for his heels'.

The non-dealer begins by playing a card from his hand face up in front of him, announcing its pip value. The dealer follows but announces the cumulative count of both cards. If this is 15, the dealer scores 2; if he plays a card of like rank ('pairs'), he also scores 2. The players continue to put a card down in turn while announcing the cumulative total. This must not exceed 31. If a player reaches 31 exactly, he scores 2. If he cannot play without passing 31 he says 'No' and the other player continues to play. When both players have declined,

Figure 2
Top-scoring hand

the last player scores 1 for 'go'. Now the players start up to 31 again with the remaining cards (if any), scoring as before. When both players have exhausted their hands, the play-off ends.

Other scoring combinations are possible in the play-off. 'Threes' – three cards of the same rank played in sequence – score 6, and 'fours' 12. (A player who scores 12 for fours has already scored 2 for pairs and his opponent 6 for threes.)

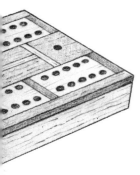

Three or more cards in sequence (a 'run') also score. They must be played consecutively but not necessarily in order – and suits do not count. For example, 6 4 5 is a run and the player to put down the third card scores 3 (three cards in run). If the second player now plays a 2 or 7 he scores 4 (four in run) and so on. A card can contribute to more than one scoring combination.

The show

In this stage, players make scoring patterns from their hands plus the starter card. Scoring combinations are as in the first stage, including 2 points for 'fifteens' but not for 31. Additionally, four cards of the same suit in hand score 4 (for a flush), and if the starter is of the same suit, 5. Finally, a player who has the Jack of the starter suit gets 1 point 'for his nob'. A hand of Q 10 5 5 (a good one) has four distinct 15-count patterns and so scores 8 ('15 – 8' is the term) plus 2 points 'for pairs'.

The dealer now turns over the crib and scores it in the same way, except that all five cards must be of the same suit to notch a flush.

In three-handed Cribbage, each player gets five cards and discards one to the crib. The four-handed game, much played in pubs, is a partnership game. Cards are as for three-handed play and scoring in both versions is as for the two-handed game. A match can be 61, 121 or 181 up. In any of the games, players may agree to 'Muggins'. In this version, you score any undeclared points of your opponents by announcing 'Muggins' – usually with relish!

STRATEGY

The skill of Cribbage lies in discarding to the crib and, particularly, in the play-off.

The most valuable cards are 5s since they can be matched with any 10-point card – almost a third of the pack. For this reason, do not lead a 5 or play a card that brings the total to 21. The average crib is worth about 5 points. As non-dealer your aim is to disrupt it: discard Ace King or King plus a spot card (not a 10), preferably of different suits. Do not discard 5s or Jacks or cards in sequence. As dealer, this advice does not apply because you inherit the crib. 5s and pairs make good contributions.

The best hand for the show scores 29 points and is rare indeed. It has 555 and the Jack of the starter suit, with the fourth 5 as starter. Score 16 for eight fifteens, 12 for fours and 1 for his nob (figure 2).

A hand of Cribbage is played out in figure 3.

Figure 3
A hand played out

A HAND OF CRIBBAGE

Deal

Player A	Player B	Starter

to crib: ♣A ♦ 7   To crib: ♣7 ♥ 7

Play-off

A	points	B	points
		'for his heels	2
♣ 3		♥ J	
♦ 2	2	♦ 4	
♠ 6		♥ 5	3
No		No	
		Go	1
♥ 8		♥ Q	
		Go	1
Show			
15/2	2	15/6	6
		Pairs	2
Crib			
	–	15/6	6
		Threes	6
	4		27

SKAT

Skat has much in common with Solo Whist but is a lot more skilful. To appreciate its depth of strategy is to understand why it is Germany's most popular card game. It also flourishes in America where a different version is played. Recommended for three players who are prepared to concentrate, Skat is a trick-taking game in which the principal object is to capture scoring cards. The bidding and reckoning are quite complicated and there are many local variants. The game is often played with four or even five players, though only three participate in a hand.

PLAY

The Skat pack is the same as for Piquet (the standard pack less the 2s to 6s) with the cards ranking ♣J ♠J ♡J ♢J, then the trump suit in the sequence A 10 K Q 9 8 7. Certain cards have values when taken in tricks. These are Ace (11), 10 (10), King (4), Queen (3), Jack (2). Other cards have no value.

The deal is 10 cards each, dealt face down 3-4-3, with two cards (the skat) placed face down to the table after the first round of three. Players bid in turn; the highest bid determines the contract with the declarer playing against the other two. Players are called forehand (eldest), middlehand and rearhand (dealer).

Bidding is based on game values which have nothing to do with card

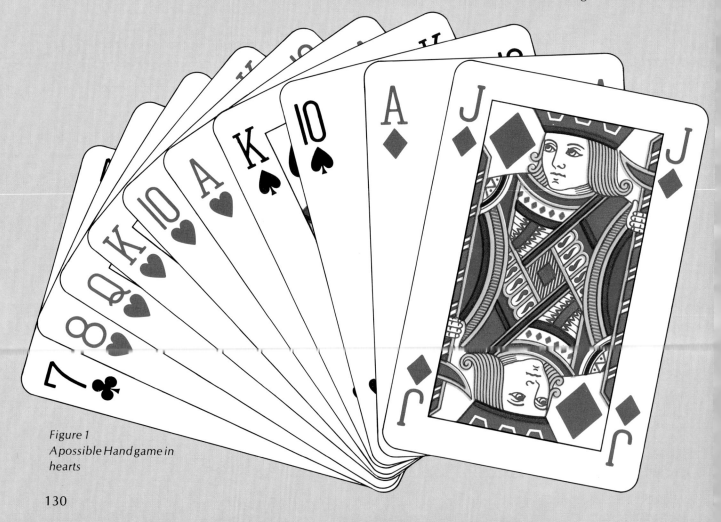

Figure 1
A possible Hand game in hearts

values. Game value, which is the highest bid you can call, is computed from your matadors, game multipliers and the base value of the suit you choose for trumps.

Matadors

The matador value of a hand is either *with* (if you hold ♣J) or *without* (if you do not). It is *with* the number of top trumps in sequence, for example, ♣J, ♠J, ♢J, etc., is 'with 2' (♣J, ♠J – the ♡J is missing); and *without* the number of trumps above the highest trump held, for example, 10 trumps high is 'without 5' (the four Jacks and the Ace). The value is based only on the number – not whether it is with or without.

Multipliers

1 *Basic (Gucki) game:* the declarer contracts to win cards with a point count of 61 (out of 120 in pack) with use of the skat.

2 *Hand game:* as Basic, but the skat is not examined until after play, when any scoring cards are added to the declarer's total.

3 *Schneider:* as for Basic game but winning 90 points or more.

4 *Schneider declared:* bid, and played from hand.

5 *Schwarz:* winning all 10 tricks.

6 *Schwarz declared:* bid, and played from hand.

7 *Ouvert:* as Schwarz declared but the bidder exposes his hand on the table before play starts.

Only the highest multiplier is counted: for example, if your contract is Schneider declared, you do not add 2 for a Hand game. (The above is necessarily a simplified explanation of scoring.)

Base values

Each suit has a base value: clubs, 12; spades, 11; hearts, 10; diamonds, 9. Alternatively, the declarer can opt for a Grand in any of the above games. In Grand, only the four Jacks are trumps. The base values are: Grand, 24; Grand Ouvert, 36.

The game value is arrived at by adding together the matador and multiplier counts and then multiplying by the base value. In the hand shown in figure 1 you might elect a Hand game in hearts, which should be an easy contract. Your matadors are without 3, your multiplier is 2 and the base value 10, so your game value is $(3 + 2) \times 10 = 50$. In play, you would probably arrange your cards with ♢J at the head of your trump suit.

Finally, a Misere call is possible in which the declarer contracts to lose all the tricks. Misere is played without trumps and with the cards ranking normally (A K Q J 10 9 8 7). There are four possible game values in Misere: Basic, 23; Basic ouvert, 46; Hand, 35; and Hand ouvert, 59.

The lowest game value, and hence bid, is 18 – a Basic game with or without one matador in diamonds. The bidding is in game values, starting with 18. The second bidder calls the next higher game value – 20 (19 is not possible) and so on, the declarer only announcing his contract when the bidding is over. The procedure is for middlehand to open ('18' or 'Pass') with forehand responding. The bidding is then a duel between these two until one or both pass, when rearhand enters the bidding.

Once you have passed you cannot bid again. Where two players have equal game values, precedence is in the order forehand, middlehand, rearhand.

It is worth repeating that bidding, based on game values, is distinct from the contract. Remember that the top bidder must declare a game at least equal in value to his call otherwise he is penalized. Here is an example of bidding:

Middlehand: 18
Forehand: Yes (he can beat it)
Middlehand: 20
Forehand: Pass
Rearhand: 22
Middlehand: Yes
Rearhand: 23
Middlehand: Yes
Rearhand: Pass

Figure 2
A Gucki hand

Middlehand must now decide whether he is going to use the skat or announce a Hand game. If he decides to use the skat, he picks it up and adds it to his hand, then rejects two cards face down to the table. He then announces his contract. Forehand leads and players must follow suit but may trump or discard if they cannot. Remember that all the Jacks are trumps. The winner of the trick leads to the next trick. At end of play, the declarer adds to his score any point count in his discards or in the skat if he played a Hand game (this does not of course apply in a Misere game).

Scoring

This is rather involved. Briefly, the declarer scores for the game he makes provided the value is not lower than the level at which he won the bidding. For example, the declarer bids a Hand game but gets over 90 points: he scores for a Schneider.

If the declarer fails to make his contract, he gets a minus score at least equal to his game value (for example, if he gets 30 points or less, his opponents make Schneider). Only the declarer scores — plus or minus.

The variable factor is the skat. Whether a game is played with or with-out it, the game value of declarer's hand is assessed after play as though it contained all 12 cards, which means that the matador count, and hence the game value of the hand, may be changed. For example: the declarer tops the bidding with 36 points, intending a Hand game 'without 3' in spades $-(2+3) \times 11 = 55$. In the play he takes cards worth 59 points. In the skat, which is then exposed, there is ♣J. This takes his count to 61, the minimum point requirement, but now his hand is 'with one' matador, not 'without 3'. So his game score is 33 — three less than his contract bid: he has lost.

STRATEGY

The skills necessary to assess the value of your hand and for the subsequent card play are not unlike those required for Solo Whist or Bridge. As an example, a void suit is worth a trick at least (and quite possibly netting an Ace for 11 points), while signalling, particularly in a Misere hand, can thwart the declarer.

The skat is an added factor. Clearly there is a chance element here but the probability is that the skat will furnish a trick in a trump game and a point count of about 8, though if you hold, say, the four

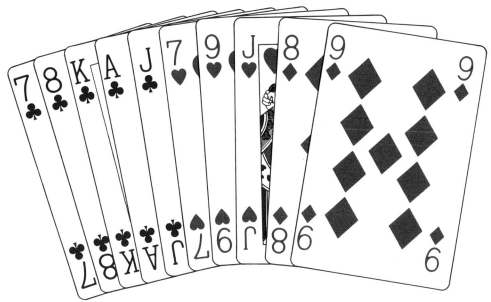

Figure 3
A Misere hand

Aces then you would not expect to find many points in the skat. In Misere hands the skat can prove a hand-winner, whether used or not. Apart from sugar in the skat, there are advantages in discarding.

Figure 2 shows a sporting Gucki hand with a better-than-even chance that one of the skat cards is a trump or an Ace to make the call in clubs confident.

A plausible Misere call could be made with the cards shown in figure 3, but only without the lead. If you get the contract, you would have to consider whether or not to take the skat. Advantage: you might improve your hand by picking up, for example, another club or heart which would permit you to discard one of the shaky diamonds. Disadvantage: you halve your profit and enhance the risk.

An easy Schneider played in Grand is shown in figure 4. Schwarz declared (but not ouvert as it will then be obvious that ♡K is the vital card) would be a gamble, perhaps not worth taking: the ♣J would draw the ♤J in Grand, and the opposition would be squeezed.

Seating is clearly important. Forehand has the advantage in most contracts as he leads to the first trick. Jacks should be used to win high-scoring cards in the play. Notice that all four Jacks, despite being the top trumps, are together not worth a single Ace in the point count.

Queens and below have little value except in trumps or in a long suit with trump control. There are only seven cards in a natural suit which means that they will go round twice at the most.

Ramsch is sometimes played in the event of all players passing. The skat is not used, the hand is played in Grand and everyone tries not to win points in tricks. There are various ways of scoring, all with modest awards or penalties.

Figure 4
A Schneider or Schwarz hand

BEZIQUE

A rather quaint card game of scoring combinations and trick-taking for two players, Bezique was much played in France a century ago and although sometimes considered old-fashioned, it is a quite fast-moving game.

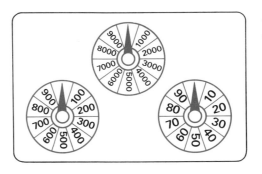

Figure 1
Scorer

EQUIPMENT

Bezique uses two Piquet packs (standard 52-card packs from which the 2s to 6s have been removed), although some variants use more. Special sets can be bought that include scorers (figure 1). Where standard packs are used they should have identical back designs.

PLAY

The cards rank Ace (high) to 7 (low) with the 10 ranking between the Ace and King (see figure 2). The deal is eight cards each, face down and distributed 3–2–3; the next card is turned up and determines trumps. The balance of the pack (placed face down) is the stock. If the turn-up card is a 7, the dealer scores 10. Game is reached when a player gains 1000 points.

The non-dealer leads. The dealer may follow suit, trump or discard at will. The best card wins the trick (if the cards are identical, the lead card wins). The winner can now declare one combination (explained below) by placing the cards from hand face up in front of him. Thereafter he may use these cards in other combinations or play them out to tricks – apart from being on view they are considered as still in hand. Whether or not he declares, the winner now draws a card from stock; the loser does likewise and the winner leads to the next trick. Play continues until the stock is exhausted: the winner of the last trick replenishes his hand with the last stock card and the loser takes the up card.

Each player now has eight cards. Any on the table are taken into hand and play continues as before, with the winner of the last trick leading off, except that now the second player must follow suit if he is

Figure 2
Card ranking

able and must trump if he can. Further, he must win the trick if he can. The winner of the final trick scores 10, and Aces and 10s ('brisques'), taken in tricks are totalled and score 10 each for the holders.

Scoring combinations

The rules governing scoring combinations (see table) are not standardized but those given here are widely accepted. A card declared in a combination may later be used in a different combination but not one of the same type. For example, a quartet of Queens cannot be broken and rebuilt, but a Queen could be extracted for a sequence or marriage or bezique, or all four Queens could subsequently be used in this way. A royal marriage may be converted to a sequence but not the reverse. A broken marriage (one card played to a trick) cannot be restored by introducing a new partner, and all four cards must be on the table at the same

SCORING COMBINATIONS

Marriages

Common (King and Queen of non-trump suit) 20
Royal (King and Queen of trump suit) 40

Quartets

Any four Jacks 40
Any four Queens 60
Any four Kings 80
Any four Aces 100

Sequence

A 10 K Q J of trump suit 250

Beziques

Single (♠ Q ♦ J) 40
Double (both ♠ Qs and both ♦ Js) 500

Trump

7 (of trump suit) 10

Figure 3
A useful hand

time to score a double bezique, though a single bezique may have been declared first.

The two 7s of trumps score 10 each if declared. The first player to declare one may exchange it for the up card. Recall that only one combination can be declared at a time and then only when a trick is won.

STRATEGY

Tricks themselves do not score, so it is only purposeful to win them if you have combinations to declare (or you believe your opponent has) or if they contain brisques. Notice that you do not score for a quartet of 10s, but these cards make useful trick winners.

Timing of declarations is important. If you expose your cards early, you give your opponent useful information. Conversely, you do not want to be left with combinations in hand when the second stage starts since they cannot then be declared. Once you have cards on the table, play them to tricks in preference to cards from hand – they talk less – provided of course you do not forsee their further use in other combinations.

Figure 3 approaches a dream hand. It contains a bezique, a common marriage, a potential double bezique and quartet of Jacks, plus a 7 of trumps – so the up card can be claimed, giving, with the Ace of trumps, two valuable brisques that should be trick winners.

There is less at stake in the second stage when your only concern is to gather brisques, but the scoring potential of these should not be undervalued: each represents a swing of 20 points. You must plan your hand during the first stage. A good trump holding is valuable: you can use it to void your opponent's trumps before you lead out your brisques. If you are attentive you may deduce which brisques your opponent is conserving for the second stage and can then try to establish voids in your hand accordingly so that you can trump in.

KALABRIASZ

Commonly called Klob or Klabberjass as well as a number of other names, Kalabriasz is a widely-played card game for two. It has strong affinities with Piquet and calls for sound judgment.

PLAY

A Piquet pack is used (a standard pack from which the 2s to 6s, and Jokers, are removed). The cards rank A 10 K Q J 9 8 7 (lowest) but in trumps the ranking is J (Jass) 9 (Menel) A 10 K Q 8 7 (lowest, curiously called Dix) except when scoring combinations (explained below).

The aim is to take tricks and to form bonus combinations. In the first part of the deal, six cards are dealt to each player, face down in threes, and the next card is turned face up on the table. Elder opens the bidding, and calls and options follow the order given in the table. Once the trump suit is accepted or another nominated the bidding ends.

Once the trump suit is established, three more cards are dealt singly so that each player has nine. If the turn-up card is in the trump suit, either player may exchange it for the Dix. Sometimes the bottom card is then taken from the pack of remaining cards (known as the talon) and placed face up on top of it to signify the deal is completed.

Combinations (melds) are now de-

BIDDING PROCEDURE

First Round

Elder	1	*Accept*	Trump suit is as exposed card
	2	*Schmeiss*	Opponent must choose between trump suit exposed or accept a new deal
	3	*Pass*	Option passes to opponent

Younger – options as for elder

Second Round

Elder	1	Nominates trump suit
	2	*Schmeiss*	Younger must nominate trump suit or accept a new deal
	3	*Pass*	Option passes to Younger

Younger	1	Nominates trump suit
	2	*Pass*

If both players pass twice there is a new deal.

clared. A meld is a sequence of three or more cards in the same suit. Normal ranking (A K Q J 10 9 8 7) is followed for melds. Elder starts by announcing the length of his sequence if he has one, or the best of his sequences if he has more than one. A three-card meld scores 20, four cards or more 50; so a meld of ♡Q J 10 is announced as 'Sequence of 20'. Younger replies 'Good' if he cannot beat it, 'No good' if he can, and 'How high?' if he equals it. The highest

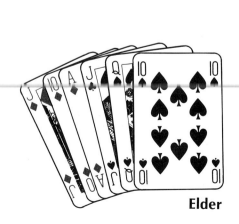

Elder

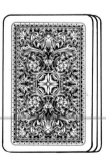

Figure 1
Initial deal

Younger

Elder **Younger**

Figure 2
Completed deal

sequence then wins. If they are of the same rank, the trump sequence wins, and if of the same rank in plain suits, elder wins.

Only one player scores for melds and he scores for all he holds, not just the one declared. Either player may undercall if he wishes.

Elder now leads to the first trick. Younger must follow suit if able and if not he must trump if able, otherwise he may discard. If a trump is led, the second player must overtrump if possible, if not he must follow suit; if he has no trumps he may discard. The winner of a trick leads to the next. If either player holds K Q of trumps he announces 'bella' when he plays out the second card, and scores 20 points. The winner of the final trick scores 10 'for last'.

Scoring

Tricks do not score but certain cards taken in them do, as follows:

Jass (trump Jack)	20 points
Menel (trump 9)	14
Ace (any suit)	11
10 (any suit)	10
King (any suit)	4
Queen (any suit)	3
Jack (any suit except trumps)	2

The remaining cards score nothing.

At the end of a hand both players add up their total scores (combinations, bonuses and card values). If the declarer scores more than the defender, both score their totals; if he scores less, the defender scores the sum of both totals; if equal, the defender only scores his own total. The winner is the first to reach 500 points.

STRATEGY

Bidding is the critical feature of the game, and the high penalty for failure signals caution. Melds represent a large chance element. A defender holding few card values may still pick up 70 points here (a '50' for a four-card and a '20' for a three-card sequence) leaving declarer a big task in the play, which is why experienced players often pass.

Strength is more important than length, particularly in trumps. The hand is likely to be won on the high cards—the Ace that beats a 10 is worth three times the King that beats a Queen.

The average hand is worth about 100 points in card values. Consider the deal in figure 1. Elder's two-suit hand with a three-card meld is most promising, while younger has prospects in clubs.

Elder decides to bluff and passes. Younger believes that elder is waiting to nominate spades or hearts and so does not wish to pass. Since elder has evinced no interest in diamonds, younger unwisely calls Schmeiss in the hope of a new deal. Elder declines, so diamonds are trumps and younger is the declarer.

The deal now has pleasant surprises for both players (see figure 2). Younger exchanges the Dix for the up-card to establish a bella, whereupon elder discloses a good sequence of 50 and also scores for his three-card meld. The only trick elder will lose will be a spade (after clearing trumps he would lead ♠9 which would fall to ♠A) so the final count will be 114 (including 10 for last) to 31 (including 20 for bella). Elder scores both, plus 70 for his melds, to gain a massive 215 points.

PIQUET

PLAY

Piquet is distinctively French and is one of the oldest of all card games. The name covers a number of closely similar games; this version, known as Rubicon Piquet, is ideal for two. Although rather elaborate, Piquet is well worth learning.

A Piquet pack has 32 cards; a standard pack from which 2s to 6s are removed can be used. Cards rank from Ace high in sequence down to 7. A game (partie) consists of six deals – three each. The object is to score points by holding certain card combinations and by winning tricks.

Each player is dealt 12 cards face down, in twos or threes, then a further eight cards are placed face down on the table to form the 'talon'. If either player has no court cards he can declare 'carte blanche' for 10 points. Both players now try to improve their hands by exchanging cards with the talon.

The non-dealer selects between one and five cards from his hand and places them face down in front of him. He then draws a like number from the talon. If he draws less than five he may look at those cards in the talon to which he was entitled. The dealer can now exchange up to the number of cards remaining in the talon – or, if he chooses, none. If he does not exchange at all, he can opt to expose or leave concealed the remainder. Discards have no further use but a player may consult his own discards at any time.

The non-dealer now declares the number of cards ('point') in his longest suit, his longest sequence (three or more consecutive cards in the same suit) and his best set (three or four cards of the same rank above a 9) in that order. To each declaration, the dealer responds 'Good', 'Not good' or 'Equal' according to whether it is better than, worse than, or equal to his own holding. The declarer or responder may undercall (but not overcall) his holding in order to conceal his strength.

The non-dealer scores at once for any combination acknowledged 'good'. At

Figure 1
A hand after exchange
The scoring would go:
A 'Point of six' (for point)
B 'Equal'
A 'Fifty-four' (pip count)
B 'Not good'
A 'Sixieme' (for sequence)
B 'Good'
A '16, and a tierce 19. Trio of Queens' (for set)
B 'Not good'

Player A

this stage the dealer does not detail his holding nor score for any combination he beats.

If point is 'good', the non-dealer scores the number of cards declared; if 'equal', pip count is compared (Ace equals 11, court cards 10); if still equal, there is no award for point.

If his 'good' sequence is three or four cards long, the non-dealer scores 3 or 4 points respectively. If it is five cards long or more, he scores the number of cards plus 10 (e.g. a seven-card sequence scores 17 points). He also scores for any other sequences he now declares. They are called tierce (three cards), quart, quint, sixieme, septieme, etc.

A 'good' set of three (trio) scores 3 points, a set of four (quatorze) 14 points. (If sets are equal, the highest rank wins.) If 'good', the non-dealer scores also for any other sets he holds.

The non-dealer now leads to the first trick and scores 1 point for doing so. The dealer then scores his winning combinations (those he replied 'no good' to) in the same way. If either player reaches 30

points before his opponent scores, he adds 60 'for repique'. In this reckoning, scoring is strictly in the sequence given: carte blanche, point, sequence, set. Now the dealer responds to the lead. There are no trumps, and the winner of the trick scores 1 point if he led to it, 2 points if he did not, and then leads to the next trick.

If in this stage of the game the non-dealer reaches 30 points and the dealer has still not scored, he gets 30 points, 'for pique'. (It is usual to keep progressive scores.) The dealer cannot score for pique because of the point for first lead. When all the tricks are played, the player with the most tricks (if not tied) scores 10 'for the cards'. If either player wins all the tricks, it is 'capot' for 40 points.

At the end of the partie (six hands), the winner scores the difference of the two scores plus 100 points for game. If his opponent has not scored 100 he is 'rubiconed' and the winner gets 100 points plus the sum of the two scores.

Figure 1 shows a hand after the exchange and explains the scoring.

After A leads (1 point), B scores 6 for point and 6 for sets. Neither player undercalled. Totals at this stage are: A – 20, B – 12. B will win eight tricks and '10 for the cards'.

Player B

STRATEGY

The non-dealer has the advantage because of his option on the talon and the advantage of the lead; they enable him to take more chances with the exchange. This is the most skilful part of Piquet since several aims must be reconciled: to score well in both combinations and trick-taking and to avoid being overrun in either. The non-dealer should usually take his quota from the talon even if it means destroying a combination, since it reduces the chances of dealer improving his hand. The dealer should keep a guard in at least two suits even if it means leaving a card in the talon. It often pays to discard high cards – remember, your opponent cannot draw them.

Suppose as non-dealer you pick up the hand in figure 2. The clubs look promising – the chances are that you will draw another from the talon. You might decide to discard the spades and two low diamonds or perhaps the pip cards of the three short suits. The ♡7 may be a good reject: you are likely to pick up a guard. Anyway, you decide rightly to exchange five cards.

If you had this hand as dealer you would exchange differently because you are defending. The stoppers in each suit should be preserved. The chance of picking up the fourth 10 is slight – and it could be beaten by a quatorze of Jacks. So discard ◇10 9 and ♣9; if you make a fortunate draw you might even win on the tricks.

Figure 2
Discarding

PATIENCE GAMES

FLOWER GARDEN

Foundations

Bouquet

A successful hand

This is a skilful patience that comes out quite often. The attractive layout adds to its appeal.

Use a standard pack, without Jokers. Deal out the cards face up in six fans or columns of six, then lay the remaining 16 cards, known as the bouquet, in a fan or row.

The aim is to build foundations in each suit from Ace up to King. All cards in the bouquet are available at any time, together with the top card from each flower-bed (fan of six). Flower-beds may be planted (added to) by moving cards from other beds or the bouquet, singly or in sequence, in descending rank and regardless of suit. An empty bed may be planted with any available card or sequence. Obviously cards cannot be uprooted from the beds to augment the bouquet.

First plan to extricate the Aces. Hold back your bouquet cards as long as possible: every one used reduces your options.

CLOCK PATIENCE

A simple game of pure chance with a 1-in-13 chance of success.

Use a standard pack, minus Jokers. A large table is necessary.

Deal 12 cards face down in a circle corresponding to the positions of the numerals on a clock, then put one card in the centre. Repeat three more times until the pack is exhausted. Now turn over one of the centre cards and place it beside the packet representing the appropriate numeral, as shown in the figure. The top card of that packet is now revealed and is placed in the same way (Aces = 1; Jacks = 11; Queens = 12). Play continues until a King is exposed, when it is put in the middle and another card there turned over. The game succeeds if the last card to be exposed is a King.

KLONDIKE

One of the most popular of all patience games, Klondike demands some skill, but success is rare.

Figure 1
Tableau for Klondike

Use a standard pack, without Jokers. Deal a row of seven cards, the first one face up and the rest face down, and overlap with successive rows, reducing by one card each time and ending with a single card face up at bottom right (see figure 1).

The aim is to end up with the suits in four piles separate from the 'tableau' and arranged in ascending order from Ace (low) to King (high). Once an Ace is exposed, it is removed from the tableau to start the foundation on which the rest of the suit can be built as cards become available.

To do this the concealed cards must be released. Exposed cards that follow one another in descending order and alternating colour may be placed accordingly, singly or in runs. If a column becomes vacant it can only be restarted with a King or a sequence headed by a King. When the bottom card of a column is face-down it can be exposed. Only the bottom cards of the columns are available. These may be moved singly to the foundations or singly or in sequence to another column.

The cards not used in the tableau are stock. Stock cards are turned over one by one on to a waste heap. The top card of the heap is available to be added to the foundations or the tableau. The patience is easier if, after you have exhausted the stock, you take up the waste pile and use it again, and so on until you succeed or are blocked. A game in progress is illustrated in figure 2.

Figure 2
A game in progress

Foundations

PARADE

An attractive patience demanding more skill than may at first appear.

Use a standard pack, without Jokers. Deal out the cards face up in four orderly rows of 13 each. Take out the four Aces and place them on the left of the rows, in order spades, hearts, diamonds, clubs, top to bottom. The object is to rearrange the cards into sequences by suits A, K . . . 2.

There are four spaces in the array created by the removal of the Aces. These are now used for moving cards. A card played into a space must be of the same suit and the rank immediately below the card on the left. The game is blocked when the four deuces precede the gaps – which usually happens. Try to relegate the deuces to the far right.

MISS MILLIGAN

This difficult patience is popular both sides of the Atlantic. The lady of the title is unrecorded.

Shuffle together two standard packs leaving out the Jokers. Deal eight cards face up in a row, removing any Aces to start foundations. The object is to build up suits (two of each) in sequence A, 2 . . . K on the foundations.

Foundations

Cards may be packed. Packing is the placing of a card so as to overlap another in a column. It must be of the rank immediately below and of the opposite colour to the card above it. Sequences, in whole or part, may be moved as single cards. An empty column, except when dealt to, may only be occupied by a King or a sequence headed by a King.

The rest of the pack is dealt out similarly in rows of eight. Only the bottom cards

of each column are available except where the bottom card is one of a sequence, when the whole or part of the sequence may be packed.

Allow yourself one grace: at any time, but preferably when you are blocked, you may lift an available card, part-sequence or sequence, and take the card beneath it.

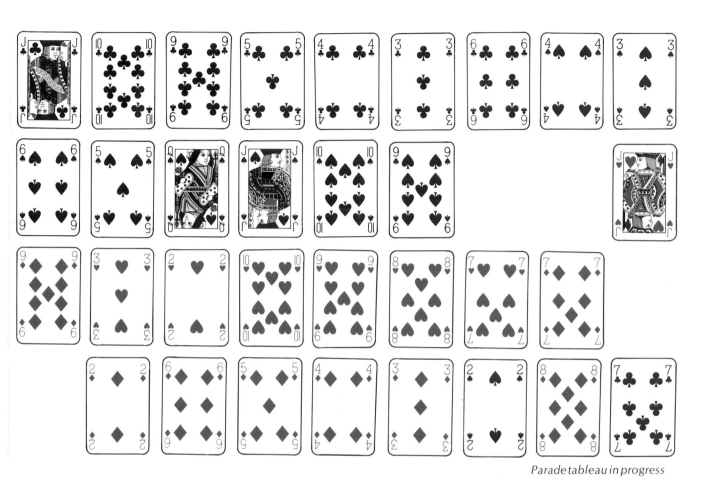

Parade tableau in progress

Miss Milligan tableau in progress

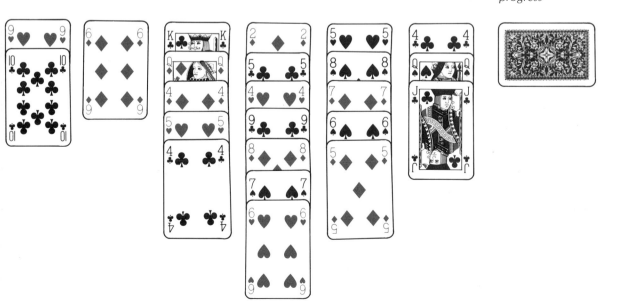

HANAFUDA

This beautiful flower-card game of Japan used to be played in the geisha houses but it is now a popular form of home entertainment. It is an ideal family game for three.

Hanafuda cards are the issue of a marriage between traditional Japanese shell-paintings and European playing cards. A number of games are played with them — Koi-Koi, Kabu, Mushi, Higu Bana and Eighty-eight (perhaps the best) — but Matching Cards, described here, is one of the simpler and more popular.

April   Wisteria

10   5

January   Pine

20   5   1   1

February   Plum

10   5   1   1

March   Cherry

20   5   1   1

May   Iris

10   5

June   Peony

10   5

July   Bush Clover

10   5

August   Pampas Grass

20   10   1   1

September   Chrysanthemum

1   1   10   5   1   1

October   Maple

1   1   10   5   1   1

November   Willow (Rain)

1   1   20   10   5   1

December   Paulownia

1   1   20   1   1   1

147

EQUIPMENT

There are 48 cards in a Hanafuda pack, which has 12 suits that correspond to the months of the year and are represented by an appropriate tree or plant. There are four cards in a suit, usually two 1-point cards and two premium cards – these are more elaborately designed, the top value card often including a picture of an animal or object, and the second value usually showing a tanzaku (paper banner). November is known as the Rain suit and has a special significance. The complete pack, with card values, is shown in the figure on the previous pages.

Hanafuda cards are small and thick and it is customary to use a soft surface, such as a large cushion, in preference to a table.

PLAY

Cards are dealt anticlockwise, four face down to each player, three face up to the table, then three down to each player and a final three up to the table, leaving the balance in stock.

The object is to make the highest score over an agreed number of rounds. Points are earned by matching cards in hand with table cards and in forming bonus combinations.

The player to the right of the dealer starts. He may take any one card from the table that matches the suit of a card he holds. He then places the pair face up in front of him. If he cannot make a match, he discards a card face up to the table. In either event, he then takes the top card from stock and exposes it. If he can match it with a card on the table he does so, placing the pair in front of him. If not, he adds the card drawn to the table. Play now passes anticlockwise to the next player, who follows the same procedure. When the stock is exhausted, play continues until all cards are matched. If at any time there are no cards on the table, the player must discard and draw from stock. If the stock card matches the discard, they may be paired.

If three cards of the same suit are dealt to the table, these are put to one side and are taken together when matched by the fourth card. If all cards of a suit are dealt to the table, it is best to re-deal.

At the end of a round players score all their matched cards plus any bonus combinations they can form from them. See the table for the scoring combinations. (Different bonuses are used in other Hanafuda games.) A card may be used in any number of combinations but combinations cannot be duplicated. For example, if you score for Five Bright you cannot also score for Four Bright.

STRATEGY

It is necessary first to familiarize yourself with the cards, since they carry no indices. Although Matching Cards has a large luck element, there is skill in the game.

A good hand is one with well-distributed suits and some premium cards. The top values are obviously the most desirable, with the Cherry 20-point (March) the best in the game.

Tanzakus are useful for bonuses. It is better to match a tanzaku on the table rather than a top-value card if by doing so you deprive another player of a bonus. Playing to spoil opponents' bonuses is a better strategy than consistently picking up the high values.

A pair of Rain cards is always a sound holding since it holds promise of a Straight Rain, and it is unwise to throw out Rain cards in the early stages. Priority for discard should be the low value of a suit in which you hold more than one card; otherwise give preference to 'Grace' (April, May, July suits).

SCORING COMBINATIONS

100 points

Five Bright
(the five 20-point cards)

60 points

Four Bright
(any four of the 20-point cards)

40 points

Seven Tanzaku
(any seven tanzaku cards, excluding November)

Red-lettered Tanzaku
(the three red-lettered tanzaku)

Purple Tanzaku
(the three purple tanzaku)

Views
(all three 'view' cards: March 20-point, August 20-point, September 10-point)

30 points

Six tanzaku
(any six tanzaku excluding November)

Three Bright
(January 20-point, February 10-point, March 20-point)

20 points

View
(any two view cards – see above)

Crane-Phoenix-Moon
(January 20-point, August 20-point, December 20-point)

Boar-Deer-Butterfly
(June 10-point, July 10-point, October 10-point)

Grass Tanzaku
(the April, May, July (plain red) tanzaku)

10 points

Straight Wisteria
(all four April cards)

Straight Paulownia
(all four December cards)

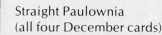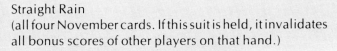

Straight Rain
(all four November cards. If this suit is held, it invalidates all bonus scores of other players on that hand.)

TAROCK

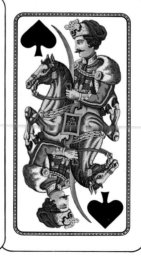

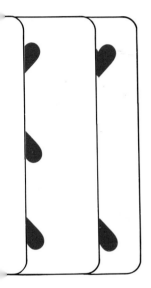

This old game, still popular in Central Europe, uses Tarot cards. It is best for three, though four may play: the dealer drops out but participates in the scoring.

PLAY

The 54-card Tarot pack is used, comprising four suits each of eight cards and a trump suit of 22. The black suits (♠ and ♣) rank downwards in order K Q C (Cavalier) J 10 9 8 7, and the red suits (♡ and ◇) rank downwards K Q C J A 2 3 4. The trumps rank from XXII (skus) – often represented as a Joker, XXI (mond) down to I (pagat).

The deal is in batches of eight to each player, then six face down to a widow (an extra hand) followed by a second round of eight. Bidding then takes place and the highest bidder plays against the other two. The object is to collect scoring cards in tricks and to form combinations (see the table overleaf).

There are only two bids that a player can make: threesome, which uses the widow, and solo, which does not. Eldest has first call; solo beats threesome, and if all abstain the deal passes.

If the call is threesome, the successful bidder takes the top three cards of the widow. He can keep them, or reject them face up and take the second three (when the game counts double) or reject these face up too and keep the first three (when the game counts treble). In each case the declarer discards three cards, but no Kings, face down to the table and

151

SCORING

Point values of cards:

Skus, mond, pagat, Kings	5
Queens	4
Cavaliers, Jacks	3

The other cards (nulls) have no value.

Trick scoring:

All scoring cards – total value less 2
Two scoring cards – total value less 1
One scoring card – card value
No scoring cards – 1 point

Scoring combinations:

(1) Skus, mond and pagat
(2) Four Kings

These are the only scoring combinations, and score 50 or 100 according to the bid.

---

declares any trumps amongst them. When play ends, the three discards belong to the declarer and the three widow cards to the opponents. When he has completed his hand, the declarer opts either for game with a commitment to win 36 points or more, or consolation, in which he elects to make not more than 35 points. Solo commits the declarer to game and the widow belongs to the opponents, who score any point cards it contains after play is over.

Combinations are announced first. Each counts 50 in a threesome and 100 in solo. The holder receives the bonus from the other two. The forehand leads and players must follow suit if able, and failing that must trump if able. The winner of a trick leads to the next trick.

If the declarer wins a game, he scores double the number of points over 35 he took in tricks (solo) and including discards (threesome) with a bonus of 100 (solo) or 50 (threesome). If he wins a consolation, he scores double the number of points he scored less than 35, plus 50 bonus. If the declarer fails, his opponents (and the dealer if sitting out) score double the number of points they take over 35, plus the bonus (50 or 100), on a game call, and double the number

of tricks declarer took over 35 in a consolation, plus 50 bonus. For example:

1 Declarer wins a consolation with a total of 29 points. He therefore scores (2 × 6) + 50 = 62.

2 Declarer loses a solo. His opponents have together 43 points, including the widow, so score (2 × 8) + 100 = 116.

If the last trick is taken by pagat, the player scores a bonus equal to the bonus value of the game. Before play starts the declarer can announce 'ultimo' to signify he intends to take the last trick with pagat. If he succeeds, he gets a bonus equal to twice the game value, otherwise he pays similarly. Either opponent may then announce 'contra-ultimo' as an undertaking to win pagat from the bidder, with quadrupled stakes.

STRATEGY

Bidding in Tarock is pleasingly simple: both sides are trying to amass as many points as possible in a game call and as few as possible in consolation. The watershed – 36 points – is just under half the total card values.

If you are playing a threesome and pick up a good widow which makes you confident of your call, it may be better to reject it the first time, look at the second three cards in the widow and reject them in turn in order to get a triple game.

Winning the bonus with pagat is not easy. It requires strength in trumps to draw them so that pagat – which is the lowest trump – is unopposed on the last trick. The lead is a decided advantage on the final rounds, otherwise pagat may be forced out to trump a lead to a void suit.

One card in three is a scoring card and the average trick is worth about 4½ points. The Cavaliers and Jacks account for a third of the total points at stake but have little trick-taking potential since a suit will only go round twice. If you control trumps they may make; otherwise discard them to the widow or, in defence, throw them on opponents' tricks.

CHILDREN'S CARD GAMES

PELMANISM

More an exercise in memory than a card game, Pelmanism is still enjoyable for any number of any age.

You need room for the game – a large table or the floor is ideal. Distribute a standard pack, without Jokers, face down at random, no cards touching. Each player in rotation turns over any two cards. If they match in rank, he keeps them and turns over another two. If the cards do not match they must be turned face down again without changing their position in the layout (purists insist their orientation must also be unchanged) and the turn ends. When the whole pack is paired off the player with the most cards is the winner.

On first turning over an untouched card, try to recall if a twin has already been turned over and, if so, its whereabouts. There are systems that can help

you remember the lie – but you have to memorize only 13 cards at most. Make the game harder by only permitting pairing of cards of like rank and colour. Young children can be brilliant at this game.

CHEAT

Several players are needed for this popular game in which dishonesty frequently pays.

Use a standard pack, without the Jokers. If only three play, remove one suit. Deal all the cards round face down and never mind the odd number.

The first player puts a card face down on the table, announcing its rank, which may or may not be its true rank. The next player puts a card face down on top of it and must announce it as the next rank above; for example, if the first player says '10', the second player must say 'Jack' whether or not it is a Jack. Play continues like this round the table and as fast as possible. The ranks are cyclical in Cheat; i.e. . . . . King, Ace, 2 . . . etc.

At any time anyone may call out

'Cheat'. The last card played is then exposed. If it is not of the rank announced, the player must take all the cards up from the table and add them to his hand, and then start the play again. If the card is as called – a Jack if a Jack is called, for example – then the accuser must pick up the cards and restart the play. In the event of two or more players shouting 'Cheat!' together, the first in order after the last player takes precedence. The first player to get rid of all his cards is the winner.

Cheat can go on for rather a long time since the game tends to be self-correcting: the less cards you have, the more likely you will be caught cheating. Players should try to conceal how many cards they have remaining.

SNAP

Two or more can play this very simple card game. Special Snap packs can be bought but an ordinary pack of cards (or two, if there are a lot of players) will do.

All the cards are distributed face down amongst the players; it does not matter if a player gets a card more or less. Each player stacks his cards face down in front of him without looking at them. The first player turns the top card of his pile over on the table beside him. Play continues like this in rotation, up-cards being placed on top of one another so that only one card is showing in each pile.

When the cards on top of any two up-piles are of the same rank, for example,

two 8s, two Queens, or are of matching design if a special Snap pack is used, the first player to call 'Snap' wins both piles. He adds them to the bottom of his own face-down pile and restarts play by turning over a card from his stack in the usual way. A player whose stock is exhausted may still call Snap provided he has at least one up card. When he has no cards at all, he drops out.

Cards must be turned over quickly and squarely so that everyone, including the player, sees them at the same time. The winner is the player who gets all the cards – if the others have not got tired of the game by then.

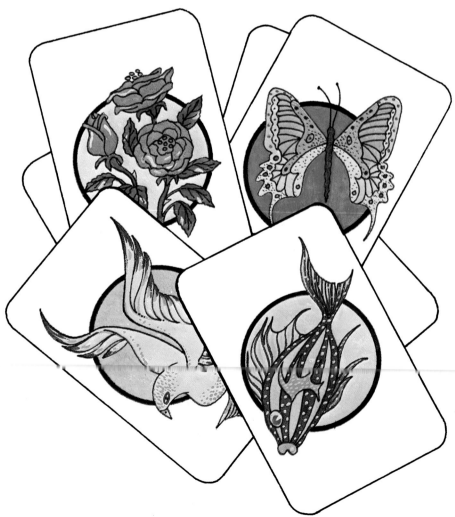

SNIP-SNAP-SNOREM

This is Snap taken a stage further. Three or more can play.

A standard pack is used, without the Jokers. Cards are dealt round face down until exhausted. Players examine their hands and the first player puts any card face up in the centre of the table. Players in turn either pass or put on the table a card of the same rank, at the same time calling out 'Snip' (second card), 'Snap' (third card), or 'Snorem' (fourth and last card of the rank).

A player may call and play more than once, either on the same or a subsequent turn, as previously agreed. For example, if a Jack is the opening lead and a player holds all three remaining Jacks, he can put them down together announcing 'Snip-Snap-Snorem'. The player who calls Snorem leads to the table. The first player to get rid of all his cards wins.

SLAPJACK

A simple but boisterous game in the Snap tradition, Slapjack is best with several players.

A standard pack is used, preferably an old one, and it need not be complete. Cards are dealt round face down and stacked in front of each player, as for Snap. The first player puts his top card face up in the middle of the table. The card should be turned over briskly, away from and not towards the player. Players continue in turn, building a pile of up-cards in the middle. Since the game is best played fast, the pile is likely to be ragged, which does not matter.

When a Jack is played, everyone tries to be the first to slap his hand on it. The player who succeeds takes all the cards in the middle and shuffles them in with his own stack, which he then replaces in front of him before putting down the first card of the next pile.

If a player slaps a card other than a Jack, he pays a forfeit of one card face down from his stack to each of the other players, who place it beneath their stacks. When a player's cards are exhausted he is allowed a chance to win the next Jack. If he fails, he is out of the game. The winner is the player who ends up with all the cards. A good umpire is an asset in Slapjack!

HAPPY FAMILIES

Special packs of cards are sold for this game, which can be played by three or more. An ordinary pack of cards may be used but it makes the game less amusing.

The whole pack is dealt out face down between the players. Each player sorts his hand into families. (If an ordinary pack is used, a family is all the cards of the same rank, for example, all the 4s.) When a player has assembled a family (four cards) he places it face down in front of him. The aim is to collect the greatest number of complete families.

The player to the left of the dealer starts by asking any one player for a card he needs, but he cannot ask for a card unless he already has at least one member of the family. If the player asked has the card, he must hand it over and the first player then again asks anyone for a card he needs. When a player is asked for a card he has not got, it becomes his turn to ask. (When using a standard pack, it is better to have the rule that a card must be asked for by suit as well as by rank.) The game ends when all the cards have been collected into families.

RACING DEMON

This is an ideal family card game, fast-moving and often hilarious. Any number can play.

Every player has a standard pack of cards (no Jokers) with distinctive backs. A large playing area is desirable.

Those taking part sit round in a circle and each deals his own tableau for Klondike (see page 142). Everyone now conducts his own patience at his own pace except that foundation cards are played to the centre of the table and are common property. Both hands may be used but a less frantic game limits the players to only one hand. The first player to go out wins. If the game is blocked, the player with the most cards in the foundations wins.

BEGGAR-MY-NEIGHBOUR

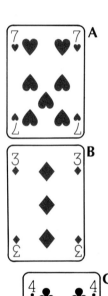

A simple card game for any number of small children, fast, good fun and zero skill.

Use the standard pack, without Jokers. If there are four or more players use two packs (the backs need not match).

Shuffle well and divide the cards between the players – roughly equal packets are good enough. No-one may look at his cards nor alter the sequence of the packets.

Players in turn take one card from the top of their packet and put it face up in the centre of the table, to form a pile, until an Ace or court card is turned. The next player must now cover it with an appropriate number of cards one after another, always from the top of their packet, thus: to an Ace, four; to a King, three; to a Queen, two; to a Jack, one. If no further Ace or court card is turned when this is done, the player whose honour was exposed gathers up all the cards in the pile, adds them to the bottom of his packet and then leads again to the table. If, in paying the tribute, the second player likewise turns over an Ace or court card, he stops and it is the next player's turn to cover the honour, and so on. A typical sequence in a four-player game is shown in the figure.

You win when you have all the cards – and that may take some time. Jacks are clearly best in this game – they offer only one chance of getting stopped.

Player B wins 10 cards

OLD MAID

This is good fun for four or five players. A commercial version, called Donkey, has matching pictures and a donkey card.

Extract the Jokers and one Queen from a standard pack. Deal the rest of the cards round singly and face down. Unless only three are playing, players will not all get the same number but this does not matter.

Players examine their hands and discard face down to the table all pairs of cards of the same rank, for example, two Aces, two 7s, four Jacks. The player with the most cards now presents his hand, fanned downwards so that all the cards are visible but the faces cannot be seen, to the player on his left, who must take one. If this matches a card in the second player's hand, he discards both to the table. Whether or not he is able to do this, he in turn fans his cards to the player on his left, who must take one, and so on round and round the table until a player is left with the odd Queen. He is the Old Maid, sex disregarded.

You are allowed to shuffle your hand and present it in any way you like – for example, with one card stuck out prominently – but all your cards must always be visible.

DONKEY

Donkey is a lively game ideal for a small party. It should be played fast.

Take from a standard pack all four cards of any denomination for each player taking part. For example, if six are playing, extract all the cards from Ace up to 6. Shuffle these and deal four to each player face down. A number of suitable tokens – matchsticks, say – are placed in the centre of the table – it is a good idea to move them a little closer to any very young players. There must be one less matchstick than the number of players.

The players pick up and look at their hands. They then select a card and place it face down on their left. When all are ready, each player picks up the card on his right. The object is to collect four cards of the same rank. The first player to do so exposes his hand and seizes one of the matchsticks. Everyone now makes a grab for a matchstick. The player who does not get one loses and the first letter of 'DONKEY' is written against his name on a score sheet. Play continues until one player loses six times, when he is of course the donkey.

CHILDREN'S GAMES

In this age of six-year-old Chess geniuses, the distinction between children's and adult games is far from clear. The days when mother and father played Backgammon or Bezique while the children amused themselves with Ludo are behind us, and many of the games elsewhere in this book can be, and often are, played by children as much as adults. The games in this section have been chosen because they are enjoyed particularly by children and have long been considered as proper entertainment for the young, often because of their simple, or apparently simple, rules. Even here, however, the picture is blurred. Solitaire and Halma, for example, are traditionally associated with children, who find them fun to play, but both these excellent games can tax the most intelligent of adults. Lotto, an old children's favourite, in which pictures sometimes replace numbers, is included here although this game appears in many guises as an adult gambling game—Bingo night has for many years been part of the social scene.

A problem can arise with children's games when children of different ages and abilities all want to take part in a game. Some of the games here, such as Snakes and Ladders or Beetle, depend entirely on luck and favour no-one, so older children may soon become bored by them. On the other hand, games of skill like Halma favour the older and brighter, and unless some sort of handicap is arranged the enthusiasm of the weaker players may quickly wane. The best solution in these circumstances is often the game that combines chance with skill, as do many of the card games, in which the best player is likely to win but not aways, so that everyone has some incentive.

BEETLE

Beetle, also known as Bug or Cootie, is a lively and relaxing little game for any number of players. It requires no skill and can be enjoyed by the very young.

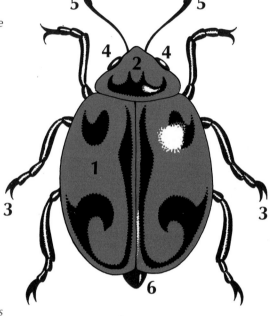

Figure 1
The numbers allotted to the parts of a beetle

Figure 2
A beetle after seven throws

PLAY

A six-sided die is necessary. A special Beetle die is the ideal: this is marked with a letter on each face, the letters representing parts of a beetle: B (body), H (head), E (eyes), L (legs), F (feelers) and T (tail). However, an ordinary die is quite adequate. Allot numbers to the various parts and draw a beetle with these marked, as a reference for the players (figure 1).

Everyone has pencil and paper. One player starts by rolling the die. If it comes up B (or 1, if a conventional die is used) then the player draws the body of a beetle on his paper; if it comes up anything else, the player's turn ends and the die is passed to the next player. Once a player has rolled a B or 1 and the body has been drawn, the head, tail and legs can be added when the appropriate letters are thrown. The eyes and feelers cannot be added until the head is on the beetle. The object is to be the first player to complete a beetle – body, head, eyes, feelers, legs and tail – 13 parts in all.

If you throw an E (4) or an F (5) you can only enter one eye or feeler, not both. If you throw an L (3) most players allow only one leg to be drawn, but since this can produce a rather tedious game, you might instead allow a pair of legs to be added each time L is thrown.

A game ends when one player completes a beetle. If several games are to be played, a points system can be used. The player who completes the beetle scores 13 points, one for each part (or if you are allowing pairs of legs, 10 points), the other players scoring for each part they have succeeded in drawing at that stage. The winner is the first to reach, say, 25 points or to have most points after some agreed time limit.

Figure 2 shows a player's beetle after seven throws (successively from the top left) using the numbering system described above. If you wish, you can allow an extra throw of the die every time a part of the beetle is added.

FOX AND GEESE

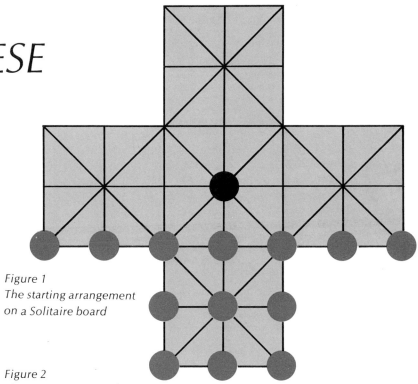

Figure 1
*The starting arrangement
on a Solitaire board*

Fox and Geese is a hunt game for two players, believed to be Scandinavian in origin. Many different versions are played, which demand some skill but are not very difficult.

PLAY

One player is the fox, the other the geese. The players have different objectives: the geese win if they surround the fox so that it cannot move; the fox wins if it breaks through the cordon or, in some games, takes enough geese to ensure its freedom.

The game is commonly played on a Solitaire board (see p.164). Figure 1 shows the starting arrangement. It is usual to allow the fox to start on any vacant point; that shown is the best. Play is on the intersections.

Both sides have the same move: one point in any direction including diagonally. The fox captures by leaping over an adjacent goose to a vacant point immediately beyond. Multiple captures are permitted. The geese cannot capture.

Other versions have more geese (15 or 17 are common) but do not allow them to move backwards. A simpler game can be played by eliminating the diagonal moves.

An easy game for young children has four geese facing one fox on a draughtsboard (figure 2). The fox may start on any white square. The geese move as draughtsmen: one square diagonally forward at a time. The fox moves like a draughts' king: one square diagonally in any direction. No capturing is allowed.

Figure 2
*The starting position for
a simple version of the game*

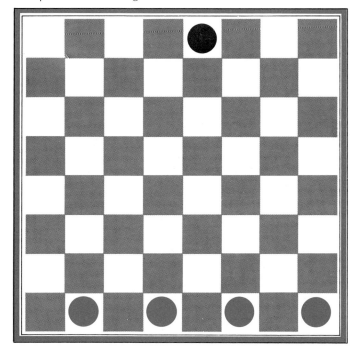

STRATEGY

In most versions, the geese should win. The tactics are to advance abreast, moving the geese farthest from the fox and avoiding gaps. The fox must try to entice weaknesses while retaining flexibility of movement.

RELATED GAMES

Games similar to Fox and Geese are common to most cultures. A great variety of boards are used and the numbers of hunters and hunted vary, as do the names – Tiger and Goats, Coyote and Chickens, Sixteen Soldiers Pursue the General, and many more. A modified version of Fox and Geese, Asalto, was popular in Victorian times.

SNAKES AND LADDERS

This simple race game for any number of players is a favourite with young children. It dates back to late Victorian times and the earliest known example has the track in the form of a spiral. Snakes and Ladders probably drew its inspiration both from the board race games popular in that period and which trace back to the sixteenth-century Game of Goose, and from a Hindu religious game used to exemplify the virtues (ladders) and the vices (snakes).

There is no skill in the game, which allows a fair distribution of the honours.

PLAY

The game is played on a board with counters, movement being governed by the rolls of a die.

The board design varies according to the manufacturer but basically it consists of a succession of numbered squares, commonly 1–100 but sometimes less. Superimposed are a number of ladders and snakes each of which links two squares. The board is usually highly coloured but this has no significance.

Each player has a counter of a different colour. Players advance by throwing the die in turn, moving their counters the number of squares indicated by the die.

If a 6 is thrown, another turn is taken.

When a player's counter ends its move on a square which contains the foot of a ladder, the counter is promptly moved to the square occupied by the top of the ladder. Similarly, a player's counter that ends its move on the head (or tail) of a snake slithers down to the square that contains the snake's tail (or head). The object is to be the first player to get to 100 (or whatever the top number is). The move must be for the exact number of the die throw; if it means overshooting the board, the counter is not moved and the player does not throw again until his next turn, though some rules require that the counter be advanced to the top and then back the necessary number of moves to complete the die score.

If a player's counter ends its move on a square occupied by the counter of another player, stacking may be permitted or the move may be judged illegal and the counter returned to its original square, the player thereby losing a turn.

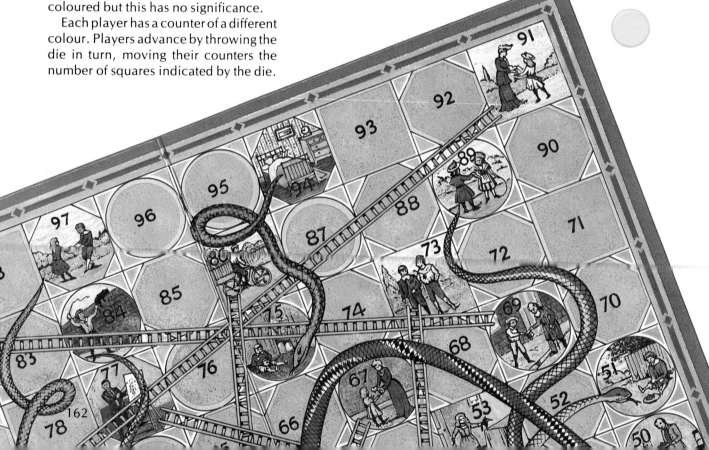

JUNGLE GAME

This is a popular game among children in the Far East, and a set can be bought very cheaply at most Chinese emporiums.

The origin of the Jungle Game is obscure. It is a board game for two players in which no luck is involved.

PLAY

The board, usually of paper, is made up of 63 regular squares in a 9 × 7 array. Each player has a den surrounded by three 'traps'. There are 12 'water' squares and the locations of each side's pieces at the start of a game are marked with appropriate drawings. Each side has eight animals, usually represented by embossed wooden counters, in order of power: elephant (strongest), lion, tiger, panther, dog, wolf, cat and rat (weakest). One side's pieces are blue, the other's red.

At the start of play pieces are placed as indicated on the board. Players move alternately, one piece at a time. All pieces move in the same way – one square forwards or backwards or to the left or right but never diagonally. Only one piece can occupy a square.

A capture is made by moving an animal to a square occupied by an enemy animal and replacing it with yours. An animal can capture any animal of equal or lower rank except that a rat can take an elephant (by entering its ear, so the logic goes). Captured animals are removed from the game.

Only rats can go in the water but a rat cannot capture an elephant by moving directly from a water square. Lions and tigers can jump the water sideways or lengthways from an adjacent land space to the nearest land space beyond but if there is a rat in the line of jump the move is not allowed.

You win by getting any animal into the opponent's den. A player may not move a piece into his own den. Traps can be entered and left freely but an animal that occupies an opponent's trap loses all its powers and any piece can capture it.

Elephant

Lion

Tiger

Dog

Panther

Wolf

Cat

Rat

STRATEGY

A lion or tiger advancing up the centre is menacing because it can leap the water to left or right. Get your rat in the water early where not only is it safe but also it can be used to block jumps. The cat is weak in attack and is best left to watch the traps, one of which must be entered by a hostile animal if the den is to be occupied.

The board and pieces

163

SOLITAIRE

Solitaire probably originated in France about two centuries ago. It is an ideal solo game for children, who can measure their progress by the number of men they can remove, and for mathematicians who will find themselves confronted with many unsolved problems.

PLAY

There are two types of board in use; the English board which has 33 holes and corresponds to that used for the older game of Fox and Geese, and the traditional French board, which has 37 holes. The boards are marked in a regular pattern, either with small shallow holes to accommodate marbles or punched to take pegs. Both boards are shown in figure 1. Notation has been added so that play may be described.

The basic Solitaire game starts with all the holes filled except the one in the centre. The object is to remove all the men (marbles or pegs) from the board except one, which should be in the centre hole.

Play is the same in all games. A man may not move except to jump, which must be over an adjacent man to an empty space immediately beyond, and the jump must be orthogonal – to left, right, up or down – never diagonal. The man jumped over is at once removed from the board. A man may continue to jump if this is possible and all jumps made on a turn count as a single move. Play is continuous, men being moved until either the goal is accomplished or two or more men remain which are isolated, when the solitaire has failed.

The shortest solution to the basic game on the English board is in 18 moves: 46–44, 65–45, 57–55, 54–56, 52–54, 73–53, 43–63, 75–73–53, 35–55, 15–35, 23–43–63–65–45–25, 37–57–55–53, 31–33, 34–32, 51–31–33, 13–15–35, 36–34–32–52–54–34, 24–44.

Following the same principle, that is starting with all holes but one filled and reducing to one man, 21 distinctly differ-

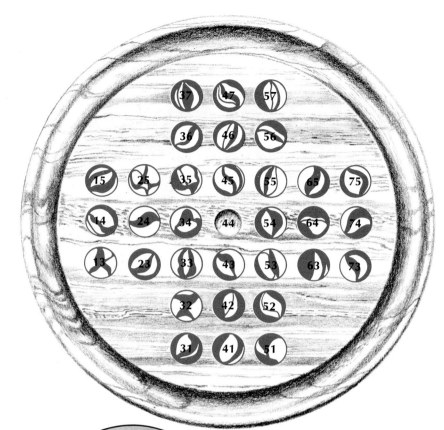

Figure 1
The two types of board:
English (above) and French
(below)

	37	47	57		
26	36	46	56	66	
15	25	35	45	55	65	75
14	24	34	44	54	64	74
13	23	33	43	53	63	73
22	32	42	52	62	
	31	41	51		

ent games are possible on the English board, the shortest of which takes 15 moves and the longest 19. The hole left empty at the start of each of these games is given first, followed by the hole to be occupied by the last man:
35/35, 35/65; 36/33, 36/36, 36/63; 37/31, 37/34, 37/37, 37/64; 45/15, 45/41, 45/45; 46/13, 46/43, 46/46; 47/14, 47/41, 47/44, 47/47.

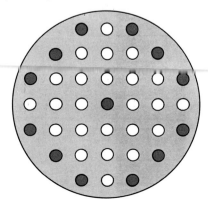

Figure 2
The Twelve Apostles

Figure 3 The seven distinct positions

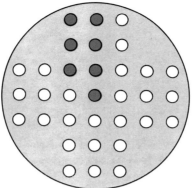

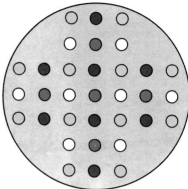

Figure 4
The four circuits
● circuit A
● circuit B
○ circuit C
○ circuit D

These games can be extended by designating the end man. In the game 46/13, for example, any of 12 men can occupy the end hole (it is impossible with the remaining 20), making 11 additional games.

It is also possible for two to play. Using any initial position, players move alternately, the first player unable to move on his turn being the loser.

Two games for the French board start, as in the basic game, with the central hole empty. In one game, the aim is to achieve the position in figure 2, known as the Twelve Apostles; the second game is identical except that holes 14, 41, 47 and 74 are also occupied. This is known as the Teacher amongst his Friends.

STRATEGY

A systematic study of board and play can reveal the potentials of this apparently simple game. In the English board, there are essentially only six different holes apart from the centre hole (figure 3). All others are rotations or reflections.

There are four independent circuits of movement and it is never possible for a man to move from one circuit to another (figure 4). On circuit A (five holes) the maximum number of jumps possible on a move is two; on circuit B or C (eight holes each: these are equivalent circuits) the maximum is nine, while on circuit D (12 holes) a total of 12 jumps is possible.

One can only clear an area by combining moves on different circuits. To remove a line of three men it is necessary

Figure 5 Removing a line of three

to have an adjacent man to act as the trigger. Consider the line of three in figure 5. The problem is to remove it, leaving a man in the trigger position. Easy: 35–37, 56–36, 37–35. Notice this cannot be done with a line where there is no adjacent hole beyond for the trigger to jump to, as is the case for example with any of the lines at the end of the arms (37/47/57 etc).

We can similarly remove a block of six, using a trigger (figure 6). Notice that the block is made up of two lines of three. Again, not difficult: 23–43, 25–23, 13–33, 43–23, 15–13–33. Unlike a line of three, a block of six can be removed from the board edge.

The holes that the trigger can occupy in order to leave a man in the trigger hole after the removal of the block are shown in figure 7. Blocks of 9, 12, 15 and 18 can be removed by combining blocks of six and lines of three. Knowing this, you are in a position to tackle any of the 21 fundamental games given above.

A version of Solitaire that uses men of six colours is a help in indicating wrong moves and also provides a range of different games—for example, removing all men of each colour in turn.

Figure 6 Removing a block of six

Figure 7
Possible positions for trigger to remove a block of six

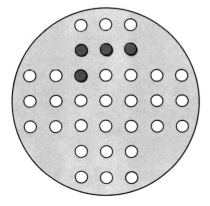

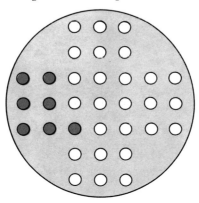

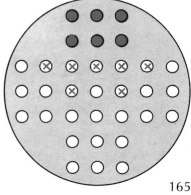

HALMA

Halma was invented during the wave of interest in board games about a century ago. Two or four can play although Chinese Checkers, a modern variant, allows any number up to six. When four take part, it is best to play in partnerships.

Halma is a game of skill but it is good fun played frivolously and can be quite absorbing. It has simple rules and is sold as a children's game but it conceals a complexity for those who seek it.

PLAY

The board is made up of an array of 16 by 16 squares, usually chequered although this has no bearing on the game. Each corner has a marked off area of 13 squares known as the court or yard. Two of the corners have a second yard which extends to 19 squares and is for use in the two-player game.

The game is played with 13 men a side (four-player game) or 19 (two-player game). The men are identical in appearance but are coloured differently for each player.

At the start, each player's men occupy a yard, partners opposite each other. In the game for two, the players are opposite each other. The board and men set up for a four-player game are shown in figure 1.

The object of the game is to move all your men into your opponent's yard before he occupies yours. In the partnership game, the aim is for the partners' forces to change places before the other side's forces do so. Players move in turn and can only move one man at a time. A square may never be occupied by more than one man and there is no capturing.

The men move one square at a time in any direction, including diagonally. A man may, however, leap over *any* adjacent man (his own, his partner's or an opponent's man) to an empty square immediately beyond it in the same line, again either moving orthogonally (in straight lines forwards, backwards or sideways) or diagonally, and he may

continue to leap in this fashion over any number of men if able to do so. Thus a player on his turn may move a man a single square or undertake a leap or succession of leaps, but he cannot do both. All moves are optional, so a player may end his move after one leap although further leaps are possible with the same man.

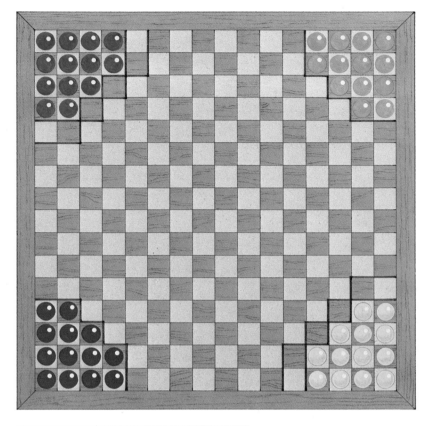

Figure 1
The board with the men in the starting position for a four-player game

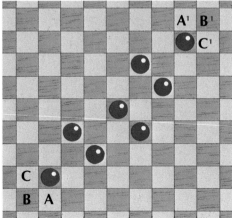

Figure 2
Advance via a ladder

Figure 3
Advance in a group

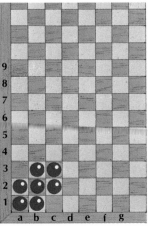

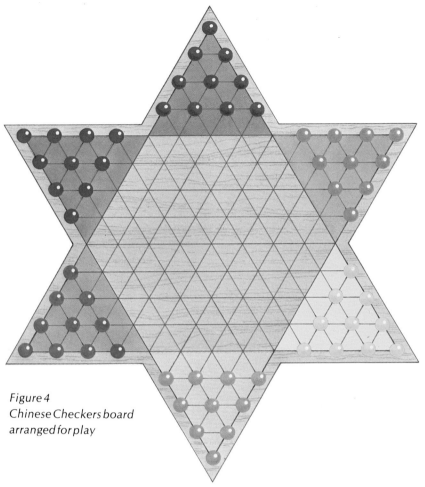

*Figure 4
Chinese Checkers board
arranged for play*

advanced rapidly by jumping. One such ladder, made up of men of one colour, is shown in figure 2. Here a player can bring a man from A, B or C to A1, B1, or C1 respectively in a succession of leaps, an advance which, without support, would take at least nine moves.

However, ladders have disadvantages; a man has to be brought to the foot and moved away from the top to clear the way for the next man, and this takes valuable moves. Forming ladders takes time too and they can be used by or easily disrupted by the opponent.

An alternative method of movement is the group or team. In this, a cluster of men advance, each with the help of the others. Consider the group of seven in figure 3. It takes only 10 moves to advance the whole group four squares diagonally: 1. b2 − d4; 2. c3 − e5; 3. a1 − c3 (two routes); 4. a2 − e6; 5. b1 − f5; 6. b3 − f7; 7. c2 − g6; 8. e5 − g7 (two routes); 9. c3 − e5; 10. d4 − f6 (h8). Certain other configurations can also be moved economically. An advantage of groups is that they are less prone to interference.

A sound strategy makes use of both ladders and groups and is a compromise between rapid advance and impeding the opponent's advance. Between equal players games are often close; between experts the first move is a considerable advantage.

As the rules of the two-player game stand, a player can keep a man in his yard indefinitely and so prevent its total occupation. An additional rule is suggested: when one player vacates his yard his opponent must vacate his own yard on successive plays, that is, the opponent cannot move a man that is outside his yard until the yard is empty.

Handicaps are easily arranged. The best system allows the weaker player an agreed number of consecutive initial moves.

Halma can also be played solitaire. Using one set of men only, try to get them in the opposite yard in the least number of moves.

STRATEGY

Obviously the aim is to move your men across the board as quickly as possible. A common way to do this is to set up ladders or chains which allow men to be

RELATED GAMES

Chinese Checkers is played on the intersections of a star-shaped board, each player having 10 men. The board may be impressed to accommodate marbles or perforated for pegs but this does not change the game, which is played in exactly the same way and with the same aims as Halma. A Chinese Checkers set arranged for play is shown in figure 4.

Grasshopper is played on a draughtsboard to Halma rules each side having 10 men (8 × 8 board) or 15 men (10 × 10 board) in opposing corners.

SHUT THE BOX

This is a French game for two or more players.

The commercial equipment consists of an oblong tray into which dice are rolled, with a line of little boxes, numbered 1 to 9, along one side, each with a lid that can be slid over the number. As a simple alternative, the numbers can be written on a piece of card and counters used to cover them.

Each player's turn starts with all the numbers exposed. On his turn, a player rolls two dice and adds the number of dots shown. He then covers one or more numbers that add to the same total as his roll. For example, a first roll of 5:3 would allow the player to cover the 8 or any of these combinations: 7 and 1, 6 and 2, 5 and 3, 1, 2 and 5, or 1, 3 and 4.

The player then rolls again and continues as before except that any number covered cannot now be used. He continues to roll and to shut boxes until he throws a total that he cannot use, when his turn ends. However, if he succeeds in closing the three top boxes (7, 8 and 9), he may elect to roll only one die if he so wishes.

A player's score is the total of all exposed numbers when his turn ends. The winner is the player with the lowest score after an agreed number of rounds.

LOTTO

This game is familiar under many names, of which Housey-Housey, Tombola and Bingo are probably the best known. Any number can play – the more the better – and it requires no skill.

The equipment consists of 90 small discs or balls numbered 1 to 90, and a stock of cards and counters. Each card is marked with a different combination of 15 of the numbers on the discs.

One player acts as caller and does not take part in the game. He gives out one card and 15 counters to each player (two cards and 30 counters each if not many are playing), shakes the discs in a bag and then draws one disc at a time, calling out the number on it as he does so and placing it in front of him. The players cover the numbers on their cards with counters as they are called. The first player to cover all 15 numbers on his card ('Full house') shouts out. The caller then checks the card against the discs in front of him and, if correct, the claimant is declared the winner. If two or more players shout out together, the first to do so wins.

Shorter games can be played in which the winner is the first player to complete a line of five or some other combination previously announced by the caller.

There is a number lore that callers sometimes draw on to enliven the game. Most of the numbers have sobriquets, two of the most common being 'Unlucky for some' (13) and 'Clickety-click' (66).

10		37		58	65		85
7	26		45	56		74	
16		31	49		63		86

CONNECT FOUR

This modern two-player game is suitable for almost any age.

The playing area or board consists of a vertical screen, made up of seven slotted columns each capable of holding six or seven counters, one above the other. Each player has a stock of counters of one colour, the two colours being in contrast. The game can also be played with pencil and paper.

The game starts with the board empty. A turn consists of dropping a counter of one's own colour into any slot. If the slot is empty, the counter will fall to the bottom; but if there are already counters in the slot, it will come to rest on top of the last one played. The object is to form a line of four of one's own counters in any direction — vertical, horizontal or diagonal.

Each player on his turn has a choice of seven moves until a column is filled, when the choice is reduced to six, and so on. It is possible for the board to be filled without either player getting a line of four but this is very unusual. The player to start definitely has an advantage.

Connect Four is superficially a simple form of Go-moku (p.72) but there is one significant difference apart from the smaller board: although a player can choose which column to enter, he cannot select his position within the column — the laws of gravity determine that he occupies the lowest one vacant.

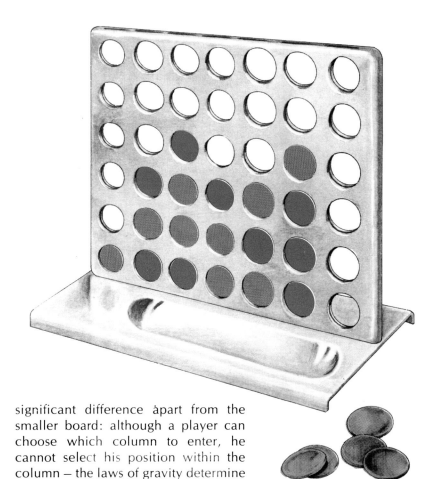

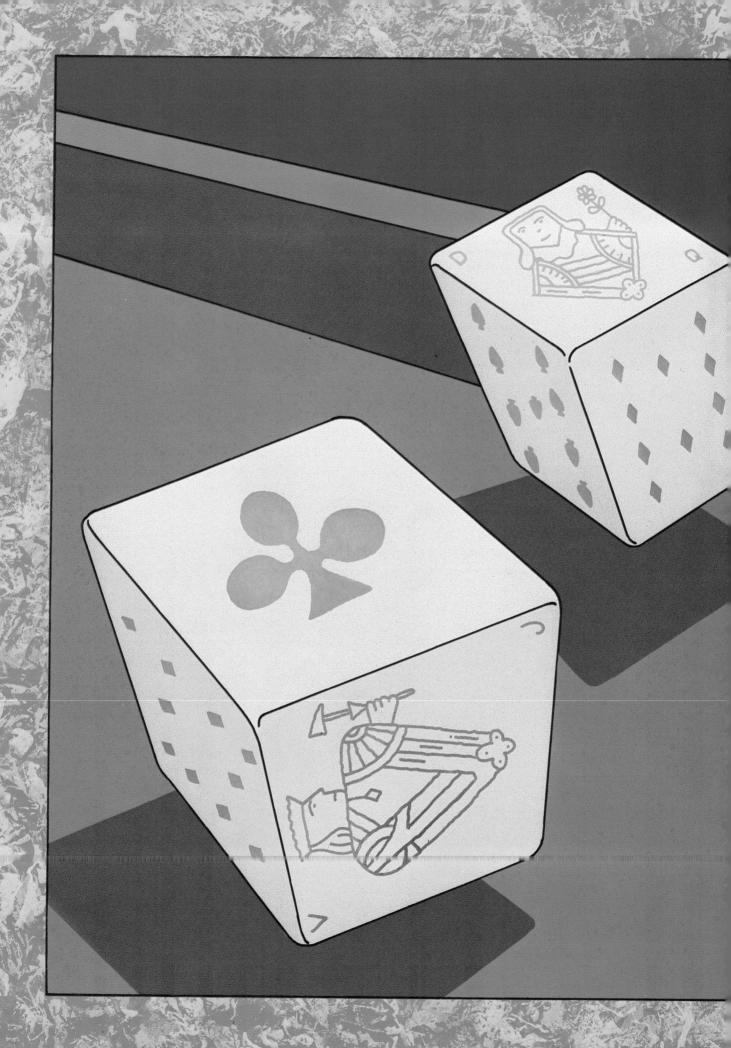

GAMBLING GAMES

Gambling has always been popular – in Rome it was considered a national vice and dice games were banned except during the festival of Saturnalia. The gambling games here are intended for harmless family entertainment and though stakes are needed if the games are not to lose their point, the stakes can be extremely modest. If wished, matchsticks or tokens can be substituted for money.

To gamble at a club or casino is another matter. There are laws governing the conduct of gambling games and these vary from country to country, and within these laws there may be house rules which, though quite legal, imperceptibly alter a game. You will almost certainly find that the games described here are not played in precisely the same way in gambling houses.

Gambling games are games of chance and serious gamblers would consider a knowledge of the laws of probability, which are more complex than may appear, essential for play. Since such knowledge is also useful to the family player, some indication of how the laws operate is included in the games here. A few of the games are pure chance – Hoggenheimer is one such – while others retain an element of skill, if only in weighing the odds and betting accordingly. Poker, however, is in a class alone. As a card game per se it is unexciting but it remains one of the best of all gambling games because it involves considerable skill. Games using a roulette wheel have not been included since the equipment and the games themselves are much more suited to gambling clubs than to the average home.

CRAPS

This is America's most popular gambling game where the dice are rolled to mystic incantations like 'Baby needs new shoes'. The game holds little interest without the betting.

PLAY

Two ordinary dice are used. One player is the shooter, who rolls the dice. He first puts down the money he is prepared to bet and the other players wager with him or amongst themselves on the outcome of the roll. The game is crowded with jargon and betting can be anarchic; the

Naturals

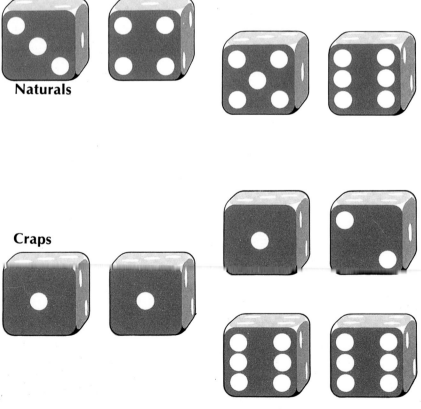

Craps

essentials, however, are quite straight-forward. The two dice are shaken in the closed hand and usually thrown ('shot') against a wall or other surface that allows the dice to rebound. The sum of the two faces uppermost on the dice determines the outcome.

The first shoot is known as the *come-out*. On the come-out:

7 or 11 is a *natural* and is a *winning decision* called a *pass*;

2, 3 or 12 is a *crap* and is a *losing decision* called a *missout*;

Any other total is the shooter's *point* and he must continue to throw the dice until he either repeats his point, when it is a pass, or he throws a 7, when it is a missout. When the shooter loses his point, he must pass the dice to the next player, but he can also pass them after any decision. The next player can decline to shoot and pass the dice on.

Odds are freely offered and can be declined or accepted by any of the players. Examples of common bets are:

Right bet This is a wager that the dice will pass.

Wrong bet This is a wager that the dice will not pass.

Centre bet Before the come-out the shooter may, but is not obliged to, bet that he will pass. This is called a centre bet. Any player who covers part or whole of the centre bet is referred to as a *fader*. All the above bets are normally offered at even money. The odds are slightly weighted in favour of a missout.

Point bet After the shooter has thrown a point, bets can be taken on a pass or missout, known as *right* point bet and *wrong* point bet respectively. The odds will depend on the point but are always against a pass:

4 or 10–2 to 1 odds
5 or 9–3 to 2 odds
6 or 8–6 to 5 odds

Craps can be fun within the family but expensive when amongst strangers – the hustlers know the odds. The casino game is played to slightly different rules to those given here.

LIAR DICE

This is very much a bar game in which an ability to deceive is the surpassing skill. Liar Dice is best with four or more players.

PLAY

A set of poker dice and a shaker are required. A poker die is an ordinary cubic die which has a small playing card engraved or printed on each of its faces. The cards are Ace, King, Queen, Jack, 10 and 9 which rank from high to low in that order. The suits are immaterial. A set is made up of five identical dice.

One player starts by rattling the five dice and turning them face down on the table beneath the shaker. He then cups his hand round the shaker before lifting it so that he alone can see the dice. He examines them and announces a poker hand, which can be the hand he has thrown or one of greater or lesser value. (For the ranking of poker hands, see Poker, p. 177). The player then replaces the shaker and, being careful not to disturb any of the dice, slides them, covered by the shaker, to the next player.

Before he lifts the shaker the second player must decide on whether he accepts or rejects the hand passed to him. If he rejects the hand, he lifts the shaker so that the dice are visible to all. If the hand revealed is less than that called, the first player loses a life, otherwise the second player loses a life. Every player starts with three lives and drops out of the game when they are lost. The last player left in wins the game.

If the call is rejected, the second player starts the next round whether he won or lost in the first. If the second player accepts the call, he in turn cups a hand round the shaker and examines the dice. He may now elect to throw none, any or all of the dice again. Suppose he decides to throw three. He covers with one hand the two he is retaining and throws the other three beneath the shaker, gathering the five dice together so that they cannot be seen by the others. He is now obliged to call a higher hand than the one he accepted before passing the dice on to the next player.

The following is an example of a short game between four players. Player A rolls and finds he has A, K, J, J, 9. He believes he can get away with a bluff so he announces 'Three 10s'. Player B accepts, and so as not to reveal that he did not receive three of a kind, he elects to roll only two dice – the K and 9. He is lucky and rolls two Jacks so that his hand is A, J, J, J, J. He undercalls his hand: 'Four 10s'. C accepts and, after careful thought, designed to mislead, passes the dice without rolling and announces 'Four Jacks'. D does not believe he will be able to roll a better hand than four Jacks even if C is not bluffing, so chooses to challenge by lifting the shaker. The four Jacks are revealed and D loses a life and rolls first in the next round.

CROWN AND ANCHOR

This is one of the simplest of all gambling games, much favoured by the hustler and popular at one time amongst seamen. Any number can play.

PLAY

The game uses a special layout (illustrated) and three cubic dice the faces of which show the six symbols of the layout. If no board is available, one can easily be drawn and ordinary dice can be used with the spots substituting for the symbols. The American game of Chuck-a-Luck, identical in every other respect with Crown and Anchor, uses a table array of the numbers 1 to 6 and three standard dice.

One player acts as banker and the others place their bets on their chosen symbols. Neither the crown nor the anchor nor the suit symbols have any special significance. When bets are placed, the banker rolls the three dice. Players who have backed symbols that

are matched by the dice are paid at even money; if a pair of dice show the same symbol, then anyone who bet on that symbol is paid at 2–1; and if all three dice are the same (it happens about once in every 36 rolls) then the payment is 3–1. The banker collects all stakes on symbols that do not come up.

Superficially it may appear that there is no profit for the banker, but in fact the banker's return averages eight per cent. If three different symbols are rolled, then the chances are indeed equal. But consider the case where a pair is rolled: if the bets have been evenly distributed, then those on one symbol are paid at 2–1, on the second symbol they are paid at evens, and the banker collects the bets off the remaining four symbols – a profit of one unit. A triple shows an even higher margin for the bank, If, for example, all symbols carry a bet of one unit and a triple anchor is rolled, that player collects three units but the banker takes in the other five.

FARO

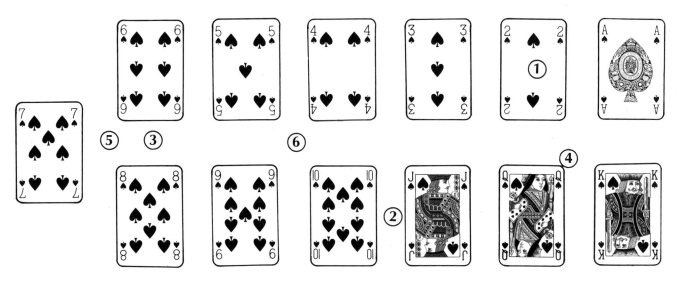

Soda and winners   **Losers**   **Pack**

Bets:
1 Single card (deuce)
2 Adjacent pair (10,J)
3 Vertical pair (6,8)
4 Diagonal pair (Q,A)
5 Corner three (6,7,8)
6 Four (4,5,9,10)

Faro has a long history and is for any number of players. Equipment, procedures and betting are simplified here.

PLAY

A standard pack of cards without Jokers is used. Players start with an equal number of chips or buy them from the dealer, who acts as banker and sets the betting limits.

One suit, usually spades, is marked on the table or borrowed from another pack and laid out. Players wager on individual cards and on card combinations. Stakes are placed in certain positions to indicate the bets. Layout and placings are shown in the figure. Players can also bet that a card or combination will lose. This is done by 'coppering' – placing a coin or token on top of the stake.

The banker puts the shuffled and cut pack face up in front of him. The top card is called soda and is dead (not used). Cards are dealt in pairs, called turns. The top card of each turn is the loser (banker wins), the second the winner (punters win). The banker starts by putting the soda to one side and the next card, the loser, near to it, thereby exposing the winner. Only denominations count: suits are irrelevant.

After each turn, any bets that win or lose are settled at even money. Notice that the first card of a combination to come up is the determinant; in a combination one is betting that the first card will be a winner (or a loser, if coppered), not that all cards in the combination will win. Bets can now be increased, reduced or withdrawn and further bets made.

The next turn proceeds in the same way with the winner from the first turn being placed on top of the soda, and so on through the pack until three cards remain. If any turn is 'split' (both cards of the same rank), the banker takes *half* the stakes on that denomination.

When the last turn is reached players can bet on the sequence that the cards will appear in addition to the usual betting. For this purpose, the banker can first look at the cards and name them. If all the cards are different denominations, the odds are 4–1, if there is a pair amongst them, 2–1. The last card, called hock, is not used except for this purpose, which is known as 'calling the turn'.

HOGGENHEIMER

This gambling game does not require skill but it can be quite exciting. It is best for several players.

PLAY

A standard pack of cards is required. The four deuces are extracted and placed face up on the table, one below the other, to indicate suits.

All cards ranking 9 and below (Aces rank high) are then discarded except for one, ideally a Joker.

Chips are distributed and one player acts as banker. The banker shuffles the cards and deals them face down in the arrangement shown in figure 1. Each suit is designated in sequence Ace, King, Queen, Jack, 10 reading from the deuce. One card is left over, the starter, which is kept concealed until the bidding is over.

Having agreed a limit, players now place their bets as they please. They are wagering that their cards will turn up before the Joker. The odds paid by the bank are:

Any one card: evens

Any marriage (King and Queen): 2 to 1

Any rank (all four cards of same denomination): 4 to 1

Any suit (all cards of a suit): 5 to 1

Chips bet on single cards are placed on the appropriate face-down card. For example, a bet on ◇ A would be placed on the card next to ◇ 2. A marriage bet is placed between the King and Queen, while rank and suit bets are positioned at the ends of rows and columns.

The banker now turns over the starter. If it is the Joker, he wins all bets and the round ends. Otherwise he puts the card face up in its proper place, transferring on to it any bets on the card. He then turns up the face-down card in that position and puts it in its correct place in the same way, continuing in this manner until the Joker is revealed, when play ceases. All bets on face-up cards are then paid by the banker who takes any stakes on face-down cards. Where a player has bet on a marriage, rank or suit, all the

Figure 1
The initial layout

Figure 2
A game in progress

cards in the bet must be face up to win.

If the Joker is the last card to turn up, the banker pays everyone   the banker has no advantage in Hoggenheimer.

A game in progress is shown in figure 2. The ♣ 10 is about to replace the face-down card at bottom right. A longer game can be had by including the 9s, 8s and 7s or as desired, and the bets can be extended to include other combinations.

POKER

Poker is justly famous as a gambling game but it plays as well at home as in a gaming club or Wild West saloon. Instead of money, use counters; the winner is the player with the most counters at the end of the evening.

Poker is best with half-a-dozen players but any number from two upwards can take part. There are two basic games, draw and stud, but in addition there are unnumbered others. In a large 'school' it is not uncommon to play 'dealer's choice' which means that the dealer nominates the game to be played — he can even invent one.

What is common to all poker games is the ranking of hands, which are always composed of five cards though in some variants more are dealt. Another common factor is that there is no play in the accepted sense — players retain the hands that they are dealt and wager on them. There is also a third factor, the human one: the best hand does not necessarily win — a good player with bad cards may succeed where a bad player with good cards fails. This is true of poker more than most card games.

PLAY

Both draw and stud poker use a standard pack. Jokers are sometimes included as 'wild' cards, that is, cards that may be substituted for any others that the holder chooses to nominate.

Cards rank from Ace down to 2, but Ace may rank low in certain hands at the option of the holder. Suits are equal.

Poker hands, in ascending order of value, are shown in figure 1. If a hand lacks even a pair, its value is that of the highest card in it. Where hands match, the first higher card wins. For example, if Player A has a diamond flush A Q 10 7 5 and Player B has a club flush A Q 10 9 2, B wins because his 9 beats A's 7.

Hands take precedence according to card ranks. Thus a full house of three 9s and two 3s beats a hand of three 8s and two Aces.

**Pair
(plus 3 unmatched cards)**

**Three of a kind
(plus 2 unmatched cards)**

Flush

**Four of a kind
(plus 1 unmatched card)**

**Two pairs
(plus 1 unmatched card)**

Straight

Full house

Straight flush

*Figure 1
Poker hands in ascending
order of value from the top
left reading across*

It is customary in all poker games to start with an 'ante': each player contributes an agreed stake before the deal (a counter will do) to establish a pot or pool which the winner will take.

Draw poker

Five cards are dealt singly face down to each player. Players examine their hands and bet on them, Elder starting. He can fold or stack – throw in his cards face down and drop out of the play, in which case all he has lost is his ante; he can check, which means he stays in the game but does not bet; or he can bet, in which case he announces how much and contributes accordingly to the pot. The option now passes clockwise. On his turn a player may always fold but he may only check if no previous player has bet. If he elects to bet, he must equal the previous highest bet. He may raise it, and if he does so a player, to stay in the game, must at least equal the raise.

The betting goes on as many rounds as necessary. For example: A checks; B bets 2; C bets 3 (raise of 1); D drops out; A bets 3 (equalling C's bet); B bets 2 (equalling C's bet and raising 1); C bets 1 (equalling B); A bets 1: end of betting.

When all have bet or dropped out, the remaining players may change as many cards as they please, or none, starting with Elder. Discards are placed face down on the table and the dealer gives the appropriate number off the top of the pack to each player, starting with Elder and finally himself.

The second round of betting now takes place. The player who bet first in the first round starts; if he has folded, the next player in sequence starts. Each player who bets does so because he thinks he may have the best hand or because he plans to bluff the other players into thinking that he has so that they will drop out.

When the betting has been equalized, hands are shown and the highest takes the pot. If one player continues to raise the betting and the others drop out, he

A

C

takes the pot without showing his hand.

In draw poker, it is common to play 'Jackpot', which means that to open the betting a player must have a pair of Jacks or better. If all pass, a further counter is contributed to the ante and there is another deal. The player who opens is obliged at the end of the game to reveal his 'openers'. For example, a player who started the betting with three Queens need only show two of them if his hand is

Figure 2
A hand of stud poker

B

D

opens. If there is a tie, the player on the left of the dealer takes precedence and thereafter in sequence clockwise.

Three more cards are dealt singly face up to each player. Each round of cards is followed by a round of betting which is always opened by the player with the best visible hand: highest matched cards, or failing any, highest card. The dealer indicates the player to open by announcing, say, 'Pair of 10s bets'.

The final round of betting, when each player has one down card and four up cards, determines who takes the pot. If all but one player drop out of the betting, the winner does not reveal his hole card. If more than one player remains, the players reveal their hole cards and the one with the best hand takes the pot. As in draw poker, players may drop out (fold or stack) at any time.

STRATEGY

The only habit you should form is to be inconsistent – and do not bluff too often. The poker face is a myth: it is quite in order to attempt to deceive by facial expressions or mannerisms, but do not overdo these. Psychology and bluff play a big part in poker but the skilled player is first a mathematician: playing with the odds is more rewarding than playing against them. The chance element adds spice to the game.

Notice how many cards each player exchanges in draw poker. In any poker game, do not bet too high on a good hand – you may scare the other players into folding when a small bet could have enticed them to stay in.

Figure 2 shows a game of stud poker with four players left in. Obviously, all depends on the hole cards. The best exposed hand is A's – a pair of 6s. He could have three of a kind or two pairs with the hole card. B may have a high pair to beat A. There is one chance in five that C has a flush but D is most unlikely to have a straight – he needs an 8 and there are two on the table.

not called in play. Once a player opens at Jackpot anyone may bet regardless of holding.

Stud poker

Each player is dealt one card face down, then a second card face up. Players examine their down or 'hole' cards but do not reveal them. A round of betting now takes place, as in draw poker. The player with the highest-ranking up card

PONTOON

This popular gambling game is also known as Blackjack and Vingt-et-Un and a few other names. The game is little affected by the many different sets of rules, imposed or preferred. Any number can play and each deal is complete in itself.

PLAY

One player acts as banker and retains the deal as long as he remains so. Play for money, matchsticks or anything, but agree beforehand on maximum and minimum stakes.

The standard pack is used, without Jokers. Suits are disregarded. Cards are not ranked but instead are given point values as follows:

Ace – 11 or 1, at holder's choice

All court cards – 10

Pip cards (10s – 2s) – pip value

The object of the game is to score 21 points or as near to, but not over, as possible with two or more cards. An Ace and a 10 or court card score exactly 21 with two cards. This is known as Pontoon.

The dealer distributes one card face down to each player including himself. Players (but not the dealer) look at their cards and bet on them, placing their stakes in front of them. The dealer now

distributes a further card face down to everyone and again the players (but not the dealer) look at their cards. Now the banker (dealer) completes the play with each player in turn, starting with Elder. A player has three options:

1 He can 'stick', i.e. he declines further cards, provided his card count is not less than 16;

2 He can buy, i.e. he adds to his stake a sum not greater than his original stake (it may be less) for which he receives a card face down;

3 He can 'twist', when no addition is made to his stake and banker gives him a card face up.

After electing for (2), the player has the same three options open to him again but after electing for (3) he no longer has option (2). A player who buys more than one card may not increase his bet.

Each player continues until he is satisfied with his hand or until his cards, face-up and face-down, exceed a count of 21, when he is 'bust', declares this and drops out, losing his stakes to the banker.

Cards are usually left on the table during play but players always have the right to examine their face-down cards. If a player gets pontoon he discloses this by turning over one of his cards (some people insist on the Ace).

When all have played, the banker

Figure 1
First round deal and betting

A B C D **Banker**

Figure 2 Second round deal

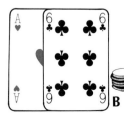
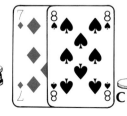

A B C D **Banker**

Banker

Figure 3
The final show

turns over his two cards. If he has less than 16 points, he – like all the other players – cannot stick. He takes extra cards off the top of the pack and exposes them. If he goes 'bust', he pays all players an amount equal to their total stakes. Otherwise, he announces that he will pay to players with a card count one higher than his own card count. For example, if his card count is 18, he says 'Pay 19s'. Players now reveal their hands and those rated 19 or better are paid by the banker an amount equal to their total stakes. Those with hands scoring 18 or less lose their stakes to the bank.

Apart from pontoon, there are two special hands, one common and the other rare: five cards and three 7s. A hand of five cards totalling 21 or under – even if under 16 – is only beaten by pontoon or by three 7s. A hand of three 7s beats everything. It is often paid double or triple stakes. Where the banker has a pontoon or a five-card hand he beats any player with a similar hand.

A player whose first two cards are of the same value may split them into two hands (and again if another of the same value is then dealt). He then plays them separately just as if he were two players.

It is usual for the player who wins with a pontoon to take over the bank or at least to be given the option on it. Cards are only shuffled when the bank is changed, otherwise hands are gathered up one by one and put underneath the pack by the banker.

STRATEGY

The sure way to win at Pontoon is either to keep the bank or never to bet unless you draw an Ace or a ten-card. This does not make for much of a game so it is a good rule that everyone must bet each hand.

Skill is limited and most decisions call for little judgment. Bet the maximum on an Ace and, if you wish, on ten-cards; bet the minimum on a middle-value card. Split two Aces: the chance of getting a pontoon is high (remember that there are 16 ten-cards in the pack). As a general guide buy cards until your hand totals 12 or over, and then twist.

The banker has a definite advantage since he only pays hands that are better than his, beating hands of the same value, and since he collects from players who go bust even though he himself may subsequently go bust.

Figure 1 shows the first deal of a five-player game with the bets laid on the concealed cards. The second round of face-down cards is then dealt (figure 2). Player A, who has a count of 20, naturally sticks. B has 17 or 7 and opts to buy. He gets a 5, then a 2 and twists the last card – a 6, which gives him a five-card hand. C has an 8 and 7 so elects to twist and is busted with a ten-card. D splits a pair of fours and draws a King and 7 respectively. On the first hand he twists and receives an 8 – he is bust. On the second he buys and draws a Jack. He now sticks on 21. The banker turns his cards over – a 10 and a King (figure 3). He announces 'pay 21s'. Only B and D (second hand) get paid: the dealer takes all the other stakes.

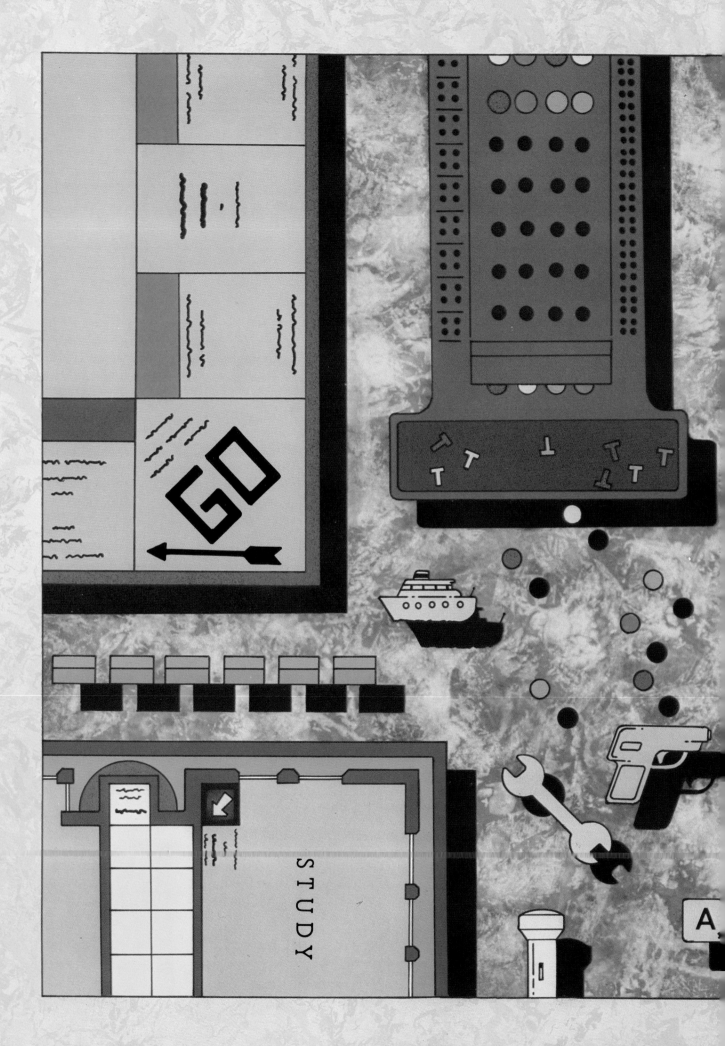

PROPRIETARY GAMES

Proprietary games are available today in remarkable variety, in contrast to 50 years ago. They are also less stereotyped and a lot more ingenious. A few will without doubt become classics, though inevitably most will pass with time.

Most proprietary games fall into one of two categories, abstract games and thematic games. Abstract games, usually contests of skill, are play ideas presented in any convenient form, commonly a board marked with a grid and simple pieces of uniform design. Mostly these are two-player games, to be taken seriously.

Thematic games parallel life in some way, however distorted. They are multi-player games and often include a chance element which qualifies them as fun games. *Monopoly* is an example of a thematic game that everyone knows. There are of course other types of game — word games, for example — and it is wise when selecting a proprietary game that you cannot inspect at least to decide on the kind you require.

The games presented here have been selected mainly for their deserved popularity, but also for their variety. One or two games that are almost unknown have been included on their merit. If a game is not mentioned, it does not follow it is not recommended: the choice is vast and space is limited.

HARE AND TORTOISE

Hare and Tortoise is a widely acclaimed modern race game without dice, invented by David Parlett. Its presentation marks it as a children's game but its strategy will challenge any adult. Handicaps are easily arranged to make Hare and Tortoise a perfect family game for two to four players.

PLAY

The board is laid out like a typical race game. Every player receives cards representing carrots and lettuces, and places a token at the start. The object is to reach the finish first, but with an important restriction: you cannot cross the line if you have any lettuces or if you have more than 20 carrots.

The race track covers 63 squares which are marked, in irregular sequence, with a hare, a tortoise, a lettuce, a bunch of carrots or a number (1, 2, 3 or 4). Tokens can be moved either forwards or backwards; moves forwards must be paid for in carrots, whilst moves backwards to tortoise squares gain carrots.

A player on his turn moves as many squares as he pleases within the rules. The faster he moves forwards, the more carrots he must consume. For example, a move forwards of a single square costs only one carrot, an advance of 10 squares on a turn requires 55 carrots — almost the entire initial allocation. Apart from moving backwards to tortoise squares, carrots can be earned by landing on lettuce squares, where you simultaneously give up a lettuce and gain carrots, or by starting a move on a number square which corresponds to your position in the race (1 = first, etc.) or by staying on carrot squares.

The only element of chance occurs when you elect to move to a hare square. You must then 'jug the hare' by rolling a die and following the instructions on the race card provided. These vary according to your position in the race as well as the number on the die, and may be favourable or unfavourable.

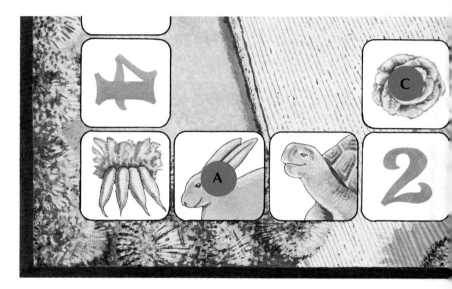

Figure 1

STRATEGY

You will not succeed at Hare and Tortoise unless you plan ahead. Because of the game's many variables, it is best to take a flexible approach. Long leaps use up a lot of carrots and thereafter limit your play, while conserving carrots by advancing gradually may leave you too far behind.

The three lettuces with which you start the race must be disposed of one at a time. There are only five lettuce squares where this can be done, so there is often congestion around these squares, and waiting means loss of time. It is a good rule to get rid of a lettuce when you can.

Number squares can be valuable carrot earners but their promise may not be fulfilled. For example, if you are last in the race and move to a 4 square with a

Figure 2

prospect of picking up 40 carrots next turn, another player may move backwards so that when your turn comes round again you are standing third, not fourth, and so get no carrots.

Number squares vary in frequency. They are fewest (and earn the fewest carrots) if you are in the lead, whereas there are three times as many that favour you if you are in second place.

Moving back to a tortoise square earns you enough carrots to carry you three or four squares beyond your previous position in a single leap but you have lost a move in the process. The ideal is to find plays that bring the greatest benefit. Thus in moving back to a tortoise square to acquire carrots, you may also be nicely placed to reach a lettuce square, while at the same time altering the race order and confounding your opponents. Do not

run short of carrots as this will limit your alternatives. Since no more than one token can occupy a square, blocking plays introduce a further factor. If your strategy fails, you can usually 'jug the hare' and hope luck will smile on you.

A game in progress is shown in figure 1. A, who has only a few carrots left, decides to move one square (spending one carrot) to earn a few more. B, who is aware that C is short of carrots, advances to 2 since he feels confident he will not be passed and so will collect 20 carrots for lying second on the next turn. C moves back to the tortoise square for 30 carrots while D, who has been accumulating them, takes the opportunity to get rid of a lettuce by leaping to the lettuce square. There is no point in his moving to the 3 square since C will pass him before his turn comes again (see figure 2).

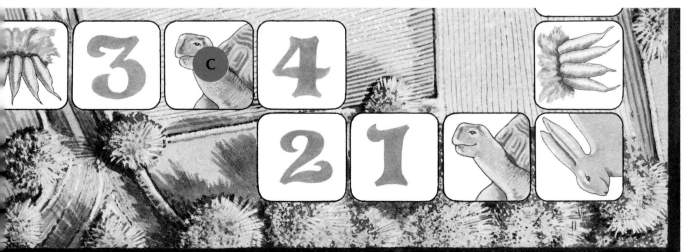

MONOPOLY

Monopoly is a board game for up to six players and it must be the world's most popular commercial game. There are many reasons for its success, not least that it is rarely boring. The game is more skilful than its presentation suggests.

PLAY

The object of Monopoly is to become the richest and eventually the only surviving player by buying and selling property and collecting rents. Equipment includes the board (illustrated here), property cards, event cards, model houses and hotels, play money, a token for each player and dice.

One player is appointed banker. He keeps bank transactions strictly separate from his own. To start, each player receives £1500 and selects a token. Tokens are moved round the board in turn according to dice rolls. A player whose token alights on unowned property may buy the title deed from the bank. Thereafter he collects rent from any player whose token lands on the property. If a player owns all the properties of one colour group he may develop them, when the rent will be sharply increased.

Properties may be auctioned, mortgaged, and traded freely. In addition to the property squares that predominate, there are a number of hazard squares which require a card to be drawn from one or other of the event packs (Chance and Community Chest) and the instructions on it implemented. There are also a few penalty squares, including jail, and the much-loved start square, known as Go, which causes the bank to pay out £200 every time it is passed.

A game can be divided roughly into three phases; the first phase, when players go round the untenanted board buying up properties as they land on them; the second phase, when most of the properties are owned (title deeds are kept in front of the owners) and players start to develop property groups by constructing houses on them; and the third

phase, when one or perhaps two players establish a firm grip on the game by developing sites to the point where rentals payable become prohibitive and bankruptcies of the remaining players are effected or pending.

A shorter game can be had by ending it when, say, two players have gone bankrupt or after a predetermined time, when the richest player, in terms of property and cash combined, is declared the winner.

STRATEGY

Monopoly is about managing money within the constraints of the game. There

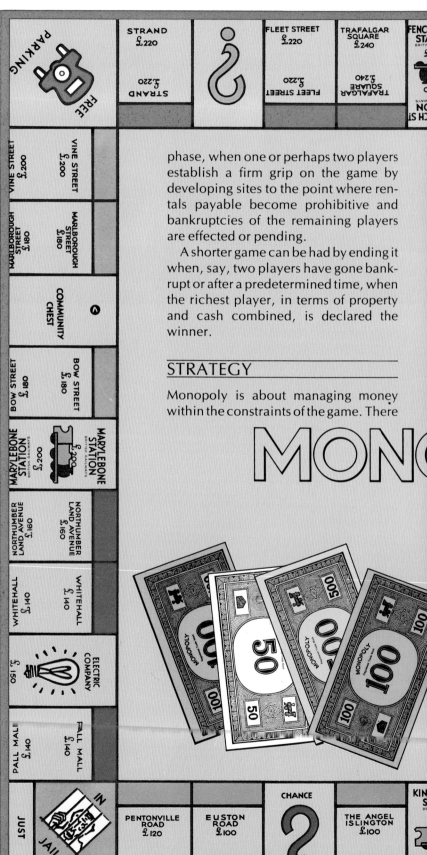

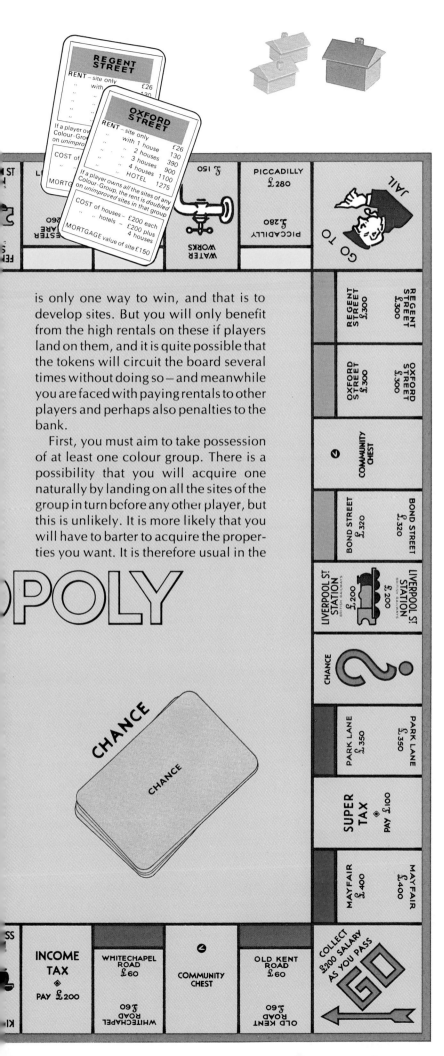

is only one way to win, and that is to develop sites. But you will only benefit from the high rentals on these if players land on them, and it is quite possible that the tokens will circuit the board several times without doing so – and meanwhile you are faced with paying rentals to other players and perhaps also penalties to the bank.

First, you must aim to take possession of at least one colour group. There is a possibility that you will acquire one naturally by landing on all the sites of the group in turn before any other player, but this is unlikely. It is more likely that you will have to barter to acquire the properties you want. It is therefore usual in the

opening stages for players to buy any property they land on because the title deed may prove a useful bargaining counter later. Until about half the property on the board has been sold and the game has started to take shape, it will not be possible to formulate a strategy. There are a number of strategies open to you, varying from conservative caution to reckless gambling, and there is the added attraction of interaction with the other players: skilled bargaining can compensate for fate's meanness.

The potential return in relation to the investment on developed properties varies considerably. If fully developed, a site in the orange and blue groups, for example, yields double the outlay every time another player lands on it, whereas the green group brings in a return of a mere 130 per cent, with the red and mauve groups only a little better. Jail is not a nice place to be when there are still unclaimed properties to be had; late in the game, however, when the board has become a nightmare of houses and hotels, there is no better place to stay.

Monopoly is unique, but its variants are many. Mostly they involve minor changes to the rules, designed either to shorten the game, like distributing a few title deeds before play begins, or to remedy its apparent shortcomings. These can be summarized as:

1 One player can mar the flow of the game by not selling or trading property;

2 One player may quickly secure a winning advantage, reducing the challenge for the others;

3 The course of the game is inflationary – rents rise swiftly as property is developed. In the later stages much time can be spent on trivial dealings, like collecting rents on undeveloped properties, which can have no bearing on the outcome;

4 The dark blue group (Mayfair and Park Lane), if developed, is considered by many players to be too powerful – a player who lands at Mayfair with a hotel on it is almost certainly ruined.

SCRABBLE

Scrabble is the best-known of all word games. An excellent game for two, it is less satisfactory for three or four players. There are Scrabble clubs and tournaments in many countries.

PLAY

Scrabble is played on a board divided into 15 × 15 small squares more than a quarter of which carry premium values. There are 98 letters in the form of tiles that fit the squares. Each letter is marked with a value inversely proportional, or nearly so, to its frequency in the language; A, E, L and T are typical 1-point letters, Q and Z are 10-point letters. The distribution of tiles matches common usage, thus there are between four and twelve of each of the 1-point letters but only one of each letter valued 5 points and above. Two blank tiles complete the

Figure 1

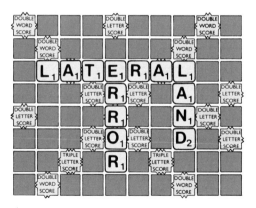

Figure 2

set. These have no point value but can be substituted for any letters.

All the tiles are shuffled face down or in a bag and each player draws seven. Racks are provided to hold these. The rest of the tiles are left on the table or in the bag to form the stock.

The first player combines two or more of the letters in his hand to form a word, which he lays on the board so that one letter covers the centre square. Thereafter each player on his turn adds one or more letters from his hand to the game array so as to form new words. Crossword principles are followed. Interlocking words are made across and down, no word may be placed in isolation and letters may not stand adjacent to one another unless they form words.

The letters of each new word made, including any letters that were previously played, are scored, the score being adjusted appropriately for any premium squares covered in play. Premium squares, which are regularly distributed about the board, are of four kinds: they double or triple the value of the letter played on them or they double or triple the score of the word(s) of which the letter forms part. The rules make clear which types of word are and are not admissible but it is as well to have a dictionary on hand to settle disputes. A bonus of 50 points is gained if a player puts down all seven of his tiles in one turn.

Instead of playing letters to the board, a player may on his turn elect to exchange any or all of his tiles for a like number from stock. Throughout the game players replenish their hands from stock after each play. The game ends when the stock of tiles is exhausted and either one player empties his rack or no player can make a word with any of his remaining tiles. A player who goes out adds the values of his opponent's unused letters to his score. It is usual to keep progressive scores in Scrabble so that players are aware of their position at any time.

Variants

The popularity of Scrabble is attested in the number of variants it has spawned. One example: players permit a blank to be taken up from the board in exchange for the letter it represents. This tends to push up scores.

Many solitaire versions of the game have been developed. One of the most satisfactory is the simplest: the rules are unchanged except that there is only one playing. The interest is in creating openings to be exploited later, and the object is to achieve the maximum possible score.

STRATEGY

The art of Scrabble, about which several books have been written, cannot be condensed into a paragraph or two.

The gulf between the average player and the expert is wide but it can be narrowed considerably by a correct approach to the game. If you simply assemble the highest-scoring word in your hand each time, look round where to place it on the board without giving thought to your opponents, the position or your next play, you will not score more than a couple of hundred points and you may wonder why the tiles were running against you. If, on the other hand, you develop a Scrabble vocabulary, examine the board as well as your hand constantly, pursue the 50-point bonus, keep account of letters still to come and maintain a flexible approach, you may hope to double that score.

The essence of a Scrabble vocabulary is two-letter words. There are nearly a hundred of them in a standard dictionary – more than twice those in common use. Their value lies in fitting parallel words, the hallmark of a skilled player. Perceptual skill is important. The biggest scores are made by grafting on letters to existing words, and the board must be studied relentlessly for these opportunities.

By getting rid of awkward letters, the chances of putting out seven tiles in one play can be maximized. Two or three bonuses in a game are not impossible – the experts achieve it regularly. The Ss and blanks are invaluable here. Never use them wantonly.

Figure 1 shows a game after three plays. A beginner, examining his rack, might be pleased to find IMPOT and even more pleased to notice that it can be overlapped with LATERAL to give two down words also (figure 2). If he had looked at the board he would have observed that the open position will allow the use of any of a number of letters already played. He might for instance have come up with TEMPLE (figure 3), which would have earned him a slightly better score, or one of a number of other words. The expert, with all two-letter words at his fingertips and hardly believing his good luck, would put down EPITOME (figure 4) for a massive 128 points. In Scrabble, high-value letters do not promise high scores nor low-value letters condemn you to low scores.

Figure 3

Figure 4

189

MASTER MIND

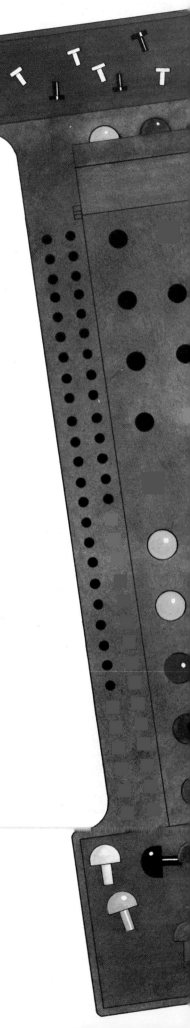

Master Mind is a proprietary adaptation of a popular two-player children's game. It was developed by Mordecai Meirowitz in 1973 and has since sold millions of copies worldwide. Many countries hold national championships and international events are also held. Part chance, but mostly skill, Master Mind is an uncomplicated code-breaking game that is quick to play, and has both visual and tactile appeal. It has the virtue of most games that combine chance and skill – the better player wins, but not every time.

PLAY

The standard equipment consists of a peg board with a screen at one end, code pegs in eight colours and small black and white marker pegs.

One player is the codemaker and the other the challenger. The codemaker starts by putting any four pegs in any colour combination in the row of holes behind the screen. This is the code.

The challenger now places a like number of pegs of his choice in the line of holes farthest from the screen. This line is then marked by the codemaker using the marker pegs. For every coloured peg that the challenger has matched in both colour and position with a peg in the code, the codemaker places one black marker peg adjacent to the line, and for every correct colour that is in the wrong position he places a white marker peg. No indication is given as to which pegs in the line the markers refer to.

For example, if the hidden code is Red, Brown, Brown, Blue, and the challenger enters Brown, Green, Yellow, Blue, the codemaker would award him one black peg (for the blue) and one white (for one of the browns).

The challenger now has certain information which he can use to formulate his second attempt. Play proceeds like this until the code is broken – that is, when the challenger has earned four black markers for a line. The aim is to break the

code in the least number of attempts.

The players now change roles. After this second game, the player who broke the opponent's code in the fewer number of lines is the winner. An example of a completed game of Master Mind is shown in figure 1.

STRATEGY

Master Mind is an exercise in deductive reasoning but there is in addition a small psychological element: the challenger may be able to develop an intuitive insight into the kind of colour combinations that appeal to or offend the codemaker. This factor can be quite noticeable between close relatives.

Follow the reasoning in a sample game. Figure 2 gives the challenger's first three attempts at breaking a code. Only the eight colours shown are in use.

The first two lines have each earned two black marker pegs, indicating that there are two correctly placed colours in each line and, since there are no white marker pegs, no correct colour is present in the wrong place.

Red and blue are in both lines but both cannot be in the code since they compete for the first position. The four remaining colours cannot make up the code because black and green equally compete for third place. Hence red or blue is in the code, and since each colour appears in a different position in each line, whichever colour is correct must be repeated in the code. If red were correct, then brown must be in the code from line 1 and green from line 2. This combination is ruled out by line three in which there are two correct colours, albeit in the wrong positions. So red is out and blue is in.

The rest is easy. Blue must be in first and second position and since red is out, black must earn the other marker peg in line 1 which from line 2 leaves yellow in fourth position. The code has been broken in four attempts, which is one better than average.

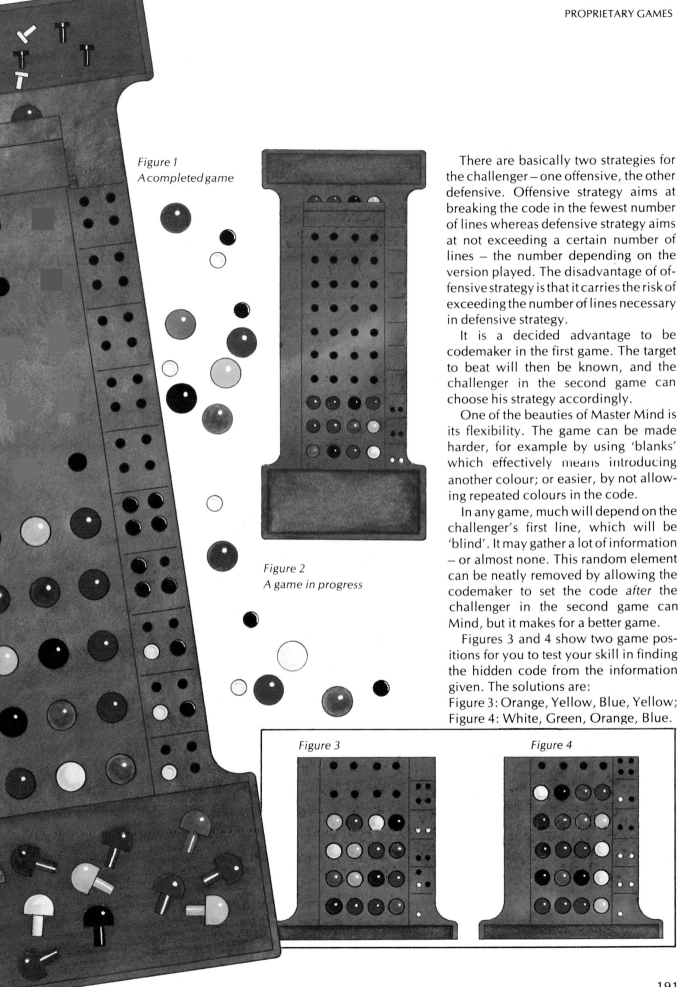

Figure 1
A completed game

Figure 2
A game in progress

Figure 3

Figure 4

There are basically two strategies for the challenger – one offensive, the other defensive. Offensive strategy aims at breaking the code in the fewest number of lines whereas defensive strategy aims at not exceeding a certain number of lines – the number depending on the version played. The disadvantage of offensive strategy is that it carries the risk of exceeding the number of lines necessary in defensive strategy.

It is a decided advantage to be codemaker in the first game. The target to beat will then be known, and the challenger in the second game can choose his strategy accordingly.

One of the beauties of Master Mind is its flexibility. The game can be made harder, for example by using 'blanks' which effectively means introducing another colour; or easier, by not allowing repeated colours in the code.

In any game, much will depend on the challenger's first line, which will be 'blind'. It may gather a lot of information – or almost none. This random element can be neatly removed by allowing the codemaker to set the code after the challenger in the second game can Mind, but it makes for a better game.

Figures 3 and 4 show two game positions for you to test your skill in finding the hidden code from the information given. The solutions are:
Figure 3: Orange, Yellow, Blue, Yellow;
Figure 4: White, Green, Orange, Blue.

CLUEDO

Cluedo is a lively deduction game for two to six players. It offers a pleasing balance of chance and skill.

PLAY

The game starts with an ending – Dr Black has been murdered in his home at Tudor Close. There are six suspects, six possible murder weapons and nine rooms in which the crime could have been committed. A playing card, suitably illustrated, represents each of these possibilities, making 21 cards in all.

The cards are separated into the three groups, turned face-down, and one card is drawn from each group and placed unseen in an envelope. This establishes the murderer, the weapon and the lo-cation. The rest of the cards are then shuffled and divided, face down, between the players.

Cluedo is played on a board portraying the nine rooms of the house and the passages between them. Small replicas of the weapons are placed on the board, one in each of six rooms. Each player has a token and assumes the role of one of the suspects. Tokens for unrepresented suspects are also placed on the board.

Moves are determined by dice rolls. When his token reaches a room, a player can summon any suspect, transfer any weapon to the room, and link the three in a 'suggestion' – 'I suggest that the murder was committed in the Study by Colonel Mustard with the Candlestick.' The next player must show *one* of the three corresponding cards, if he has any, to the player who made the suggestion and to no-one else; otherwise this requirement passes to the following player, and so on. Notepads are provided so that all the players can record these incidents. In this way players gradually accumulate information.

At some stage a player will decide that he knows all the circumstances of the crime and makes an 'accusation' by writing down the name of the murderer, the weapon and the room, and comparing them with the cards in the envelope. If he is right, he has won; if not, he replaces the cards in the envelope and thereafter assumes a passive role.

STRATEGY

The best cards to pick up are rooms since you have to eliminate eight of these against only five each of suspects and weapons. For this reason, it is usually wrong to make a suggestion where you hold the room card, though often wise to do so where you have one or both of the others in order to bluff your opponents.

If you are required to show a card and have an option, it is better to show one that you have shown before – you can never be asked for a specific card.

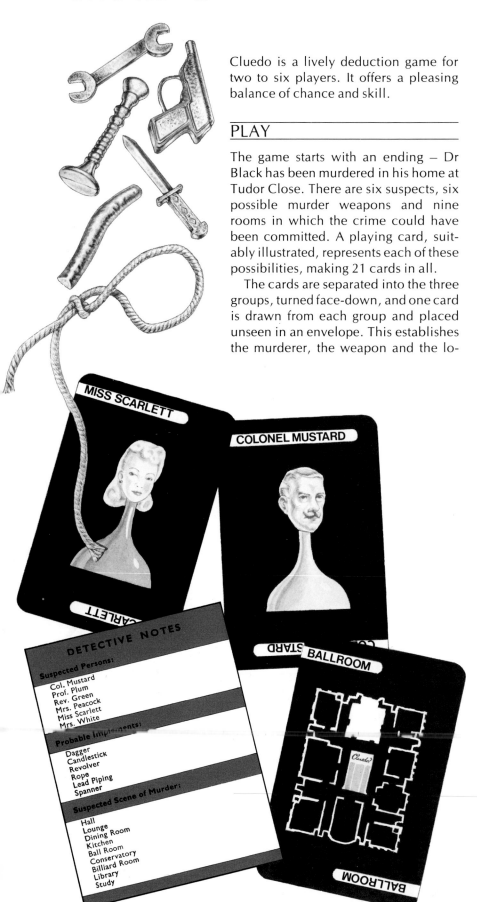

Rummikub, as its name suggests, is a variant of the card game Rummy and makes for a compulsive family game. A Rummikub set comprises 106 tiles. Each tile bears a number from 1 to 13 in four distinct colours and is duplicated. Two Jokers complete the set. The tiles thus correspond to two packs of cards so it follows that a number of games can be played with them. However, the tiles are peculiarly suited to one game, called the Sabra version, which is the game that is everywhere referred to simply as Rummikub.

The tiles are shuffled and each player (four is the ideal) draws 14 face down. Racks are provided to hold the hands. The object is to make sets. These are either groups – three or four tiles of the same value but in different colours – or runs, three or more tiles of the same colour in sequence. The first player to dispose of all his tiles is the winner. The other players are penalized for tiles still in hand.

Sets are placed face up on the table and are then common property. A player on his turn, provided he has already put down the minimum set requirement, may alter or add to any of the sets on the table as well as adding any further sets from his hand. It is this freedom to manipulate sets that makes Rummikub such an excellent game. A skilled player may transform the table array in order to dispose of one or two tiles!

Focus and **Twixt** are abstract games. Focus is for two or four players and uses an octagonal board. Each player puts his distinctively coloured pieces on the board in the prescribed pattern before play begins (18 pieces each in the two-player game, 13 each in the four-player version).

Movement is orthogonal, either to an empty space or on top of a piece or a column of pieces – colours are disregarded. A move is over as many spaces as there are pieces in the column moved. When a pile exceeds five pieces, any in excess of five are removed from the bottom; the opponents' pieces are captured while friendly pieces are put into reserve and are later re-entered. The player or side unable to move loses.

Twixt has a 24 × 24 hole pegboard. Two play and the object is to join opposite sides of the board with a continuous chain of pieces of one's own colour, opponents playing at right angles to each other (compare Hex, p.81). A turn consists of putting a peg of one's own colour into any vacant hole. If there is a peg of like colour a knight's move away (see Chess, pp.43–4, for how the knight moves) then a span is laid across to link the two pegs. Links cannot cross one another. Apparently a simple game, Twixt is full of subtleties.

Diplomacy is a sophisticated adult game remarkable for its play system. Its weakness is that to use its full potential, seven players and several hours of playing time are necessary.

The board is a stylized political map of Europe at the start of the twentieth century. Each player assumes the role of one of the major powers that then dominated the continent. There are 34 supply centres spread around the board and the first player to gain control of 18 of them is the winner. Players deploy units, which are either armies or fleets, corresponding to the number of supply centres they control. Units can advance and support one another but they may also be forced to retreat or disband.

The game has two distinctive features. One is simultaneous movement. Players write down their unit orders, which are read out and executed together. The second feature motivates the whole game. Between each movement phase there is a diplomacy period which usually lasts about 15 minutes. In this time the players negotiate among themselves. Secret pacts are made, ultimatums delivered, and plots are hatched. Almost anything is legal; bluff, bribery and bullying are all popular tactics. Fortune tends to favour the most skilful diplomat.

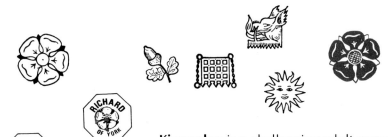

Kingmaker is a challenging adult game that requires several players. The scene is England on the eve of the Wars of the Roses. The board depicts the country with geographical and political features. Pieces represent nobles, royalty – either Lancastrian or Yorkist, and ships, which can be used to transport the nobles and royalty round the coasts. Two packs of cards are used: a Crown pack of 72 cards representing nobles, titles and offices, and an Event pack of 80 cards. Action is both military and political and the rules are rather elaborate. The winner is the player who controls the last surviving crowned piece. Kingmaker is not a game for the lazy.

Acquire is a clever property game marred by its abstract presentation. Hotels are represented by tiles and the aim is to create chains and mergers by linking tiles on the board. The chainmaker receives founder's stock in his property and stock may also be bought and sold using the play money provided. Compensation is paid to major shareholders when a chain is absorbed by a merger.

The game ends when one player announces that all chains have 11 or more hotels or that one chain has 41 or more hotels. The player with the most money wins. This is another game that demands concentration.

L-game This invention of Edward de Bono's is a thought-provoking way for two players to pass a few minutes. It was created in response to a challenge to design a simple but skilful game.

The playing area is a 4 by 4 square grid. Each player has an L-shaped piece that exactly covers four squares of the grid and there are two neutral pieces that occupy one square each. The starting position is shown in figure 1.

Players move in turn. A turn requires the player to pick up his L-piece and move it to a new position. The piece may be turned round or over, but when placed back on the grid it must cover at least one square that it did not cover at the start of the turn. The player is then free to move one of the neutral pieces to a new square if desired. The object is to leave the opponent without a move for his L-piece. In the position in figure 2, Black has won since Brown is unable to move his L-piece.

There are 15 basic winning positions and many more from which a win can be forced. With best play on both sides the game is always drawn. Tip: do not play your L-piece into a corner.

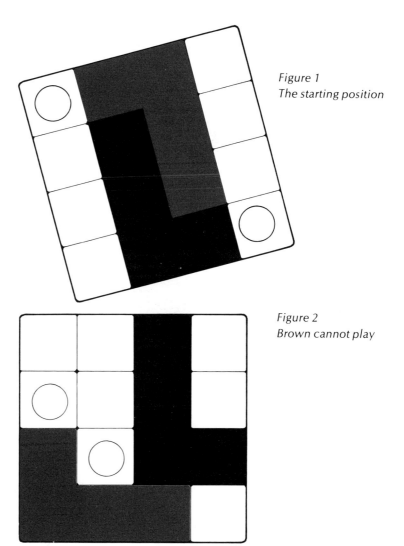

Figure 1
The starting position

Figure 2
Brown cannot play

Black Box is a deduction game that makes use of a modern conception – the container whose external workings can be observed but whose internal structure is unknown.

One player, the challenger, arranges four or five atoms in a replica of the box (which is in the form of an 8 by 8 square grid). The second player, the experimenter, injects imaginary rays into the box, announcing their points of entry (the perimeter squares are numbered for reference). The challenger plots the passage of the rays through the box (the rays behave in certain known ways when adjacent to or striking an atom) and announces where they emerge, if at all. The experimenter uses this information to locate the atoms. There is a scoring system to determine the winner.

Pit is a party game for three, or preferably more, players. It is exhausting but fun and children in particular enjoy it. The equipment consists of a pack of cards, each depicting one of five commodities commonly traded on the American Corn Exchange, plus a Bull (bonus) and Bear (penalty) card, and a hand-bell.

Each player is dealt nine cards face down. The object is to trade cards until you have all of one commodity (rye, for example). You decide from your hand which commodity to go for — probably the one of which you hold most cards.

The bell opens the trading, which quickly develops into a frenzied free-for-all. Players offer between one and four cards face down that they do not want ('Trade three! three! three!'), with everyone shouting at once. Two players offering the same number exchange cards and then offer again. The more you trade the better chance you have of cornering the market. Commodities have different point values and a game is made up of a number of hands.

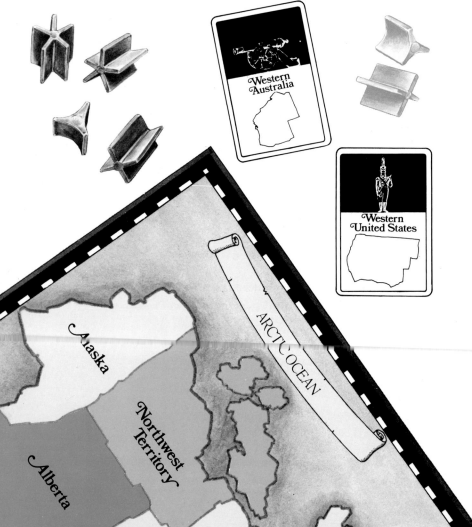

Risk is described as 'the world conquest game' and it should appeal to the ruthless. It is also colourful and fun to play, and its encouragement to aggression should not be overstressed. It makes a good family game for up to six players.

The board is a map of the world, distorted for playability. Each continent is of a distinctive colour and its various regions are distinguished by shading. There are 42 cards, one for each region on the board, a number of mission cards and six boxes of playing pieces in contrasting colours to represent armies.

Each player starts by drawing a mission card, which is the player's objective in the game and is not disclosed to the other players until the end. The region cards are dealt round and each player receives an allocation of armies which he then distributes amongst the regions he has drawn. Play turns consist of forming new armies and attacking armies in neighbouring regions in pursuit of one's mission. Dice are used to resolve conflict. Despite the fortunes of the draw and the dice rolls, there is a lot of strategy in the game.

Marrakesh is almost unknown outside the western United States but it deserves wider recognition. It has charm and balance, demands skill and plays fast.

Marrakesh is for two players. It combines card play (special cards are used) with the bearing-off stage of Backgammon. A half Backgammon board, again with special features, is the play area. The chance element in the card play combined with the use of dice for the disposition of the men makes this also a splendid gambling game.

The cards played dictate movement and the aim is for a player to bear off his men in one of the favourable patterns while preventing his opponent doing likewise. It is definitely a game for adults.

Lexicon is an old-established word card game which is a good game for children learning to spell and for crossword addicts, who will appreciate the subtle strategies that Lexicon offers. Every card is marked with a letter of the alphabet, with common letters repeated, and each letter has a point value – the more frequent the letter, the higher the value. In addition there is a master card that can be substituted for any letter.

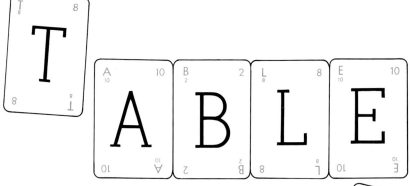

Ten cards are dealt face down to each player. The remainder forms the stockpile and the top card is turned face up beside it. The object of the game is to get rid of all one's cards by forming words. When one player achieves this the round ends and the other players are penalized according to the values of the cards they hold. When a player's score reaches 100 he drops out and the last player in is the winner.

After the deal players examine their hands and the player to the left of the dealer starts. He has two options:
1 He can put down any number of cards face up on the table to form a word: or
2 He can throw out a card from hand and replace it with either the up card or the top card off the stockpile.

When a word has been played on the table, players subsequently have two further options:
1 A card or cards can be inserted in the exposed word, without disturbing the letter order, to form a new word;
2 One or more letters can be exchanged from hand with a like number of letters from the exposed word to make a new word, again without disturbing the letter order.

One option only can – and must – be exercised on a turn. Words may be challenged with a 10-point penalty to the loser.

INDEX